TO WAR WITH THE 4TH

TO WAR WITH
THE 4TH

A Century of Frontline Combat with the US 4th Infantry
Division, from the Argonne to the Ardennes to Afghanistan

MARTIN KING
MICHAEL COLLINS &
LT. COL. JASON NULTON, USAF (RET'D)

🜨 CASEMATE | publishers
Philadelphia & Oxford

Published in the United States of America and Great Britain in 2016 by
CASEMATE PUBLISHERS
1950 Lawrence Road, Havertown, PA 19083, USA
and
10 Hythe Bridge Street, Oxford OX1 2EW, UK

Hardcover Edition: ISBN 978-1-61200-399-3
Digital Edition: ISBN 978-1-61200-400-6

A CIP record for this book is available from the Library of Congress and the British Library

Printed and bound in the United States of America

For a complete list of Casemate titles, please contact:

CASEMATE PUBLISHERS (US)
Telephone (610) 853-9131
Fax (610) 853-9146
Email: casemate@casematepublishers.com
www.casematepublishers.com

CASEMATE PUBLISHERS (UK)
Telephone (01865) 241249
Fax (01865) 794449
Email: casemate-uk@casematepublishers.co.uk
www.casematepublishers.co.uk

CONTENTS

PART 4: GLOBAL WAR ON TERROR

FOREWORD

The long and proud history of the 4th Infantry Division is unknown by most people. Although it is among the oldest divisions in the American Army, our history has not been as widely reported and followed as that of some divisions.

As we approach the 100th birthday of the 4th Infantry Division (4ID) on December 10, 2017, it is timely that the authors have tackled this project of combining the 4th Infantry Division's history in five wars—World War I, World War II, the Cold War, Vietnam, and the War on Terror—into one very readable document.

In World War I, the 4ID was the only American division to fight in the French, British, and German sectors. They finished that war with the first five battle streamers on their Colors, along with one recipient of the Medal of Honor.

Reactivated in 1940 as the storm clouds of World War II hung over the globe, the 4ID became an experimental motorized division before being selected as the spearhead division to attack Utah Beach on D-Day, June 6, 1944. Fighting on foot across Europe, five more battle streamers were added to their Colors, along with five Medal of Honor recipients. The 4ID had the distinction of being the first seaborne division to land on D-Day, led the breakout at St. Lô, and were the first American troops into Paris and onto the soil of the German homeland. They fought for a month in the bloody Hürtgen Forest, held the southern shoulder of the German attack in the Battle of the Bulge, fought back through the

Siegfried Line and into the heart of Germany. When the war in Europe was over, the 4ID was sent back to the States to prepare to participate in the invasion of Japan.

When the Russians threatened Europe in what became the Cold War, the 4ID was the first division reactivated and sent back to Germany to stand steadfast against the Russian threat, from 1950 to 1956.

A decade later, in 1966 to 1970, loyal 4ID soldiers fought for four and a half years in the jungles of Vietnam's central highlands. They returned to the US having added an additional ten battle streamers to their Colors, along with 17 of their soldiers having earned the Medal of Honor.

The latter years of the 20th century were spent preparing for war against the Soviet Union, once again serving as the experimental division of the Army (Force XXI) where they became the most technologically advanced and lethal division in the world, and prepared to fight any battle they were called on to fight—anywhere in the world. In 2003, they were tapped for the invasion of Iraq. They continue to fight in the War on Terror, spending four long tours in Iraq between 2003 and 2011, multiple deployments to Afghanistan from 2009 through the time of the writing of this book (where three 4ID soldiers have earned the Medal of Honor), and have once again picked up the mission of standing against the rising Russian threat in Europe.

It has been a busy and successful hundred years for the 4th Infantry Division. The following pages expand on this brief summary—history that has never before been encapsulated as it has in this one book. Fellow veterans and family members of the 4th Infantry Division will swell with pride as they read our history. Others will come to realize that this mighty division, which never sought publicity or glory, has always lived up to our motto in service to our country—Steadfast and Loyal.

Robert O. Babcock
President and Historian
National 4th Infantry Division Association
May 1, 2016
www.4thinfantry.org

ACKNOWLEDGMENTS

This volume is dedicated to my wife Freya for her continued support despite all the adversity. Posthumous thanks to my late grandfather Private 4829 Joseph Henry Pumford who fought at Passchendaele in World War One and provided invaluable inspiration for all my early interest in military history. He was promoted to corporal but then demoted for punching out a sergeant. He was unique in managing to terrify both sides in that particular conflict. Also and not forgetting offspring Allycia and Ashley Rae, brother Graham, sisters Sandra and Debbie, brother in law Mark, nephews Ben and Jake and niece Rachel. Not forgetting cousins Alan Pumford, Sue Ellis, Dean Ellis, treasured friends Andy Kirton, Dirk de Groof …always there.

Many thanks to Ruth Sheppard, Tara Lichterman and the tremendous staff at Casemate including former editor Steve Smith who always inspired.

Special thanks to my dear friends, Mike Edwards, Mike Collins, Lt. Col. Jason Nulton (ret'd), Commander Jeffrey Barta (ret'd) and General Graham Hollands (ret'd) Betsy Jackson, for their wonderful support and encouragement. Grateful thanks to my dear friend Mr. Roland Gaul at the National Military Museum Diekirch and Helen Patton.

Thank you also to Mrs. Carol Fish and the staff at the United States Military Academy at West Point, Rudy Beckers and Greg Hanlon at Joint Base McGuire, Dix, Lakehurst for their wonderful ongoing support. Joseph Schram at the American Legion Flanders. Many thanks to

Doug McCabe former curator of the Cornelius Ryan Collection Ohio University, my friends Brian Dick, Jerome Sheridan, Julia and Dale Dye, Ken Johnson, veteran John Schaffner and Madam Ambassador Denise Campbell Bauer.

Martin King

I would like to dedicate this book to my son, Daniel Edward, who is always smiling and making me realize how precious life is every single day. Thank you my co-authors Martin King and Lt. Col. Jason Nulton for your support and hard work. To my parents, John and Joanne Collins for your continued support in this wild ride of research, my brothers John and Chris, my sisters-in-law Melissa and Maria, nieces and nephew, Morgan, Katie, Keira, Margo and Henry. To the King and Nulton families, for their support and understanding during the writing of this book. My friends Michael Aliotta, Christopher Begley, Howard Liddic, John Vallely, Sean Conley, Christian Pettinger, Dirk De Groof, Rudy Aerts, and all those who support me during my many travels. To Kathleen Reilly and Ann-Marie Harris and the staff in the Local History Department at the Berkshire Athenaeum who continue to support and teach me about research. I would also like to thank Robert Babcock for his help with this book. Thank you to the staff at Casemate and editor Ruth Sheppard for your continued professional work and help throughout the publishing process. Finally to the members of the 4th Infantry Division, both past, present, and future, thank you for your service over the last 100 years, and continue to be steadfast and loyal.

Michael Collins

This book is for my truest loves: my children, Wyatt and Amelia. Without the support of the two of them, my parents Dave and Lynn Nulton, and my sisters Jennifer and Julia, my work on this book would not have been possible. My longtime friend Martin King also deserves my humble thanks for agreeing to gamble and let a crusty and cynical retired military officer like me get involved in chronicling these incredible stories with him. He gave me this shot, mentored me and coached me, and I'm forever grateful for it. My professional colleagues and friends deserve recognition as well: Mike Collins, Mike Edwards, Ken Johnson, Dr. Dan Blair and his staff at Ohio Valley University, Lauren Katzenberg from Task & Purpose, and members of the Military Writers Guild. I also extend humble thanks to those who gave me their valuable time to provide war stories and views on their personal combat experiences: Congressman Steve Russell, Lt General (retired) Don Campbell and his wife Ann, Colonel Desmond "Dez" Bailey, Cody Hoefer, Chris Darden, Antonio Salinas, Korey Staley, and Brian Bennett from the LA Times. Finally, work like this can't be done without significant input and backing from friends, and mine are no exception. Special thanks to Jim and Sabrina Vant, Scott and Eva Whitfield, my lifelong friend Tom Martin, Kim Cowgill, Tina Hutchison, and my old Air Force colleagues and friends Jeff Garner and Sandy Scott who were constant sources of encouragement, humor and support. Last and certainly not least is my thanks to God above for endowing me with the patience to take on this project and make sure these amazing American stories get the attention they deserve.

Jason Nulton

INTRODUCTION

There have been many books written about many US divisions over the years but how many of those divisions saw action and were awarded battle honors in almost every major conflict of the last 100 years? The 4th Infantry Division is one of the exceptions because it saw action from World War I to Afghanistan and then some. To the men who served and are still serving with the 4th Infantry Division that distinctive "four ivy leaf" patch is not just an emblem. It is much, much more than that. It is a symbol of dedication, valor, fortitude, and enduring loyalty that surpasses all other considerations. They were always ready, they were always "steadfast and loyal," and they were always there.

On September 14, 1918, when the men of the 4th Division stood to in their trenches and prepared to attack, they would have had little idea that they were in close proximity to men whose names were destined to become synonymous with 20th-century warfare. Not far from their position were George Patton and Douglas MacArthur. On the German side fighter ace Herman Goering was flying around while Erwin Rommel studied maps and prepared his men for battle.

It would be one of the first times that American divisions would operate autonomously, unencumbered by British or French interference. They would go over the top on uneven ground, their young bodies would be mutilated by German artillery and they would fall in their hundreds to the percussive spitting of lethal German machine guns. The 4th Infantry Division was there.

In World War II on D-Day, June 6, they scrambled ashore across the sands of Utah Beach and remained in Europe until it was all over. They would participate in the Normandy campaign, see the hell of the Hürtgen Forest, memorably described by Ernest Hemingway as the equivalent of the Great War's bloody battle of Passchendaele, except "with tree bursts," and then they would feel temperatures plummet during the Battle of the Bulge and stand their ground against overwhelming odds. No other American division suffered more casualties in the European theater than the 4th, and no other division accomplished as much.

In Vietnam they would execute precarious "search and destroy" missions in dense jungles against a determined and resourceful enemy and experience a series of major engagements that would entail 33 consecutive days of vicious, close-quarter combat in the battle of Dak To in 1967. They would receive no fewer than 11 Medals of Honor, the 4th Infantry Division was there.

On December 13, 2003, during Operation *Red Dawn*, an American military operation was conducted in the town of ad-Dawr, Iraq, near Tikrit, which led to the capture of Iraqi president Saddam Hussein. The 4th Infantry Division was directly involved.

In May 2009 at the height of Operation *Enduring Freedom X*, the 4th Infantry Brigade Combat Team was deployed to Afghanistan for a 12-month combat rotation mission. They operated in the birthplace of the Taliban in the Maiwand and Zhari districts along the Arghandab River Valley, west of Kandahar City, an area often ominously referred to as "The Heart of Darkness." In their role as part of Task Force 1-12 they had to operate in a highly complex combat environment due to notoriously dense grape fields that gave excellent cover and concealment to the insurgents as they conducted repeated attacks on coalition forces. The 2nd Battalion 12th Infantry Regiment saw heavy combat throughout the area when they were deployed to Regional Command East and were based in the Pech River Valley in Kunar Province.

In this volume we will once more attempt to provide as many first-hand veteran accounts as we can that refer to all these conflicts. If you want to know about a division that knows about war in all its grotesque manifestations, then you have to know the 4th Infantry Division.

PREFACE

In our past volumes we have introduced many unsung heroes to our readers and this volume will be no exception but the challenge here is to condense the events of a whole century into one volume? It isn't possible to cover every single military engagement that involved the 4th Infantry Division because they are simply too numerous. However, each war had its own distinct character and the purpose here is to present that character through the eyes, ears, hearts, and words of some of those who were there. To present the evolution of warfare spanning almost 100 years rather than presenting a comprehensive analysis of each individual action that involved the 4th. Where there are surviving veterans, with firsthand witness accounts we will present them as we have done in the past.

In time-honored style we will depict the details of some of the battles that the 4th Infantry Division were involved in and then leave it to the veterans to tell you what it was really like for those in the field. This information will empower you, the reader, to draw your own conclusions based on the information presented. To facilitate this objective, the book will be divided into four parts accordingly and focus on the major engagements of each conflict from World War I, to World War II, Vietnam, and finally Iraq/Afghanistan. Each chapter will be augmented with veteran accounts, after-action reports and medal roll calls.

To cover a division's history spanning almost a hundred years is quite an undertaking but we believe that the Ivy men are more than worthy of this treatment. It is our aspiration to present a tribute to an incredible division, nurture a greater appreciation of their accomplishments over the last 100 years, and inspire the reader to look at other published materials about the 4th.

2015 saw the 97th reunion of the National 4th Infantry (IVY) Division Association, which took place at the Hilton Hotel, Springfield, Illinois from September 26 until October 4. To be able to have had 97 reunions is no mean feat but sadly, as with most veteran organizations, the numbers of World War II survivors are dwindling at an alarming rate. This makes our task even more of an imperative, to record the experiences of these indomitable veterans before they finally leave us, and one doesn't need to be an author to do this. We would encourage anyone who knows a veteran to record their stories and experiences, if only for posterity.

Our goal from the outset has always been to direct attention and give credit where credit is due to those divisions that we feel had been slightly overlooked by history. That said none of this would be possible without the assistance and cooperation of Bob Babcock, CEO of Deeds Publishing LLC and currently the President/Historian of the 4ID Association "surviving veterans of the conflicts." Bob is a veteran of the Vietnam War and his personal veteran interviews formed an integral part of this volume.

In conclusion, we sincerely hope you will join us on this journey with the Ivy men from the trenches of the Western Front to the hills of Afghanistan and through some of the most devastating conflicts ever unleashed on, and perpetrated by mankind.

PART I

THE GREAT WAR

CHAPTER I

"THE IVY MEN ARE ON THE WAY"

On April 2, 1917, President Woodrow Wilson approached a joint session of Congress to request a declaration of war against Germany. He cited Germany's violation of its pledge to suspend unrestricted submarine warfare in the North Atlantic and the Mediterranean, as well as its attempts to entice Mexico into an alliance against the United States. These were, in his opinion, grounded reasons to declare war and Congress agreed. Two days later the US Senate voted in support of the measure and on April 6, 1917 the United States officially declared war on the German Empire. There was no turning back.

President Woodrow personally appointed General John J. Pershing (also known as "Black Jack" after he commanded the famous 10th Cavalry in the 1890s) with the task of leading the AEF (American Expeditionary Force). When Pershing left for Europe he had a specific mandate from Wilson to cooperate with Allied forces to the fullest extent, but Wilson was quick to demur that this cooperation would be conditional. He insisted that the forces of the United States would remain a separate and distinct component of the combined forces and that they would retain their own identity. This meant in essence that there would be no wholesale merging of American soldiers into the British and French armies as reserves troops and cannon fodder, which was essentially what the Allied commanders had hoped for. The United States would fight under its own flag and answer only to its own leadership. This factor eventually proved to be a bone of contention among the Allies for the remainder of the war.

On November 17, 1917, the 4th Division was activated at Camp Greene, North Carolina. The ranks were compiled mostly from recent draftees. The insignia, consisting of four green ivy leaves on a khaki background, was adopted by its first appointed commanding general Major General George H. Cameron. Born in 1861, Cameron had graduated from West Point in the class of 1883, and brought with him a wealth of experience and the highest traditions of the United States Army. Using his inimitable knowledge and tact, his understanding of men and their motives, his military ability, his justice, his humanity, his willingness to give credit, he commanded not only the respect of his officers and men but their affection as well. He gave the 4th Division a spirit and breathed life into what might have been otherwise just another division. Above all he was fiercely loyal to his Division, and this loyalty was reciprocated all the way down the line. An earnest student of his profession he had a keen appreciation of military situations and the courage to construct and convey orders with the ultimate conviction.

The 4th quickly became known as the "Ivy" Division because the Roman numeral for the number 4 is IV. The Division's motto is "Steadfast and Loyal." They would have only 17 days of outdoor training before being thrust into action in World War I but they would rise to the challenge.

> The 4th Infantry Division is built around three of the oldest and most distinguished infantry regiments of the United States Army. It is heir to the history of the 4th Division in World War I. Based on these traditions; we have been building a tradition of our own, one of accomplishment of assigned missions in spite of enemy, weather, fatigue or shortages of personnel or supplies. "We never failed."
>
> H. W. Blakeley
> Major General Commanding

The regiments selected for service in the 4th Division were created out of some of the most famous regiments of the old US Army. The 58th and 59th Infantry were formed from the old 4th Regiment, which almost dated back to the Revolutionary War and carried on its regimental colors no fewer than 111 battle honors. The 47th Infantry was an offspring of the old 9th Regiment, formed just before the Civil War and famous for distinguished service in Indian Campaigns, in Cuba, and in the Philippines; it had even participated in suppressing the Boxer Rebellion. The 39th Infantry was formed from the 30th, which, after fighting in the Philippines, had been returned to the Pacific Coast and had rendered valuable service during the San Francisco earthquake and fire of 1906. The 77th Field Artillery, originally the 9th Cavalry, could trace its lineage to the 2nd Cavalry (the old 2nd Dragoons) which, organized for the Seminole Campaign in Florida, had run the gamut of army history through the Mexican and Civil Wars, the Indian Campaigns, and the Spanish-American War. The infantry came from Gettysburg, Pennsylvania, and from Syracuse, New York, the artillery from camps and training stations in Texas, Wisconsin and Vermont.

These elementary organizations had been fleshed out to some extent by the voluntary enlistment of men who were gripped by patriotic fervor and anxious to go to the front as quickly as possible. Like those of other combatant nations these young Americans, imbibed with a passion for adventure and combat, were spurred on by jingoistic dialogue and were doubtless the pride of the nation's youth. They quickly absorbed the spirit of the old regular units in which they were to train and fight. Nevertheless they would soon learn that mere enthusiasm for adventure wasn't enough to sustain one in combat.

When they embarked for France in April 1918 they would become the only American combat force to serve with both the French and the British in their respective sectors, as well as with the rest of the AEF in the American sector, and they would definitely learn a thing or two from these veterans.

Between March 1 and 21, 1917 around 10,000 men poured in from Camps Custer, Grant, Lewis, Travis, and Pike to fill the ranks of the 4th Division but this was still insufficient to constitute a full division. Voluntary recruits added to the numbers. They usually arrived at Camp Greene in their civilian clothing and presented a very nondescript appearance. Most of these men were undisciplined and untrained. The men from the training camps arrived in uniform, and had already received several weeks or months of instruction. All were willing workers and anxious to learn. It was soon discovered that many of the men drafted under the regulations of the "Selective Service Act" were totally unfit, mentally and physically, to be sent overseas. The Selective Service Act or Selective Draft enacted May 18, 1917 authorized the federal government to raise a national army for the American entry into World War I through compulsory enlistment. The ones deemed unfit for combat duty were transferred out of the Division to a section at Camp Greene to be retained in service for mainly menial tasks.

Allocating the men to particular functions was an added burden for the division psychiatrist who had the job of examining each man sent to the Division and recommending him not only for acceptance or rejection but also for the special duty to which he was best suited. The criteria he used to determine whether or not a man would make a good "machine gunner" or expert "trench raider" has never been entirely revealed so it's safe to say that he worked on instinct.

French and British instructors were brought over the Atlantic to provide vigorous instruction on hand-grenade throwing techniques and bayonet practice. It should be noted that throwing grenades didn't come naturally to these men and it took a lot of persuasion and coercion to discourage the natural inclination of the men to pitch a grenade like a baseball. Despite this, once they had grasped the advantages of the overhead lob, they quickly became proficient. Learning the ferocious thrust and twist of bayonet training proved to be equally problematic. Despite the fact that most of the men drafted had never struck a blow in anger in their lives, the primary purpose of the instructors was to embue them with the determination to close with adversaries and dispatch accordingly. Although the rigorous bayonet drill instilled an aggressive spirit and provided the men with individual impetus, it should be noted that it was never really popular.

The 4th Division soon discovered the real value of professional training and the marked positive psychological effect it could instill in the troops. On March 5 and 6 Colonel Applin, a British Army officer, arrived in Charlotte and delivered two landmark lectures to 1,700 officers and 1,100 sergeants. During World War I, Applin became an instructor in the use of the machine gun, and was attached to the Machine Gun Corps Training Centre in July 1916. In November 1916 he was appointed temporary lieutenant colonel, and commanded the machine guns of II ANZAC Corps at the battles of Messines and Passchendaele. With the entry of the United States into the war, Applin was part of a British mission to the country. His remarkable ability to communicate would hold him in good stead for his future vocation as a Conservative politician. The first of his lectures covered "Discipline and Training," and the others focused on "the tactical handling of machine guns." These lectures made a great impression on the men because they were entertaining as well as instructive and were not only enjoyed but remembered by all who were present.

The 4th Division would soon be on its way to France. Speaking in Baltimore, President Wilson said: "Germany has once more said that force and force alone shall decide whether justice and peace shall reign in the affairs of men; whether right as we conceive it or dominion as she conceives it shall determine the destiny of mankind. There is therefore but one response possible from us, force, force to the utmost, force without stint or limit, the righteous and triumphant force that shall make right the law of the world and cast every selfish dominion down in the dust."

Between April 21 and 28, the Ivy Division, less its artillery, was moved by rail from Camp Greene to the New Jersey and New York camps. Some of the units had their journey broken at Washington and enjoyed a two-hour period of marching, for exercise, through the outlying streets of the capital. Some realization of what moving a division means, even under what were virtually peacetime conditions, may be gathered from the fact that when the 4th Division moved it took along some 24,000 pieces of freight, 35,000 of heavy baggage and 6,000 of light baggage, without counting the hundreds of vehicles, which are the indispensable paraphernalia of the modern fighting unit.

The 4th Engineers were the first troops of the Ivy Division to sail. The regiment embarked on April 29 at New York and landed at Bordeaux on May 12. On the same day a battalion of the 59th Infantry reached

Liverpool on the *Olympic* and 48 hours later the machine gun company of the regiment, and the 12th Machine Gun Battalion, made the same port aboard the *Aquitania*—both of these great liners had made the dash across the Atlantic in seven days without convoy protection.

The Division Headquarters, and the remainder of the 8th Brigade, with the exception of the 58th Infantry, left New York on May 3 and disembarked at Liverpool on May 15. They were initially escorted out of New York by the USS *San Diego*, which was sent to the bottom by a mine a few days later. The 7th Brigade, with some artillery units, arrived at Brest on the coast of France as part of a 16-ship convoy that transported 35,000 men. They had set off from Hoboken, New York, and endured a 13-day journey across the Atlantic. The Ivy men were on their way and by June 5 the whole 4th Division, with a few minor exceptions, was on French soil.

CHAPTER 2

"THE IVY MEN ARE HERE!"

There was no greater tragedy in World War I than the callous, multitudinous sacrifice of a generation of healthy young men on the Western Front, and there couldn't have been a more petrifying prospect than waiting in those godforsaken trenches to go over the top. Waiting to hear the whistle that could signal one's almost inevitable demise by machine-gun bullet or shrapnel. Many of the men would in effect be waiting to die, in the vain hope that it would be a quick and painless death. Heads would cower and flinch at the percussive blasts of enemy artillery shaking one's soul to the core then stomach muscles would tighten and contract before they obediently ascended the trench ladders and launched themselves into "No Man's Land," an undulating, skeletal terrain, pockmarked with shell holes, laced with barbed wire, shattered remnants of bodies and almost unimaginable horror. Their eyes would absorb a scene of unequivocal destruction and death.

The first casualties that the 4th Division incurred as the result of enemy action actually happened while they were still crossing the Atlantic. The converted British ship *Moldavia*, an armed merchant cruiser operating as a troopship, sailed from Halifax on May 11, 1917 as an ocean escort to a convoy. It was transporting Companies "A" and "B" of the 58th Infantry when it was torpedoed and sunk by a German submarine with the loss of 56 men, all of whom with one exception were from Company "B." This occurred at 0240 hours on the morning of May 23, 1918, in the English Channel approximately midway between Land's End and the Isle of Wight, just off Beachy Head. The *Moldavia* was leading her convoy of five ships, while five British destroyers, which had joined them the previous day, darted around and between them. On the day she got hit the sky was overcast and the night was very dark. Under normal circumstances these were ideal conditions for outwitting the predatory German U-boats but not on this fateful occasion.

A sudden break in the clouds made the moon visible for perhaps five minutes, during which short time the periscope enabled the commander of *UB-57* to glimpse his prey and launch a single torpedo that crashed into the 9,500-ton vessel.

The explosion tore a gaping hole in the port side of the hull and shattered the compartment where the "B" Company men were sleeping. The explosion killed nearly all the men in the compartment outright. The listing of the ship to port undoubtedly saved those who survived the explosion, enabling them to utilize the uneven surface of the sloping compartment walls in climbing to the deck above, and from there to the boat deck and rescue. Fortunately, the explosion did not damage the engines, and the bursting of a starboard bulkhead caused the ship to resume an even keel. An attempt was made to reach shore, but the water gained rapidly and within an hour it had stilled the ship's throbbing engines. Contrary to orders, many of the men had undressed before going to bed in the belief that the submarine danger was practically over, as land had been visible throughout the entire day. In the darkness and confusion many of them, unable to find their clothes, were forced to go to their boat stations in little more than their underwear, while some were even less suitably attired.

Upon arrival in France, 4th Division troops were first sent to the British Army to get "trained up" and made "battle ready." The first qualm registered by the Americans was noted by their reluctance to consume the nutritionally questionable British cuisine and the glaring absence of coffee. The latter almost induced a riot. For a start the United States hadn't been subject to sugar rationing like the British had and this was reflected in the daily menu. Thankfully the 4th Division only had to spend three days at the British camp in Calais before being transported south to train with the French Army.

En route the 4th would have passed the historic battlefields of Agincourt and Crécy where their erstwhile allies had once been committed adversaries in medieval battles. It was in these picturesque little French villages that the men gleaned their first experience of French billets. Many of them discovered that a barn, even one in which it was rumored Napoleon had stabled his horses, was worse than no barn at all.

During that turbulent summer, under the glaring June sunshine commanding officers acquiesced to the many requests made by the doughboys to be allowed to bivouac in the open field. They were staying in places that they could hardly pronounce, such as Desvres, Deaudeauville, and Bernieville, but in no time at all the French people became endeared by the cheerful smiles of these young American soldiers who, in the midst of searching for water drawn from wells 400 feet deep, found time to entertain the local children and attempt to pick up a few useful French phrases.

This scene of rustic harmony was in fact deceptive because in the distance the portentous, bass booms of life-shattering artillery would have been audible to the troops. Despite the welcome distractions provided by war-weary French villagers the 4th would have been made fully aware that the industrial-scale war machine was preparing to mercilessly consume and destroy their innocence for all eternity. They may have been reasonably well trained but they were far from battle hardened.

During the first months of 1918 the Western Front became more mobile and fluid, nevertheless trench warfare still existed along the line that ran from Neiuwpoort on the Belgian coast all the way through Belgium and France down to the Swiss border.

The last great German offensive was launched on March 21, 1918. During this "spring offensive" innovative German "stormtrooper" tactics proved to be very effective. The purpose of the offensive was to finish off the British and French before the Americans arrived. After the precursory bombardment stormtroopers attacked, but unlike the standard infantry units used at the beginning of the war, these men were equipped with a wide variety of weapons, rather than just using the standard issue bolt-action rifle. Wire-cutting and explosives engineers created gaps in the barbed wire belts followed up by grenade throwers, flame throwers, machine gunners, and mortar crews to infiltrate the enemy positions. Then they would be followed by up to four waves of infantry. The attacking troops were not confined to fixed objectives and bypassed pockets of concerted resistance, leaving them for supporting troops to deal with. By the third day of this offensive the Germans had opened a 50-mile-wide gap and were pouring into open country after completing an unprecedented 40-mile advance. However, the troops leading the attack ran short of vital supplies—what was initially hailed as a tactical masterpiece dissipated into a strategic failure as supply lines struggled to keep pace with the advance.

The tactics may have been innovative in some ways but in all fairness they were not entirely new. The British Army had already begun experimenting with alternatives to the standard "everybody over the top" system that had been so costly in human lives almost from the outset. In the latter months of the war there were some similarities between British and German infantry tactics but the British held the critically important advantages regarding their use of counter-battery fire, tanks, and ground support aircraft. The use of these improvements ultimately gave the British and their allies the means by which they could defeat the German forces in the later months of 1917 and check the German spring offensive in 1918.

It is well documented that once American troops began to enter the trenches, Allied morale soared and German morale plummeted. The psychological effect on the Germans became all too apparent when the Allies went on the offensive. Despite this, the most pervading problem was that once General Pershing had extricated all American units from British and French command control, little effort was made to adapt new battle tactics and it was observed on more than one occasion that their assault formations were too dense and lacking in flexibility. Moreover a glaring lack of accurate reconnaissance frequently impaired an already bad situation. The result was that although the AEF (American Expeditionary Force) achieved and contributed to some notable victories in the latter half of 1918, they incurred terrible casualties.

A 4th Division World War One soldier was inducted into the Hall of Heroes at the Pentagon, June 3, one day after the upgrade of his Distinguished Service Cross to Medal of Honor, posthumously. The President awarded the Medal of Honor to Sgt. William Shemin, Company G, 2nd Battalion, 47th Infantry Regiment (Raiders), 4th Infantry Division for actions during World War I.

From Aug. 7–9, 1918, during the Aisne-Marne Offensive in France, Shemin distinguished himself conspicuously by gallantry above and beyond the call of duty. His Distinguished Service Cross (DSC), citation reads:

"For extraordinary heroism in action on the Vesle River, near Bazoches, August 7, 8, 9, 1918. Sergeant Shemin, upon three different occasions, left (cover) and crossed an open space of 150 yards, exposed to heavy machine-gun fire to rescue the wounded. After officers and senior noncommissioned officers had become causalities, Sergeant Shemin took command of the platoon and displayed great initiative under fire until wounded August 9."

Shemin was born in Bayonne, New Jersey, in 1896. In 1917, he joined the Army during World War I. He was assigned as a rifleman in Company G, 47th Infantry Regiment, which moved from New York to North Carolina, becoming part of the 4th Division. The division was part of the American Expeditionary Forces in France.

The 47th Infantry Regiment was assigned to the 7th Brigade, 4th Infantry Division. The regiment took part in four European campaigns during World War I with 40 of its members receiving the DSC.

"With the most utter disregard for his own safety, (Shemin) sprang from his position in his platoon trench, dashed out across the open in full sight of the Germans, who opened and maintained a furious burst of machine gun and rifle fire," said Capt. Rupert Purdon, one of Shemin's supervisors.

Shemin survived that moment with only shrapnel injuries. Later, Shemin was hit in the head with a bullet from a machine gun. This along with his prior injuries saw Shemin hospitalized for three months. He received the DSC and Purple Heart Dec. 29, 1919, for his actions.

Shemin was honorably discharged from the Army in 1919. From there he went to Syracuse University where he played lacrosse and football while earning a degree from the New York State College of Forestry. After graduating, he opened a greenhouse and landscaping business and raised three children with his wife, Bertha. He died in 1973 and was buried in Staten Island, New York.

French and British observers of American attacks were amazed by the almost suicidal zeal that these young men displayed as they moved out to confront the enemy. There may have been no shortage of admiration but there were also serious questions concerning American tactics at that stage of the war.

America's build up for the war had been slow and laborious but by the spring of 1918 the "Doughboys" had 420,000 men at the front and ready for action. The Allies supplied most of their equipment such as the distinctive "British" helmet. The 4th Division was raring to go and wouldn't have to wait long to see and participate in the anticipated "action."

CHAPTER 3

"BAPTISM ON THE AISNE-MARNE"

During the night of July 14 somnambulant Parisians were unceremoniously jolted from their slumbers by the dull stomach-churning thuds of 84 German batteries pounding away from the direction of the Marne River. Crown Prince Wilhelm of Prussia was executing his threat to attack Paris by launching 29 divisions in what would be the ultimate concerted German offensive of World War I.

The impending offensive would be defined by two attacks launched against the Fourth French Army commencing east of Rheims. This would be augmented by a secondary attack between Chateau-Thierry and Rheims against a combined force of French and Americans. On the morning of July 15 the German artillery piece known as Big Bertha opened fire with its 820 kg (1,807 lb) shells on Paris while another sizeable siege gun mounted on a turntable near Brecy, shelled Meaux, Coulommiers and La Fert-sous-Jouarre. The German bombardment, which preceded the attack in the Champagne region, was particularly intense and persisted for more than ten hours but, unbeknown to the German high command, the French Brigadier-General Gouraud was ready and waiting. On the night before the attack he had ordered and executed a daring raid, which had provided him with such valuable intelligence that he managed to almost curtail the German offensive in its tracks.

German prisoners taken during this night raid freely revealed the plan along with their orders. They revealed to their captors how there would be an artillery barrage would precede thousands of Germans leaving their trenches to swarm toward the Allied lines. Gouraud wasted no time in formulating a plan to counter this move. The French artillery was immediately informed of the impending assault and half an hour before the German artillery opened, the French anticipated it with a concentrated barrage on the German positions, sowing misery and mayhem among enemy troops anxiously preparing to go over the top. It was obvious to the German commanders that their plan had been intercepted but in time-honored World War I style they went ahead regardless, even though it took them over three hours to reach the French positions because Gouraud had withdrawn his forces from the front line to his principal second line of defense, leaving behind only a token force to provide a delaying action.

The German attack was inevitably welcomed by a ferocious onslaught of machine gun and artillery fire, but despite this the Germans pushed forward with the relentless and derisible desperation so characteristic of these battles. As it raged on throughout the day and while crucially holding some 80km of the front around Champagne, Gouraud coldly issued his renowned "stand or die" command to his army, which included men of the AEF. By sunset German hopes of taking Chalons and Epernay had faded and the attack continued to dissolve until it finally lost all momentum.

Meanwhile, between Chateau-Thierry and Dormans, the Germans had managed to successfully cross the Marne River but as soon as the failure of the drive east of Rheims was realized they were ordered to pull back and stand down. At this time the 4th Division was positioned just northwest of Chateau-Thierry and now it was their turn to go "over the top."

The French commander Field Marshal Foch now ordered an all-out counteroffensive to rout the battered Germans. The 4th Division would advance as part of the French 6th Army under the command of General Degoutte.

So between July 18 and August 17, the 4th Division went on the attack in the Aisne Marne offensive (also referred to as the second battle of the Marne). The 4th Division didn't function as an autonomous unit at this time, remaining under French command for the duration. Some units were attached to II French Corps while the rest were sent to VII French Corps.

The tension was palpable as Companies A and C of the 11th Machine Gun Battalion, 39th Regiment 4th Division proceeded to move into communications trenches in preparation for the approaching counterattack.

The night before the attack troops were subjected to a heavy downpour and a thunderstorm that was so intense that it competed for attention with the sound of trench mortars and artillery. At 0430 hours the French artillery launched an eardrum-shattering 70-gun barrage as their troops extricated themselves from the trenches and moved out. Zero hour for the 39th Regiment of the 4th Division was 0530 hours, July 17. As the first timorous beams of light permeated the dawn air, Company A braced for the advance.

Peering tenuously over the parapet with periscopes, the company officers would have seen a veritable inferno of flame and smoke as French artillery shells rained onto the German positions roughly 400 yards away. Suddenly the whole line was ordered to "Stand to!" and "Fix bayonets!" When this was done the men would have exchanged reassuring glances and then stared at the parapet in anticipation. Then suddenly whistles blew down the line. As soon as the men emerged from their rain-drenched trenches and clambered up the trench ladders into hell they were immediately raked by two German machine gunners camouflaged in a wood pile on their left flank. After wading through a quagmire reminiscent of the battle of Passchendaele, a sergeant discovered one of the nests, rushed it single handedly and lobbed over a hand grenade. Seconds later an explosion sent wood splinters flying through the air as the woodpile fell over revealing the two startled gunners. Before they could throw up their hands to surrender they were peppered with bullets.

Then the men moved steadily eastward, meeting only sporadic rifle and machine-gun fire from a handful of Germans who held the southern face of the woods. Soon thereafter the whole battalion proceeded through the woods, on a gradient that led up to their pre-determined objective. Within two hours, more than 100 Germans had been taken prisoner, along with several of their machine guns. When the 3rd Battalion advanced at 0900 hours, they discovered that the 1st had already cleared the front.

At 1600 hours, 2nd Battalion commanded by Major Manton C. Mitchell moved out of their trenches. They had sustained numerous casualties while waiting to go over the top due to German artillery, so when the time came it was practically a relief to the men to launch into No Man's Land. Their advance met with hardly any resistance, but in their eagerness to get to the enemy they inadvertently crossed battalion boundaries and became intermixed with other Allied units.

Meanwhile the French hadn't progressed as rapidly as they had expected and by the afternoon no French troops had managed to reach their pre-selected objectives. As the day wore on, the Germans recovered from the initial onslaught and stiffened their resistance. Companies A and C of the 11th Machine Gun Battalion received a lot of praise from their regiment for their contribution to what was widely regarded as a substantial Allied victory. Lieutenant Quentin Roosevelt, son of Theodore Roosevelt, was killed during this assault flying in support of the Allies during the Aisne-Marne offensive.

John Luebke, B Company, 47th Infantry Regiment, 7th Brigade

Aisne Marne Offensive, Action on the Ourcq: *Crown Prince Wilhelm of Germany launched the last great German drive for Paris on the evening of the La Fête Nationale against General Gouraud of France east of Rheims with 29 German combat divisions. A smaller drive was against General Degoutte of France southwest of Rheims with 21 German divisions. We extended from Ancienville to Hautevesnes and lay west of the main highway from Soissons to Chateau-Thierry.*

The next day we moved to the area of the reserve trenches and marched to Cheneviere Farm, Boullareee and to Neufchelles on the Ourcq front, returning the next day to our regular stations. The "alert" maneuver was a necessary part of the training for the difficult task of placing a unit in line at night.

At night, the Fourth Division moved by camions to the Ourcq area. The going was slow, trying to stay on the road, because of the mud. A strong wind drove the rain through my clothing and blinded my eyes. The lightning helped us to see the road better. The poor horses! What a mess in this terrible weather! What am I doing here in this kind of weather when I could be near the nice warm stove at home. If mother knew what was happening to me, she would surely die. I knew she was thinking of me all the time, praying I would return.

On the 12th day of July, 1918, the French infantry troops withdrew from the front lines, and the American infantry took over at night. Everything was on the quiet side, and we got in place where the French were situated. In the evening of July 14th, we withdrew some distance and received word that a large offensive was going to launch east of Chateau-Thierry on the morning of July 15th by our own command. We soldiers of the Ivy Division would occupy the northern sector. The zero hour was set for the French at 4:30 a.m. and for the Americans at 5:30 a.m. The bursting shells were flying overhead, and the machine-gun fire swept the ground until daylight. It seemed to me that nothing could stay alive with those shells bursting. I looked over the top of the trenches, and I could see the bursting shell dirt flying all over and smoke going up in the air.

Then came the time to move forward, and we were met with machine-gun fire from the Germans, which held us back. The German machine guns were so well concealed that it had to be a direct hit to stop them. They gave us lots of trouble. We could not see where they were situated and had to wait until they ran out of ammunition and food. This gave the Germans time to go back and then take up a new front.

Advancing was slow with that much resistance, and we could not move around much in the daytime as the Germans could see so well. They would use high-explosive shells and sometimes gas shells on our little Stokes Mortar. Our one-pound guns did not amount to much in such a large combat.

During this action, the Fourth Division did not function as a unit. The Division Commander exercised no command, and the units of the Division were brigaded with French troops. Our Ivy Division was now attached to the II French Corps and the rest of the Division with the VII French Corps.

Then the Ivy Division was sent to the village of Chateau-Thierry on the River Marne. This was the first ruins I had seen in the middle of July, 1918. The whole village was bombed, and I was thinking of the French people coming back to their living quarters. How sad it must have been! The bloodiest fighting took place around the Chateau-Thierry salient.

A terrible tragedy happened when the Fourth Division was on the move in the valley of the Ourcq. A message reached our commnder that the French changed the time of the attack, and that a barrage was to precede it. However, the runnaers were too late to relay the message to the French that the position was already taken by the 39th Infantry, and to advance the barrage. The French shells came thick and fast and caused many casualties among the Americans.

The 39th moved forward, and the Germans were shelling heavily. The Second Battalion on the right passed through small but dense patches of woods and advancing was difficult. Before it lay the marshes, hills, woods and the winding valley of the Ourcq. The left of the battalion became immersed in a swamp and suffered enemy machine-gun fire. A platoon was sent forward, and they captured the machine guns in front so our soldiers could move out of the swamp. It was not only the troops in the front line, but also those like the 47th where I was serving and also the 59th serving at this time as reserve battalions, that had other important duties in the rear, who suffered casualties on that day. At this time, we were behind the front lines through thick and through thin. If they lost too many men and needed replacements or a rest, we were right there to take over. Our closest support units were the 39th and 59th Infantry.

As we advanced from time to time, the Germans left behind much of their equipment like field artillery, machine guns, and minenwerfer which were small guns like we had. Our ammunition gave out, but that did not stop us as we were looking for the enemy with our bayonets. I never got to see a German casualty or a wounded one, as they had enough time to take care of their own soldiers.

I got within ten steps of a German machine gun before I saw it. It was placed so well in the ground. The top of the cover was camouflaged. My heart sank, but I tried to act bravely as a soldier should. I thought to myself, "I just made it." Soon the ammunition had given out, and the firing from the enemy doubled in volume. Then the advance was temporarily stopped for rest and reorganization. Resting behind a crest, a French soldier was found shining his shoes with American polish. He said, "I have found this polish. It is good polish, and I may not get another chance to use it." A little farther on, an American soldier dug a pit in the side of a bank and was calmly seated with his back to the enemy. He was shaving from his tin cup.

A Frenchman remarked, "Had I not seen it with my own eyes, I would never have believed that green troops would advance under such fire. This is not war. This is worse than battle." The Frenchman valued their lives until replacements arrived, but the Americans brought new tactics to the war.

I estimated there were about 25 miles of fighting front. That took lots of ammunition and food to keep it going. Many soldiers and horses were brought to the front lines, and it always had to be done in the dark. The casualties among the officer and men had been heavy.

James Platt, C Company, 12th Machine Gun Battalion, 8th Brigade

…In no time we were out in the oat and wheat fields of the rolling countryside. The sun was shining bright. It was hot and the fog of early morning was gone. The company was in line of squads, each squad a gun section, each spaced about 25 feet from the next squad so a shell would not wipe out too many men. We advanced slowly up the gentle slope, through grain nearly to our waists. I kept near Captain Hoopes and Headquarters squad. The squad was few in numbers as the three cooks, the Mess Sergeant, clerk and all mule

drivers were left in safety, in our rear. We went very slowly, just a few steps, then laid down, straightened up and another few steps—we could go no faster than the infantry, and they were held up by gun fire.

As we reached the top of the slight hill, really just before we reached it, the Germans could see the grain waving and, of course, knew American soldiers were making it wave, so they opened a barrage of shells right on top of the hill. The advance stopped and everyone hunted for a hole. It is an awful experience to lie with only a bit of ground to protect you and hear those shells coming in, and exploding all around. Each shell sounded as if it were aimed at your person. It is a mystery to me how so many shells can fall all around a bunch of men and yet hit so few.

I found myself and a young boy in a shallow hole. We were hugging the bottom of that place, and he was Catholic, for he was praying to Mother of God to save him. He was promising all sorts of things if he got away from there in one piece. I got the same kind of ideas, only I didn't know what to promise if that barrage would just leave me alone—now laugh—but the idea came to me that I would promise to go back to teaching when I, and if I, returned to the States. That shows how much I liked the occupation. It wasn't what I had intended to spend my life doing, but perhaps from that shell hole my whole future life was planned. Talk about jumping from the frying pan into the fire. I did it right then for I heard Captain Hoopes yelling my name, he was in the next shell hole, hiding from the shells, just like the rest. I didn't like to get out of my safe (?) hole, but did manage to crawl over to where he was sheltering himself. He told me to go over to a sunken road, about 100 yards to our left, and keep in the ditch and get down the road far enough to see what was going on. In other words, he wanted firsthand information about the advance of the infantry we were following.

If I was ever frightened, if I ever wanted to be about the size of an ant, it was when I crawled through that shellfire and slid over onto that sunken road. I slid into every hole I could find, but the trouble was that nearly all holes were crowded, and no one welcomed me. In the sunken road, it was the same, the ditches were occupied. In my wiggling down that ditch I found a culvert that was across the road, about 2 feet in diameter. But there was room for no more, as infantry was just jammed in it. The road ran right down into German-occupied territory. I felt as if every German down there was watching and laughing to see me keeping as low as I could. I asked several men if there was any sign of an advance. "Advance in the face of this barrage, I guess not," was the general answer. I squirmed down the road until I had a clear view as far forward to the place where the German shells were being fired from and could see no signs of American uniforms going forward, but did see some dodging back. Believe me, I didn't stay there long to look at the scenery. I was in too prominent a place. Another thing, it didn't take me long to crawl back the way I had come. By now I was getting the hang of making progress on hands and knees or at moving at a crouch. In all my trips around the firing line, I crawled many miles, I am sure.

When I turned in my report to Captain Hoopes, he didn't seem pleased, acted almost as if I had made it up. I didn't care what he thought, I wanted only to get back to my home in my shell hole, and did so at once. Queer how safe one can feel with a bit of dirt between you and the enemy. My knees were sore, my back was creaking, my clothes were dirty, but I was not touched.

The casualties were indeed heavy and many American mothers and wives received letters such as this one:

> Mrs. Ackerman –
>
> *Your husband, Sergeant Lloyd C. Ackerman, was in my company, and was the best sergeant I ever had. I thought a lot of him, and was greatly grieved when he was killed. He was right at my side when he was killed. We were in a wheat field about 5 miles northwest of Chateau-Thierry, and your husband is buried right there. Your husband died a hero. He was right in the front line advancing on the Germans, when some machine guns opened up on us and killed many of our men.*
>
> *Sgt. Ackerman was the best drill sergeant I ever had, and was cool under fire. The company and regiment lost a very valuable man when he was killed, and I personally feel it very deeply. I cannot speak too highly of him...*
>
> Captain W. F. Marshall, 318th Inf., 4th Division

They continued to advance until July 22. By August 2 the 4th Division had subsequently re-assembled to relieve the 42nd "Rainbow" Division in the salient along the line of the Vesle River, and by August 6 the battle front had stabilized.

John Luebke, B Company, 47th Infantry Regiment, 7th Brigade

> Aisne Marne Offensive, Valley of the Vesle: *General Cameron was the commander of our Fourth Division and General Poore commanded our 7th Infantry Brigade in the Fourth Division at this time. Our 47th Infantry of the Fourth Division was passing through the Forty-Second Division on to the front line and operating for the first time under our own commanders, not the French, and continuing to dive as far as the Vesle.*
>
> *On August 3, 1918, another big drive was to be made towards the Vesle River. There again the front-line troops were withdrawn some distance. We were moving forward through the thickly wooded country on the way to the Vesle.*
>
> *Early in the morning, heavy artillery fire was next to the German front line and also on the German artillery guns in the back. With such heavy bombardment, the Germans were forced to retreat but left behind many machine guns, which were not hit. The enemy guys were so well concealed that our shooting had to be a direct hit in order to stop those German soldiers who were staying with their guns until the ammunition was gone. Advancing was always slow, because we had to wait for that. Because of this, the*

Germans could go back to a better position among the hills along the Vesle River where they could see a long ways.

The enemy aviators were controlling the air and preventing our planes from getting any information that we needed. Because of the frequent destruction of telephone wires, many messages were delivered by runners who had to dodge in and out of the shell holes to escape the enemy fire. Also our last hope was the pigeons that flew to the Headquarters carrying messages attached to themselves. Some arrived wounded.

A heavy rain came that slowed everything. The ground got muddy, and it was hard to move artillery guns around by night. The artillery horses could not pull the guns through the mud, so the deepest holes were filled with whatever could be found such as stumps, stones, branches, etc. The Ivy Division was going from Sergy where we had "mopped up" to Mareu-il-en-Dole, leading through the Forest de Nesles in knee-deep mud. This was more than I bargained for.

Little by little we got to the Vesle River. We noticed marshes on each side of the banks. We met with much machine-gun fire from the Germans. We came to a stop until more reinforcements were brought. Again, it was hard moving the artillery in that mud! Coming closer to the river, we noticed there was no bridge, and the river was full of barbed wire. Some of the men swam and waded, and some used trees which had fallen across the river. In crossing the river, many of the gas masks were rendered useless when soaked. We tried very hard not to get them wet.

The rest of us waited until the engineers could build a bridge across the river. This was not so easily done as the resistance was too much. A lot of artillery fire was used to quiet down those German guns so that the engineers could get a bridge across the river. On August 5th a bridge was laid across the river with much difficulty and with many casualties. We tried to cross the bridge but were always met with much resistance from the Germans, because they could see so well.

Our Battalion Commander was one hour late reaching the river. During this time gas shells were thrown by the enemy followed by shrapnel, high explosives, and artillery from their planes coming from St. Thibaut, on the south band of the Vesle River. The barrage had passed on when the Commander arrived. He was lucky he was one hour late, because he could have been killed.

It took until August 9th before any amount of men could go across the bridge. By the time I got to cross, it was somewhat easier. It took a few days to get settled on the other side in a protected area. I took care of myself as well as I could and was pretty much on my own.

After fighting in St. Thibaut on the south bank of the Vesle River, our soldiers fought heavily in Bazooches on the north side of the river. A German shell came whistling though the air and landed squarely on the muzzle of a gun. The lieutenant's right arm tore off near the shoulder. He remarked, "The Boches haven't got me—I write with my left hand."

We spent 26 days in combat duty this time, and to me it seemed like a long time in mud and much rain. Hardly a night had passed without shelling by using high explosives. As soon as we advanced, the enemy withdrew further north, and we gained the railroad.

> On the 12th day of August, orders were received to relieve the units of the Fourth
> Division from duty in the front line. The good news came that we were going to be relieved
> by the 305th Infantry of the 77th Division. That night at midnight, we started walking
> back from the front lines. A much-needed rest awaiting us.
>
> I don't know how I made it through all this so far, but I feel that God was with me
> through all those narrow escapes I encountered. I never prayed so hard in my life, and I read
> my prayer book whenever I had a chance. The Chaplain who was available all the while,
> prayed many times with all of us. We looked up to him like he was a messenger of God.
> Now my thoughts turned back to the fighting again. The total losses of the Fourth Division
> during the operations from July 18th to August 17th, 1918 were 6,923 casualties.

James Platt, C Company, 12th Machine Gun Battalion, 8th Brigade

> One fellow I knew very well, by name Threet, who was one of the regular army men in the
> company and had been in China before being placed in our company, had a toothache and
> was pacing up and down trying to stand the aches and pains when the fireworks started. He
> lost control of himself completely, started to shake and shiver, so he couldn't stand by himself.
> He almost had convulsions. He couldn't stop laughing. Some of us took turns holding him
> and walking with him the rest of the night. The next morning an ambulance took him back
> to a hospital. This was the first case of shell shock most of us had experienced. Threet came
> back to the company about a month later, but he was not cured, for the first time he was
> under fire he went off again, and had to be sent back to the rear lines where no shells were
> going off near him. I am sure he didn't put on an act as he wasn't that kind.
>   …We walked along for a couple of miles, sometimes in woods and at other times in the
> open. Finally we reached an open spot on a slight hill, and [Captain Hoopes] said it would
> be far enough, and for me to make a sketch of the forward terrain. I sat down on a rock and
> he stood looking through glasses, when all at once there was the shrill whistle of incoming
> shells. I rolled over behind the rock I had been sitting on just as they exploded, half stuffing
> me. When I finally looked about, there was Captain Hoopes lying on the ground, but no
> one would have known who it was, one of those shells had hit him high in the chest and
> practically decapitated him. He never knew what hit him.
>   I was pretty well unnerved, not only by his death but by the fix it left us in. He was
> the only commissioned officer we had left. The others were either transferred or had been
> wounded…

The AEF were now up against several German armies who were defending a series of fortified trenches in their section. The trench boundaries
started in the French area southeast of the infamous town of Verdun,
and jutted south toward St. Mihiel, and then east to Pont-Au-Mousson.

A vigorous, somewhat opinionated young officer called George S. Patton Jr. was present at this battle. He and his subordinate officers fervently believed that by rapidly adapting to a situation and through their personal leadership they could influence events on the battlefield. That still remained to be seen as the AEF became embroiled in the complexities and murderous consequences of trench warfare. The worst was yet to come.

CHAPTER 4

"HELL IN ST. MIHIEL"

The salient at St. Mihiel had been formed four years previously in September 1914 when German forces had counterattacked after the first battle of the Marne. They had shattered French defenses and captured the two important positions, the Camp des Romains, just south of St. Mihiel, and Mont Sec, 3 kilometers east of it. This placed the main railroad from Paris to Nancy precariously within range of German artillery and prevented the use of a vitally important canal route that ran alongside the Meuse River. Consequently communications between Paris and the Lorraine front were greatly impeded.

The reduction of this salient was the first task assigned by Marshal Foch to General Pershing, who gathered together 15 American divisions for the attack. Of these, nine were earmarked for the assault and six were retained as tactical reserve. Marshal Foch added four French divisions to this force. Some of the worst casualties incurred by 4th Division occurred during the harrowing St. Mihiel offensive that began September 12, 1918. Two American corps launched the main attack against the south of the line. The second wave was provided by the (French) 26th Division, the French 15th Colonial Division, the 8th Brigade, and elements of the 4th Division in line with the rest of the 4th held in reserve.

At St. Mihiel between September 12 and 16, 1918, the Western Front in France would experience one of the most significant battles of World War I. The engagement was the first battle in which American-led forces used concise and comprehensive operations orders that allowed independent initiative from their front-line commanders. The battle of St. Mihiel was a learning curve for modern tactical commanders. It emphasized the necessity to issue clear and concise orders that would allow small unit leaders the autonomy to effectively execute their commander's plans during the battle.

Although the Western armies had numerical superiority over the Germans, by the summer of 1918 the strategic situation was becoming less fluid and devolving once again into a murderous war of attrition. Despite this General Pershing believed, somewhat optimistically, that if the Allies could launch a successful attack in the region of St. Mihiel, Metz, and Verdun, this would psychologically break the German will to fight. Pershing was aware that the AEF's primary objective demanded clearing all rail and road communications into Verdun, and the capture of the Germans' key rail center at Metz. Once this had been achieved the AEF could establish new bases closer to the Rhine River and organize further offensives into Germany to mop up the remnants.

As in previous WWI battles the terrain was to play a vital part in the strategy and tactics employed by the Allies. The area here wasn't flat as it was in Flanders. It was hilly, uneven terrain that demanded different tactics. Prior to the first attacks, the ground had been soaked with five days of incessant rain, making it almost inaccessible to both the tanks and infantry alike. Some commanders were beginning to make unpromising comparisons with the terrible battle of Passchendaele that had occurred the previous year further north in Flanders. The weather report provided by I Corps at the time said that visibility was restricted due to heavy driving wind and torrential rain, and it went on to say that the roads in the vicinity were very muddy. This was an understatement.

A further detriment to the American operation was the many in-depth series of trenches, wire obstacles, and machine-gun nests that the Germans had installed to augment their defensive positions. The available Renault tanks, which were designed to cross 6-foot trenches in dry weather, were being forced by their crews to traverse through veritable quagmires and go up against line after line of trenches that were 8 feet deep and in some places 10–14 feet wide.

The basic plan was to simultaneously attack the two flanks of the salient and form a bottleneck in the center to isolate German positions there and ensure the complete envelopment of the German positions near St. Mihiel. To achieve this aim the American forces would breach the trenches and then advance along the enemy's logistical road network toward their goals. Fourteen AEF divisions would be attacking 10 enemy divisions, consisting of mainly Austro-Hungarian troops belonging to the German 5th Army.

During the night of September 5/6, men of the 59th Infantry Regiment and the 12th Machine Gun Battalion, who had been moved up to the line by bus, began the relief of French troops just southeast of the infamous town of Verdun. This sector was relatively dormant at that time but it had experienced some bitter fighting during 1917 and it constituted the extreme northwestern edge of the salient. The Germans had stoically held the line there continuously since 1914. Consequently their trench positions were well established. They were equipped with all the latest homicidal devices along with reinforced trench walls, electric lighting, modern communications and reinforced concrete dugouts large enough to hold up to 40 men.

Despite all the modernity, the troops that occupied these trenches still had to contend with large, voracious rats and the ever-present fear of instant obliteration. Most of the AEF had been meticulously trained in the art of trench warfare before shipping overseas but the reality still came as a shock. The first 24 hours were the worst. Acclimatizing to the new environment and all the horrific attributes thereof came at a price. Despite all the modern accouterments the trenches were still vulnerable to artillery shells, mortars and trench raids. Death was always in close proximity and the troops were constantly reminded of this by the bilious stench of decomposing corpses that permeated the whole area. Anyone daring to peer above the parapet would immediately become a target for vigilant enemy snipers.

Life was reduced to a continuous series of terrified moments interjected by vain attempts to impose a semblance of normality. Even the veterans displayed visible signs of strain. Nighttime brought little comfort to the occupants. This was when the rats were at their most vigorous, their familiarity with the dead having made them fearless and contemptuous of the living as they scurried along the trench floors and walls making off with every discarded morsel of food. These audacious vermin would crawl over the bodies of sleeping soldiers taking food from their hands and pockets and gnawing at the decomposing remains of the abundant corpses. Another problem that soldiers had to contend with was lice. Lice caused a condition that became known as "Trench Fever," a nasty and agonizing disease that began suddenly with severe pain followed by high fever. Although it wasn't considered life threatening, Trench Fever was debilitating, and required a recovery period of two to three months. It wasn't until 1918 that doctors discovered that these lice transmitted Trench Fever. Apart from the incessant itching and discomfort they caused, they sucked the blood of infected hosts and would then spread the fever.

By 1918 St. Mihiel was the last great salient on the Western Front. Due to the incessant shelling, the terrain in No Man's Land resembled a moonscape, with craters in such close proximity to each other that in most places they overlapped. The roads had almost completely disappeared and surrounding hills had been plundered of every blade of grass. Former woodlands were now skeletal wastelands with the odd protruding bullet and shrapnel-raked tree stump standing forlorn and abandoned among the regurgitated white chalk subsoil. This was the apocalyptic sight that met the wearied eyes of the Ivy men when they first encountered this battlefield.

The night of the 11/12 was deathly quiet but the air was filled with the pregnant expectation of the impending barrage. At exactly 0100 hours on the morning of September 12 the greatest artillery concentration ever assembled on the Western Front erupted in unison with a pugnacious, deafening roar that shook the earth to its very core. A few seconds later innumerable tons of explosives were being launched and lobbed into the German front-line positions. While the gas and smoke created an eerie mist the whole sky appeared to ignite with the reflecting flashes of the thousands of guns that amalgamated into one another, highlighting the horizon with an eerie red orange glow. As timid crepuscular rays of light began to hail the dawn the barrage increased in intensity. Cowering below the parapets, ankle deep in filthy, putrid black water, the men of the 4th Division stood held firm and stood fast, awaiting their orders.

During the course of the afternoon the first patrol left the 8th Brigade trenches and headed towards the German lines. At 1610 hours a further patrol set forth to reach what remained of the small town of Manheulles, just beyond on the Paris–Metz road. They were quickly spotted by rapacious German machine guns that raked their number and forced them to return to their trenches. Throughout the ensuing night and the next day patrols were kept low as they attempted to determine the exact movements of the enemy. On September 14 at 1000 hours the reserve company of each battalion left the trenches to press home the attack.

They advanced behind a creeping barrage before reaching their objectives. The creeping or rolling barrage was a carefully timed slow-moving artillery attack that kept the enemy's heads low and acted as a defensive curtain for advancing infantry who followed closely behind. Using this tactic the reserve companies managed to capture prisoners, and from this position they could see many of their German comrades absconding from the rear of the town. It was at this juncture that the Ivy men made an unexpected but pleasant discovery. In their haste to escape, the Germans had abandoned their kitchens, where they had been preparing the midday meal. Good roast beef, fried potatoes, sauerkraut, coffee, sugar, bread, and beer were among the delicacies that the Germans had left behind.

Meanwhile the 7th Brigade marched to the junction of the Grand Tranchee de Calonne and the Mouilly–Les Eparges road where it was joined by the 10th Machine Gun Battalion on the morning of September 13. This force was retained as the V Corps reserve and did not participate in the action.

It was around this time that General Pershing wrote:

At dawn on September 12th, after four hours of violent artillery fire of preparation and accompanied by small tanks, the Infantry of the First and Fourth Corps advanced. The Infantry of the Fifth Corps commenced its advance at 0800 hours. The operation was carried out with entire precision. Just after daylight on September 13, elements of the First and Twenty-sixth Divisions made a junction near Hattonchatel and Vigneulles, 18 kilometers northeast of St. Mihiel. The rapidity with which our divisions advanced overwhelmed the enemy and all objectives were reached by the afternoon of September 13th. The enemy had apparently started to withdraw some of his troops from the tip of the salient on the eve of our attack, but had been unable to carry it through. We captured nearly 16,000 prisoners, 443 guns and large stores of materiel and supplies. The energy and swiftness with which the operation was carried out enabled us to smother opposition to such an extent that we suffered less than 7,000 casualties during the actual period of the advance.

John Luebke, B Company, 47th Infantry Regiment, 7th Brigade

St. Mihiel Offensive, Marne Salient: *On September 12, 1918, a big drive was being made by General Pershing with fifteen American Divisions. Of these, nine were in the assaulting line and six in reserve. Four French divisions were added by Marshal Foch to this force in the Mihiel sector. The objective was fixed as the line Vigneulles-Thiaucourt-Regnieville.*

During the march, we noticed the French women, children and old men at work, as the younger men had all been taken away for the war. They tilled the fields, gathered the crops, and made it possible for the men to carry on in the war. No one ever heard them complain.

When we of the Ivy Division were walking to our destination in the woods east of Haudainville, we noticed shell holes so thick that here and there they overlapped one another. The roads in many places had completely disappeared, and nothing was growing. St. Mihiel, in the plain of the Woevre, was the last salient left on the Western Front. We heard of many weird adventures of patrols roaming about at night in the wire of No Man's Land, or they were forced to lie for hours in shell holes half full of water. Many thoughts went through my head. I was thinking, "What are we getting ourselves into?"

I don't know where the gray rats came from, but they were always in our trenches. It seemed the darker the nights became, the bigger the rats looked. The soldier on night duty jumped when a rat caved in the side of the trench and ran over his shoes. They were hungry and carried off our hard tack, bully beef, our rifle grenades, mess kits and whatever was available. If we couldn't find something, the rats were blamed. I could put up with the enemy more so than with the terrible rats, but the rain was the #1 killer.

General Pershing hastened the operation because of five continual days of rain. The soldiers had to carry the ammunition up by hand with two shells on their shoulders because of the difficulty of moving guns over the muddy roads. In the dark it was impossible to see, so two men at each trench would help him. One would cry "Jump" and the other would catch him in order to keep his balance.

At 3 o'clock in the morning the great attack was being made with intensive artillery fire using both small and big guns; also long-range naval guns (75s) and French, British, and

American airplanes. We made much headway and the fighting lasted only two days as the enemy retreated very much. In their haste to escape, they left their kitchens on as the noon meal was being prepared. They certainly knew how to cook!

The American offensive had been a resounding success. The salient had been cauterized and back at the Allied HQ heads nodded in admiration because this was one of those all-too-rare occasions—when the line was secured, it exceeded the preplanned objective by roughly 5 kilometers. The success was also due in some part to the effectiveness and accuracy of the supporting artillery units. While taking up position their progress was hampered to such an extent by the muddy, almost indiscernible roads that in many cases shells had to be carried two at a time on the backs of weary artillerymen. The strain proved so great that they had to be rested after five or six journeys.

During the night of September 14/15 a section of the 59th Infantry was relieved by the French and on the following morning the rest followed suit. Consequently the 8th Brigade was withdrawn from the front line and bivouacked in the woods between Haudainville and Sommedieue. The Ivy men were congratulated on their efforts and reliably informed that their mission had been effectively accomplished beyond expectations, but celebrations would have to be delayed because another even greater and more daunting task lay ahead.

Time was now of the essence as Pershing hastily prepared plans to engage the Germans yet again. He wanted to get all the preparations completed as fast as possible before the expected fall rains turned the whole area into a rancid quagmire. What the 4th Division was about to face would overshadow their experiences at St. Mihiel and would firmly establish their rightful place in the annals of American military history.

CHAPTER 5

THE MEUSE-ARGONNE OFFENSIVE: PART ONE

The battle of the Meuse-Argonne was essentially fought in two phases. The plan for the first phase commencing on September 26 entailed the First Army advancing through most of the southern Meuse-Argonne region, capturing enemy strongpoints and seizing the first two German defense lines. The second phase would offer a different story. The Argonne is a 300-meter high forested ridge that lies between Aisne and Meuse rivers in northern France, where it extends along the plains of Champagne and to the north of the Ardennes region. For General Pershing and the AEF this was going to be their greatest battle to date and the one in which they would incur the most casualties. The Allies would employ a "limited objective" strategy that would ultimately be to their detriment.

The German high command knew that another battle was imminent but there was disparity as to precisely where the Allies would mount their next offensive. A secret order issued by German 5th Army Commander General Von Marwitz at the time stated:

> *According to information in our hands the enemy intends to attack the Fifth Army east of the Meuse in order reach Longuyon. The objective of this attack is the cutting of the railroad line Longuyon–Sedan which is the main line of communication of the Western Army. Furthermore the enemy hopes to compel us to discontinue the exploitation of the iron mines of Briey, the possession of which is a great factor in our steel production.*
>
> *The Fifth Army once again may have to bear the brunt of the fighting of the coming weeks on which the security of the Fatherland may depend. The fate of a large portion of the Western Front, perhaps of our nation, depends on the firm holding of the Verdun front.*

The Fatherland believes that every commander and every soldier realizes the greatness of his task and that everyone will fulfill his duty to the utmost. If this is done the enemy's attack will be shattered.

The Allies were equally unaware that the Germans were feeling compromised and cornered. Although the reduction of the salients had affected the German fighting spirit on the Western Front, they were now well dug in behind strong defensive lines. The presumed door to breaking these lines was firmly shut and bolted but its hinges hung on the Meuse River, east of the Argonne forest. The plan was now to push open this proverbial door by throwing forces against it all along the line and simultaneously smash it off its hinges by battering through on the Meuse-Argonne front.

Marshal Foch assigned the task of breaching these formidable German defenses to General Pershing. Pershing had requested control of this sector so that he could organize the attacks and operate autonomously, outside British and French control. The 4th Division was the only American division to serve in both the French and British sectors on the Western Front. Pershing was made well aware of the gravity of the situation by other Allied commanders who informed him that the Germans were going to rigorously attempt to hold this section with all the strength with every available means at their disposal.

Marshal Foch said to the American commander-in-chief that "The Meuse-Argonne is a hard nut to crack, and there are great obstacles to be overcome. But it is all right, your men have the devil's own punch. They will succeed despite everything. Go to it."

There was no disagreement among the Allies that along the Western Front the Meuse-Argonne was the region where German defenses were at their strongest and in the closest proximity to one another. Moreover, the AEF would also have to contend with uneven and precarious terrain, which provided a natural advantage to the defenders. To the Germans the reinforced concrete and barbed-wire fortified defensive lines in this area were known as the Hagen Stellung, the Volker Stellwag, the Kriemhilde Stellung (which constituted part of the Hindenburg line) and the Freya Stellung, which hadn't been completed at the time of the battle. All these lines traversed the Argonne heights. To the north of these positions there is a series of rolling hills adorned with a smattering of wooded areas. It was generally acknowledged that the Meuse-Argonne area would be more desperately defended than any other part of the front because if it was breached it had the potential to isolate the German armies there and prevent a general retreat to the Rhine, which would inevitable force the Germans to sue for peace or surrender.

A railroad in this vicinity was absolutely essential to the Germans and if it were severed before any retreat could be effectively organized it would inevitably lead to their collapse. During the final days of September 1918, The German High Command had gradually woken up to the fact that any feasible hope of victory was now rapidly diminishing. They were demoralized and battle weary, but they weren't finished yet.

The AEF moved up to a 35-kilometer stretch of lines in the Meuse-Argonne sector almost completely ignorant, firstly of the magnitude of the task that lay before them, and secondly of the terrain. The latter detail and the lack of sufficient reconnaissance of the area would be to their detriment in the coming battle.

For days leading up to the attack, the supply lines that stretched to the Meuse-Argonne area were a veritable hive of activity as men and munitions were laboriously brought up to the front, sometimes in pitch darkness, along every road, trail and donkey track in the area. Extended, organized columns of trucks and men sweated, cursed and weaved apprehensively along these lines to the front. It was duly noted by Allied command that the AEF performed this task with consummate skill and precision until every artillery piece and every man was in place and ready for action.

The 4th Division was allocated to the Third Army where the 33rd Division had just arrived from the Somme where they'd been fighting alongside the British. The newly arrived 80th Division, which was also with them, was as green as could be and had never fired a shot in anger. When they arrived at the front line, to the right of the 4th Division's position was the 79th Division which was part of V Corps and also untried in battle.

The general plan was for the AEF to press northward together with the French on their left toward the Mezieres–Sedan–Carignan railroad leaving the Argonne Forest itself to be sealed shut by driving troops up each flank and meeting around its northernmost extremity. The night preceding the attack, five German divisions and part of a sixth were in line directly opposite the Americans and they had been keeping a close eye on their movements. The Germans were in a high state of alert and had been able to make some preparations for the impending assault.

On September 25, the Ivy Division moved its HQ from Lemmes to two dugouts on a steep hill overlooking Montzeville, which would afford them a panoramic view of the battlefield area. The 7th Brigade was the first unit to reach the front line and was designated to launch the initial attack. The Artillery Brigade and then the 8th Brigade would follow it. On the night of September 25 the troops of the 7th Brigade marched to their positions in the trenches west of Dead Man's Hill, which had featured quite predominantly during the battles for Verdun. The 8th Brigade similarly took up initial positions in reserve in the trenches north and west of Vigneville.

Within the sector that the 4th Division eventually occupied there was only one road leading up to the front. It ran from Montzeville to Esnes, and along this all the troops had to pass. The night before the drive commenced was dark and murky. The scarcity of roads and the density of the transport, together with the unfamiliar surroundings, contributed to making travel a problem that required a lot of patience and skill to compromise before the men could reach the selected positions ahead of zero hour. Before the preliminary barrage commenced, literally miles of convoys, ammunition trains, guns and troops competed with one another in their anxiety to reach their destination. The night air resounded to the sound of boots on the march, equipment rattling along to the exasperated shouts of officers and non-commissioned officers attempting to keep the lines flowing. As the Ivy men trudged along through the inky darkness the predatory hum of biplane engines overhead and the trail of tracer bullets reminded them that the Germans were keeping a close eye on the situation.

Eventually the 7th Brigade settled into their positions with two regiments lined up side by side. At 0230 hours on the morning of September 26, the ground suddenly began to shake and tremble to the thunderous, angry roar of artillery shells whizzing over the heads of the anxious Ivy men as they stood or sat with eyes raised aloft. By 0530 hours the shells were raking No Man's Land in an attempt to smash the lines of barbed wire and machine-gun nests along the German defenses. 4th Division officers stood beside their trench ladders and studied the hands of their watches before giving the order to "Fix bayonets."

The area that lay before them was shrouded in dense mist, which made it impossible to see more than 50 feet ahead. The leading elements of the 47th and 39th Regiments were lined up on taped lines that had been placed during the night by the engineers. They had cut wide lanes through the barbed-wire entanglements in front of the American lines. Detachments of engineers equipped with heavy wire cutters also preceded the infantry to cut the German wire that remained intact. At the appointed hour the men advanced. An engineer officer or sergeant who carried a compass with an illuminated dial accompanied each front-line company commander.

As they scrambled out of the deep trenches, the 10th Machine Gun Battalion and two companies of the 11th Machine Gun Battalion added to the roar of battle by enfilading the enemy front line. This kept the Germans low and prevented them returning fire until the creeping artillery barrage reached them. The fog proved quite fortuitous to the advancing Ivy men by providing excellent cover but it did cause some difficulties in maintaining liaison. As they approached the German positions 4th Division engineers were called on to place ladders over the swampy terrain. As the advancing troops ascended a hill in front of the German trenches they discovered that these positions had been mangled and blown to smithereens by the violent and consecutive artillery barrages.

The men of the 39th and 47th Infantry dove in to what remained of the trenches and began impatiently searching for the occupants. Within moments German soldiers began timidly emerging from their dugouts ready and willing to surrender and spend the rest of the war in captivity. A solitary American soldier was sufficient to accompany them back to the MPs who promptly marched them away. Up until that juncture the fog had obscured all noticeable landmarks and it wasn't until the fog dissolved some time later that the troops realized that they had passed right through the Volker Stellung. Further along the German line things had not gone as smoothly. The 39th's 1st Battalion incurred heavy losses as machine guns poured withering fire into their lines. It was around 1500 hours that they extricated themselves from this situation.

To the left of the 4th Division, V Corps hadn't reached their targets but regardless of this the 4th were instructed to press home the advantage and continue advancing. Without artillery support, in approaching darkness, and in the face of increased German defense they quickly ground to a shuddering halt approximately along the line of the corps objective. The problem the Ivy men now encountered was symptomatic of many previous attacks on the Western Front. They had paused too long after reaching their initial targets, which had given the Germans ample time to reorganize and orchestrate a more concerted defense of their positions.

At 0845 hours that same morning, the 8th Brigade had been moved from the reserve trenches to the front-line trenches on Hill 304, and instructed to hold that position in case of a determined German counterattack. At 1600 hours they were moved forward again to occupy the German intermediate positions south of the town of Cuisy. It was there that they endured a horrendous night of continuous shelling. As daylight crept onto the horizon squally rain began falling and drenching the troops to the skin. The trenches they now occupied were so cramped and uncomfortable that the men abandoned them, preferring to take their chances out in the open despite the inclement weather and German artillery. The Germans may have been reeling from the shock of the initial onslaught but they were far from beaten. The following days would reveal how determined they could still be despite the overwhelming advantage the Allies now had in manpower and machinery. Despite the initial successes against somewhat demoralized adversaries, different tactics would now be employed but the results would be less than satisfactory.

The commander-in-chief of the Allied forces later admitted the effectiveness of the limited objective strategy in open warfare against a traumatized enemy was a fallacy. On October 26 Marshal Foch sent General Pershing the following memorandum and requested that it be transmitted to the units under his orders:

Operation plans of the 4th French Army as well as those of the 1st American Army, prescribe for those armies a method of attack by limited objectives. Such a plan, which was very much used during the war of position, can still be useful in certain special cases, when only a restricted result is contemplated for the time being. It is not possible of general application, for the reason that it can produce only limited results. By limiting in advance the progress of the troops to lines traced on a map, and consequently by preventing these troops from taking advantage of the opportunities which always present themselves after a successful start, the high command by its restrictive orders compromises the final result— and renders it in every case more costly. Important results such as we are striving for in the present period of the war and the presence of an enemy whose strength is decreasing daily, are to be hoped for only by a progress as rapid and deep as possible. Troops thrown into the attack have only to know their direction of attack, in this direction they go as far as they can without any thought of alignment, attacking and maneuvering the enemy who resists, the most advanced units working to help those who are momentarily stopped. In this manner they operate, not toward lines indicated ahead of time according to the terrain, but against the enemy, with whom they never lose contact once they have gained it.

Under ominous deep blue grey skies and drenched by bucketing rain, elements of the 4th Division assumed their positions and prepared to venture out yet again. Concerted German resistance on the second day of the drive demanded that the front-line troops should be continuously resupplied with fresh food and ammunition. The weather conditions deteriorated hourly as rain continued to fall with no signs of abating. The men were soaked to the skin and miserable, and the roads used for the supply lines had been reduced once more to an almost impassable state. Artillery units struggled to keep pace with the infantry during those two days but eventually they managed to get their pieces in place to support the imminent assault.

The attack was resumed at 0700 hours on the morning of September 28, this time with complete artillery support. The 47th Infantry struggled through the dense undergrowth of a copse that was in their path and dispatched German machine guns in rapid succession before reaching a line close to the northern edge of these woods. It was around this location that they discovered a German ordnance storehouse that contained considerable quantities of rifles, grenades, ammunition and machine. Meanwhile the 39th Infantry progressed behind a creeping barrage toward the southeastern corner of a small wood known to the French as the Bois des Ogons.

As they came into proximity of these woods they received a withering enfilade of machine-gun bullets augmented by artillery fire emanating from the north and from east of the Meuse River. It would have been a ghastly and petrifying sight to see men literally evaporating where they stood as heads, limbs and torsos flew in all directions spattering the area with blood and fragmented flesh.

The 39th continued to press forward into the southern edge of the Bois des Ogons where it was held up again at around 1400 hours by heavy machine-gun fire from the woods in front and the clumps of trees to their immediate left. Despite harassing, hostile fire, the regiment dug in on the crest one half kilometer south of the Bois des Ogons and northern edge of the woods.

During the next four days the Ivy men faced strong resistance and very little progress was made. The Germans were so well dug in that the only means of making any progress at all was by laying down suppressing machine-gun fire and painstakingly edging forward foot by foot. The woods and heights in the vicinity were well occupied and proving difficult to clear. The Ivy men had to slog it out, dig in and wait until the artillery ammunition could be brought up to the front in preparation for another push forward.

The inclement conditions at this time put a terrible strain on the men. They had no possibility of eating warm food and were terribly exposed to the enemy and the miserable weather. During the day they were constantly targeted by machine-gun and rifle fire and at night German shells landed with alarming frequency among them. Despite all this adversity they maintained constant reconnaissance of the area to acquire a greater knowledge of the immediate terrain and to check the disposition and movements of the enemy. On October 3 the line remained static. The first phase of the battle had ended. The increasing resistance of the Germans had slowed down the advance and the congestion of the roads leading up to the front lines had forced a halt.

Full preparations were now made for a successive attack. The AEF had discovered that pushing back the Germans was more difficult than they had previously assumed and they had not progressed as rapidly as expected. Nonetheless many almost insurmountable difficulties had been compromised and they were still a force to be reckoned with. The Allies had driven the Germans back to their reserve defenses and were now facing the Hindenburg Line. The condition of the roads gave cause for anxiety but morale was still high and vigorous preparations for the second phase of the battle were under way.

On September 28, in his "Field Order No. 27," General Pershing issued the following instructions:

> The 3rd, 5th and 1st Corps will advance within their zones of action as specified in "Field Orders Nr. 20" without regard to objectives.

The reason that the advance ground to a halt after September 28 in front of the German main position was largely due to three factors. Firstly, enemy resistance, which had gradually solidified as the offensive had attempted to move forward. Secondly, the lack of training and inexperience of many AEF divisions exacerbated their failure to exploit obvious advantages. The third and most significant factor was the poor coordination that led to insufficient supplies of artillery and infantry ammunition being delivered in order to execute further advances. This lack of ammunition was the direct result of the conditions on the sole operative road in the Division's sector.

The road from Esnes to Malancourt, which carried all the traffic of the 4th Division, was partially constructed by the 4th Engineers including a further section that stretched as far as a fork in the road. The problem was that this also carried all the traffic of the 79th Division and later the 3rd Division. The congestion on this road was pitiful. From 1300 hours onward on September 26 the road remained completely congested for a full 24 hours preventing the effective delivery of necessary supplies to the front line.

It was now generally accepted at Allied HQ that the Germans were determined to make a fight of it and despite being outmanned and outgunned they were not considering surrender. The fight would go on.

CHAPTER 6

THE MEUSE-ARGONNE OFFENSIVE: PART TWO

One of the most serious problems encountered during those first few days of the offensive concerned the evacuation and hospitalization of the wounded. There can be no question that, on the first two days of the battle, the road congestion prevented prompt evacuation and unnecessary deaths occurred in the ambulances due to lack of adequate medical attention. In an attempt to remedy the situation on September 27 two field hospitals were established at Cuisy not far behind the front line. This position was in close proximity to heavy Allied artillery units, which meant the area was a target for German artillery, which wasn't necessarily conducive to the recuperation of war wounded but at least they could be tended. Seriously wounded would be operated on immediately rather than having to wait for days for a suitable transport to remove them to other field hospitals.

On September 30, the 3rd Division relieved the 79th Division that had been fighting on the left of the 4th. A few days later both of these divisions were withdrawn from the front line and the 33rd Division occupied the area. Their respite was short lived because on October 4 circumstances demanded that both divisions had to be brought back up to the front and added to III Corps. As preparations for a new offensive got under way they were now once again on the left of the 4th Division. The day before, enough material had been accumulated behind the lines to facilitate a general advance. Meanwhile a gargantuan effort had been undertaken by the whole First Army to overcome supply issues.

The Ivy Men were allocated the task of attacking and holding the northern edge of the Bois de Brieulles. They were then to push on through and turn east towards the Meuse River. They were specifically instructed to stick to the woods in the area and avoid open ground at all costs. The reason for this was that maneuvering in open terrain would make them potentially vulnerable to German artillery and machine guns. They would in effect become an easy target. Nevertheless, if they could execute this assault correctly there was a strong chance that they could constrain the evacuation of German troops and effectively annihilate their lines.

With the aim of protecting the right flank of the 4th Division, the 33rd Division would hold the line of the Meuse and the northern edge as far as Hill 280. In accordance with divisional instructions the infantry attack was launched in conjunction with a preceding artillery barrage. The 10th Machine Gun Battalion and Companies A and D of the 12th Machine Gun Battalion laid down a machine-gun barrage on the southern edge of the Bois de Pays. The heavy French artillery placed destructive fire upon the Bois de Fays and upon all known enemy artillery positions within the Division sector.

At 0525 hours on the morning of October 4, the 58th Infantry and Companies B and C of the 11th Machine Gun Battalion left their dugouts along the northwestern edge of the Bois de Brieulles and proceeded across the open ground in the direction of the southern edge of the Bois de Pays. Initially the dense morning mist veiled the advance as a creeping barrage kept the heads of the enemy low. Gradually the mist lifted to reveal the full extent of the advance then suddenly the very ground beneath the advancing troops appeared to shatter as a hail of shells and machine-gun bullets homed in from the Meuse on the right, from the Bois des Ogons on the left and from every other conceivable angle.

As bullets and shrapnel flew in all directions a noxious vapor crept menacingly across No Man's Land and settled to the ground like a swamp mist. Mustard gas was a particularly deadly and debilitating poison that was used in some form or another on many occasions by both sides in the Great War. When the Germans first used it in 1917, there was no defense against it because it had the potential to penetrate all the masks and protective materials that were available at that time. It was one of the most lethal of all the poisonous chemicals used during the war. Almost odorless it could take up to 12 hours to take effect. Detoxification procedures to reduce the effects of mustard gas were difficult to instigate because of its insolubility and also because of the drastic effects it had on the respiratory system following inhalation. During World War I, physicians had no real remedial means of treating the victims of mustard gas exposure. The only method of detoxification involved a rather extreme oxidation procedure that was by no means a guaranteed cure.

If the situation wasn't deadly enough now the Ivy men had to fight wearing their cumbersome gas masks. It was becoming worryingly apparent that the Germans had used the short hiatus between the first and second phases of the battle to reinforce and reorganize their defenses. Allied commanders now concurred that it was going to be a bitter and costly struggle to regain the impetus needed to complete the offensive.

Despite fierce and sustained opposition, the 58th Infantry advanced into the Bois de Fays and managed to gain a foothold on the southern edge, and there they remained stoic and intransigent, despite being hammered by all the artillery that the Germans could bring to bear on that position. Shells rained down with such regularity that some of the Ivy Men were asking officers if their own artillery was firing short of the target. These questions would remain ominously unanswered for the time being. Never before had the 4th been subjected to such a pummeling. The Germans maintained a tenacious grip on the situation and did everything they could to hold back the 58th Infantry Regiment at the Bois des Ogons, which owing to its strategic value the enemy was stoutly defending with all its strength.

Even though they were stunned and occasionally disorientated by a determined opposition the Ivy Men advanced and managed to infiltrate the Bois de Fays along with capturing a further objective. The Germans had cleverly concealed their machine-gun nests and were pouring destructive fire into the advancing Americans. Their only option was to press forward and seek out the machine gunners. Gradually they managed to out-maneuver their positions and force the Germans to surrender but the fighting was far from over. What now ensued would be a real endurance test.

James Platt, C Company, 12th Machine Gun Battalion, 8th Brigade

No rations were available, except our emergency ones, canned corned beef and hard biscuits. Of course everyone wanted coffee. Our Top Sergeant Virgin was especially loud about his coffee. He said we could go along without food if we had coffee and that the next morning if none came up, he was going to personally go back and haze up our rear echelon to get some for us. He did too, for he was gone before the men got up that morning. He said we were not going far the next day, how true that statement was.

There being no coffee, everyone was thirsty and the water canteens were empty. There was a spring of good water just a short way back in the woods, but the Captain would not allow anyone to go to it until after dark, as the Germans were watching that spring in hope some soldier would be tempted to go for water. They had already shot some of the men from our infantry.

There were numerous shell craters where we stopped. I imagine from our own guns, so for shelter this night, all hands crawled into a shell hole. About four men could lie half in and half out of one hole. No one bothered about unrolling packs. In fact not many of us had anything in our packs. As I have said before, that was one thing that I had learned, get rid of all the unnecessary items. The machine gun and ammunition was weighty enough without any packs to carry.

Even if I knew that Germans might be all around, I slept soundly. At daybreak a number of shells fell in our vicinity. Company D was on our right. They had come in and made themselves as comfortable as conditions would allow, after Headquarters had done so. They were scattered about in shell holes as we were. However, they seemed to receive more shells than we did. Very foolishly, most of their officers slept in or near one hole and a shell fell into that hole killing or wounding four of their officers.

I was hungry, and started to eat some of my iron rations, standing up to do so. I should have known better, for when someone called, "See the German army is in behind us," I should have dropped to the ground. Remember that the woods had underbrush about shoulder high all around our little clearing, so the German army did infiltrate around us. Sure enough, there was a row of coal shuttle German helmets moving above the brush, moving at a trot, as they were bobbing up and down. I couldn't see the faces. The helmets were about 10 feet away. Not thinking, but on impulse, I drew a revolver and still standing, commenced to fire at the helmets, aiming not just underneath, but right at any head I could see. What I should have done, was to throw myself on the ground, but no, I had "buck fever" and just like the fellow who sees a deer for the first time, just aimed and pulled the trigger as fast as I could. I was not alone in firing, for the rest of men were doing the same, but not standing up.

I shall never know if I hit any of the Germans, for suddenly my revolver would not fire, all the shells had been fired off. I started to put in a new clip when something hit me with a blow like a sledge hammer in the left shoulder. It was such a blow that it hurled around and dropped me to the ground. There was no pain, but when I tried to lift myself up I found there was no help from my left arm. It just flopped around.

The 58th filtered into an exposed area they had been instructed to avoid and were decimated. Their numbers dwindled in seconds and they were forced to order a bitter retreat, falling back about half a kilometer to occupy three sides of a wooded area, which formed a kind of salient. Almost as soon as they had occupied this peculiar position around 400 Germans attacked it.

Undaunted the Ivy men hastily retracted the bolts on their Springfield rifles, aimed and prepared their machine guns, and then waited. They waited in hushed, expectant silence and allowed the Germans to advance to within 200 meters of their position before the order to "open fire" resonated along the ranks. Immediately they discharged their weapons and unleashed a crushing volley of lead that stopped the Germans in their tracks. The air was suddenly rendered by the nightmarish screams of men falling dead and wounded as jets of blood spouted and the ground became lathered in brains and stomachs. Then all fell silent save the desperate moans of the few survivors who crawled or slid away.

During the night of October 3 the 59th Infantry Regiment were taken out of the line and replaced by the 1st and 3rd Battalions of the 47th Infantry, reinforced by the 37mm guns and Stokes mortars of the regiment, two companies of the 11th Machine Gun Battalion and two guns from the 16th Field Artillery. This force was given the commission to hold the woods, repel counterattacks and neutralize the fire from a strong enemy position about roughly 4 kilometers southwest of Bois de Brieulles.

After being taken out of the line the 59th Infantry had been allocated as a reserve for the 8th Brigade who occupied the southwest part of the Bois de Brieulles. While two battalions remained south of Bois de Fays, near the western edge of the Bois de Brieulles the other one was sent into the Bois de Fays to assist the decimated 58th Infantry. The 4th Division line now extended from Hill 280 along the northern edge of the Bois de Brieulles, along the eastern edge of the Bois de Fays, to where it joined the right of the 80th Division.

Throughout the day the 80th Division had also contended with fierce resistance from the Bois de Ogons and like the 4th they had suffered from German artillery fire from east of the Meuse. A German letter dated October 6 gives an informative insight into the tenacity of the men of the 4th Division:

Army Group of von Gallwitz

> Between the Argonne and the Meuse the Americans continued their powerful attacks. E. of Exermont they succeeded in pushing forward to the top of the wooded heights about a kilometer N. of this place, but gained nothing further by their renewed attacks in the afternoon. On both sides of the road from Charpentry to Romagne their attacks were once more completely shattered against the line of Westphalian and Alsatian-Lorrainian regiments. Further east the enemy penetrated into the du Fays wood, but was everywhere else repulsed.

All infantry and machine-gun units in the Bois de Fays were beginning to feel the tremendous strain of continual enemy bombardment as they attempted to shelter in what cover they could find. Among the tree stumps and undergrowth they had excavated a precarious line of foxholes that were far from adequate. Incessant rain and dampness only served to exacerbate an already miserable situation. Nevertheless they were determined to hold the salient.

Lighting fires was strictly prohibited and even the glow of a cigarette could tempt a lethal sniper's bullet. Those in the trenches were advised to "Never take the third light from a match." Noxious gas seeped through the woods and welled into bomb craters and dugouts, mingling with the putrid stench of decaying human cadavers. Holding this position demanded all the resilience and tenacity that they could marshal. Quiet heroism had never been in greater demand. When dark came no one attempted to sleep because the night was punctuated by small groups of German soldiers attempting to infiltrate the line and cause even further anxiety to the Ivy men. This demanded more vigilance and resolution than anything that they had endured up that point, this was hell like they'd never experienced. Even though minds were dulled by sleep-lessness and the threat of imminent attack they held on. On October 6 the 58th Infantry Regiment and one battalion of the 59th Infantry Regiment were pulled out of the woods at Bois Fays and taken to a rest area near Cuisy.

While the remaining units of the 8th Brigade were withdrawn from the Bois de Fays to rest, other units of the 4th Division now prepared for action. The 7th Brigade, reinforced by one battalion of the 59th Infantry and one battalion and the machine gun company of 132nd Infantry, 33rd Division were designated to organize the next attack. The 4th Division's 47th Infantry was directed to hold the northern edge of the Bois de Brieulles along with Hill 280 as far the divisional sector extended to include everything between the western boundary and the Meuse River.

The 39th Infantry would lead the assault. The battalions of each regiment were subsequently arranged in three lines, the 3rd Battalion on point with the 2nd Battalion in support and the 1st in reserve. Each battalion was suitably furnished with a machine gun company but the preparations, as always, lacked any innovative plans. Orders were issued to the effect that other attached units of the brigade would remain in the Bois de Fays. Zero hour would depend entirely on the progress of V Corps. At 1030 hours the 3rd Battalion, 39th Infantry settled down in foxholes, south of the Fond de Ville aux Bois, to await the signal to advance.

By this time the Bois de Fays and surrounding area had become a veritable death trap. Some confusion arose at 4th Division HQ when they registered the fact that the 80th Division, who were near the north-ern edge of the Bois des Ogons, which is west of the southern edge of the Bois de Fays, was going to advance behind a creeping barrage. Consequently they would not be expected to reach the 4th Division positions for well over one hour and forty minutes. Precise timing would be essential to the success of the advance. If the 39th left their positions too soon they could become prone to friendly artillery fire, too late and they would expose their flank. Nervous hours passed as the 4th waited to receive the go ahead. Finally at 1500 hours a coded message was received informing the waiting Division that H-Hour would be 1530 hours.

The information was promptly transmitted. The 3rd Battalion, already demoralized after being ravaged by German artillery shells, would move out at 1700 hours. The Germans were well aware of the plan on this occasion. They knew precisely where the 4th Division was and that the 80th Division was advancing. At 1640 hours rolling funnels of smoke and a dark orange glow on the skyline announced that a colossal concentration of German artillery fire was being landed on the northern half of the Bois de Fays, most of the shells were filled with mustard gas.

Much of the artillery fire emanated from east of the River Meuse, which made the 4th Division think that they were indeed being fired on by their own cannons. This began to severely affect their morale. Men scattered in all directions and the officers had to work to gather them back together to re-form for the impending attack. As the light began to fade the men advanced through thick undergrowth wearing gas masks. Then, as German machine guns opened up and spat death the front ranks fell, but the rest pushed on stumbling over the bodies of their comrades as they struggled to negotiate barbed wire and shell holes. Progress was labored and staggered but they pressed on until suddenly the word was passed around to halt the advance and retreat. All the commanding officers were compelled to concede that the attack had been a miserable and costly failure. Regardless of the tactical blunders that had transpired, the attack was resumed at 0700 hours the very next morning. The 2nd and 1st Battalions of the 39th had been surreptitiously moved into the Bois de Fays after midnight under cover of darkness.

Now that the 1st Battalion had been almost put out of commission, the 2nd Battalion was handed the baton and placed in the front line with the 1st Battalion in support. The 3rd Battalion, augmented by two companies from the 132nd Infantry, was placed in reserve. Advancing behind a preliminary barrage and regardless of a repetition of the massed artillery, machine gun, and trench mortar resistance they had witnessed only one day previous, the 2nd Battalion crossed the Bois de Malaumont.

As they progressed their flanks came up against heavy machine-gun fire. Combined with accurate rifle fire pouring into the front ranks the line began to disintegrate and fall back to the Bois de Malaumont to regroup. Supporting artillery fire was requested and promptly provided as the battalion got to their feet and advanced again only to face a terrifying repetition of the previous day's activities. The lines were now thinning out dramatically because all the officers and sergeants had been either killed or wounded and a corporal was commanding one company. The gallantry and courage of these men was unquestionable but the methods employed and the military planning left much to be desired. Once again lack of imagination and attention to tactical detail was negligible to the point of shambolic.

On the morning of October 12 a further company from the 132nd Infantry, 33rd Division, was dispatched to the front line to reinforce the left flank of the 2nd Battalion, 39th Infantry. A patrol of 15 men from this company crawled across the open ground where they reached a small copse about 200 yards south of the top of Hill 299 and remained there in observation for the entire day. Sometime around 1230 hours prolonged and heavy artillery fire rained down on the heads of men in the front line, which was being held by the 2nd and 1st Battalions of the 39th and the 132nd Regiment. This bombardment caused terrible casualties among the ranks and inflicted such severe damage that 200 men were either killed or wounded.

It was later discovered that some of the artillery fire that they had endured was indeed the result of friendly fire. This had been previously suspected but never confirmed. Although various complaints were lodged no investigation was undertaken and no conclusions were ever drawn. The only indisputable fact was that the shelling didn't come from 4th Division artillery.

Under normal circumstances, troops were subjected to a 12-day rotation system. Their time would be divided equally between three lines, the front line, the support line, and the reserve line. They would then have short rest period before resuming the cycle. Time spent in each section varied from sector to sector. During a sustained offensive the soldiers would spend far longer in the front line than prescribed and less time than usual at rest. The Ivy men withstood 17 days at constant risk of being killed, maimed or incapacitated by bullets, high-explosive shells and gas, during which time they were the target of sustained machine-gun and sniper fire. This was enough to test any man's courage and stamina. Momentary respites from the fighting were not enough to combat the sleeplessness, cold and almost constant rain, and consequently many were on the verge of total collapse from exhaustion.

The mere notion that some of the shells that had blasted their positions were from American artillery was devastating to the morale of these battle-weary troops. To be shelled by American artillery was beyond the pale for many of them. The remaining officers gave the order to fall back until the artillery fire had ceased but this was only a temporary measure because they were soon back in their hard-fought positions on the edge of the woods. This was a testament to the fighting spirit and resolve of the Ivy men.

Due to some miscommunication, an attack planned for October 12 failed to materialize. It had been agreed at HQ that a support battalion, formed from the 47th Infantry and the 132nd Infantry Regiment, would attack toward Bois de Fort under the protection of a barrage. This was mainly intended as a mopping-up operation to remove any remaining Germans from those woods. The barrage went in but for some unfathomable reason the infantry remained static. This was the result of incoherent orders and general mismanagement of the situation and by no means the fault of the troops who were prepped and ready to go at the blow of a whistle. No further attacks were ordered for that day. It was agreed that the 5th Division would replace the 4th in the front line. Then in typical World War I style this order was almost immediately retracted by III Corps, who insisted on preliminary reconnaissance being conducted before the Ivy men could be taken out of the line.

They had performed admirably under the circumstances. They had secured and consolidated their position and were awaiting further orders. Ahead of them lay Hill 299 and this would be the most northerly point that they would reach during the ferocious battles of the Meuse Argonne.

John Luebke, B Company, 47th Infantry Regiment, 7th Brigade

Meuse-Argonne Offensive, Argonne Forest: *Training had to be done before going into the Meuse-Argonne because the defensive lines were stronger and closer together here than anywhere else on the front. We of the Ivy Division, were sent to the III Army Corps, and special training in liaison was established. Division Headquarters was quartered at Lemmes.*

All of a sudden we got orders at 11 o'clock at night to move to Verdun Hill 378, and we arrived there at 7 o'clock in the morning. We had made good headway, and a small batch of prisoners was passing by us to the rear. The march took 11 miles in seven and one-half hours and most of the time in the rain. The night was very dark, and this made the going difficult. We were staying in a wooded area supporting the front lines. I was pretty well pooped out from walking all night and stayed in that wooded area. I walked around to find the best place to rest and to be at ease for a few days. The rest was well needed, and we ate food like hard tack, bully beef and water. I don't know how everything became quiet. It seemed like the war was over, but I knew better.

All at once we moved, but we did not know where. Walking along at ease, I could see during the daytime that the ground was war-torn. Towards evening we stopped and got a supply of field rations and rested a little. When darkness approached we were on our way to the front-line trenches, northeast of Verdun Hill 304. Here the ground was really disturbed with trenches and big shell holes. I could hardly see a place where the ground had not been moved.

The French and Americans knew a large attack was going to be made on September 26, 1918, on the Meuse-Argonne front. The 7th Brigade was marching to their positions, where were located in the trenches north of and around Hill 304, north of Esnes, and west of Dead Man's Hill.

Miles of the camion moved in utmost secrecy in the dark. All night long we struggled along the road from Montzeville to Esnes. Swear words and cries of warning were heard from the officers to stay on the road. The mule drivers thought the world of their animals and treated them in a charming way. They talked to them gently, mostly in French. We gained 11 kilometers before night to Hill 304. We arrived at the front on September 24, 1918. Behind us in the far distance was the citadel of Verdun.

Our Generals arrived on time, and were so tired they slept in the drizzling rain. We men got so extremely tired that we just collapsed anywhere at any time, despite the noise of war.

We got into the trenches and everything seemed on the quiet side. We had one more day to stay here, hoping that everything would go as planned. We lay for hours in trenches half full of water. Our time was set at 5:30 in the morning to jump out of the trenches. I could hear the artillery gun firing a long time before, at least for an hour or more. When 5:30 came, we jumped out of the trenches. We noticed the ground was muddy from the rain, and the weather was very foggy and dark. I didn't know if that was good or not. We of the

47th were advancing across "No Man's Land." We couldn't see more than 50 feet ahead, because the entire valley was filled with a thick mist. The fog had swallowed all landmarks. We were walking along at a very slow pace with the artillery firing over us more than ever before. Gas shelling was so frequent in this territory that we had to fight in gas masks. The way it seemed to me, the enemy's army had grown stronger in strength. During the summer months they met with no resistance all day, because they were firing those guns.

The enemy kept on going until those guns could not shoot over us anymore. During the last 2 miles without our artillery support, we reached our objective by mid-afternoon and came to a halt in a wooded area where we stayed for the night. Our Division Headquarters moved to Cuisy.

The next morning at 5:30 came an instruction to move forward without that artillery support. This will be suicide I thought, and my mind was minimal. The artillery could not move up so fast in that muddy ground, so no progress was made that day. Everything quieted down for the night.

On the 28th day of September, the attack was certain to resume without that artillery support. We were in the woods with a lot of tangled brush filled with wire. Now the Germans were active with machine guns. We never knew what was going to happen next. Two days went by with not many results, but we suffered some losses.

On the night of September 30th we got back in the reserve which was a lot easier, but we had to be on the lookout at all times, being under shell fire all the while. We were not very strong without that artillery support, and our field rations were very low. The men's minds were getting somewhat disturbed from the high command asking us to go forward without that artillery support. A day went by, and we just kept in place and rested as much as we could. In the morning when the supplies came, I could hear the firing of artillery guns. It must have been difficult to move the artillery and supplies up in the dark in that muddy ground.

After a few days staying there to catch up on rest, we were called back to the front lines, relieving the 39th Infantry in our own Fourth Division. We found much resistance from the German, but we had good artillery support and a good supply of field rations. This improved the morale of our men who were still in the woods in all that underbrush.

The fighting in the forests of Bois de Fays and Bois de Brieulles was a battle of horror for us in the Ivy Division. We found out later that the German units in front of us were the 236th Division, Fifth Pioneer Storm Battalion, the Fifth Bavarian Reserve Division, together with a sprinkling of other units. Gas, artillery shells and machine-gun bullets had rained on us, and also rockets were fired. Machine guns were fired on us from different directions. In the tangled underbrush we were trying to hear our officer's voice. I couldn't see much through the goggles of my gas mask during the daytime, and at night it was unbearable. I had one last hope that God would get me though this living hell. The bitterest battle in the Argonne in World War I took place in this area.

We could not see what was going on and at the same time kept low for protection. Every so often a German shell fell among us, and the losses became heavy. As time went on, we were making no headway as the resistance was too much. We just stayed in place and let the artillery fire. They sure did! We spent two days there. Smoke and gas reeked though the woods and airplanes bombed us at frequent times. The smell of dead bodies was unbearable. We went back somewhat, stumbling over bodies trying not to look at them for fear we would know someone. Then the 39th Infantry relieved us.

I saw some of our men, who could not take the pressure anymore, climbing the trees shouting, "Oh God, take me." They were shot down by enemy fire. This was certainly "Worse than battle. It was hell!" I held myself together, but I didn't know how I did it. Words can't describe how I felt—more than horrified. God and my German heritage must be keeping me alive. The infantry units were always relieving one another which helped a lot.

On October 4, 1918, a change came, and things were letting up. We were staying here just like always, but our field rations were running low. When evening came, we withdrew some distance and received a new supply of field rations. We were walking some distance and stayed there for the night, getting a good rest. Another day went by, and then came orders that another attack was going to be made on the 9th day of October.

That evening we started to walk, getting in place before midnight. Our time was set to move forward at 5 o'clock the next morning. I could hear the artillery firing long before that time. The enemy was smart enough to leave a town unoccupied during the daytime but defended it strongly at night. We did some advancing that day but met with too much machine-gun fire. Our casualties became heavy as some got in the wrong place at the wrong time. The fighting carried on for three days until the 12th day of October, and it sure got on my nerves, looking for a safe place when there wasn't any. Besides, the supplies were running low. Enemy aviators dropped twice as many bombs and were more active.

We were shelled by our own artillery. This was almost too much to handle. A heavy artillery barrage was dropped on the front line which caused many losses. According to the officers and men in the line that suffered, this artillery fire came from their left rear. There is no other explanation than the shells were fired by the artillery of another division. The firing was suspended for all of our divisional guns for a definite period.

The whole 47th Regiment was pretty well beaten up with dead, wounded, and missing men. This was 26 days of hard fighting in the cold and wet weather. The German line was still not broken in the Argonne. From then on for some days our regiment marched by night and rested and policed by day. We wore raincoats, which made it harder than ever. The weather was as bad as can possibly be imagined. It rained almost continually for day, and even in the densest woods the soil was changed to a think, sticky mud. Every shell hole was filled with water. When it came to the Ivy Division, the weather was certainly against us. The patrols that went out at night could hear the enemy talking German across the river.

At this time the advance stopped. The attack failed, and the fighting had been a hopeless cause. The losses here heavy and the lines were getting thin. Some companies were commanded by corporals, because every officer and sergeant were killed or wounded.

Now it took some time to walk a distance before finding a rest area because of the war-torn area. On the way, we walked to the towns of Bois de Septsarges and Nantillois and saw the losses in animals as they lay dead everywhere. Water carts lay scattered about the towns with their horses dead in harness. The poor horses even had to go through the fighting, and I shuddered to look at them.

This was 26 days of heavy combat duty. We were in need of a long rest and good food, but we all know that was impossible. Everybody wanted it to be over before winter. We finally were within sight of our goal at Sedan, France. The goal of the Fifth German Army led by General von Marwitz depended on the firm holding of the Verdun front.

The Battle of the Meuse-Argonne in which General Pershing had engaged 631,000 American troops and suffered 119,000 casualties was over. It had lasted 47 days, penetrated the enemy lines to a depth of 55 kilometers, liberated 150 towns and villages for France and freed 1,650 square kilometers of territory.

The Fourth Division was withdrawn from the battle line on October 18, 1918 at midnight. We soldiers left the front at night and hiked five days until October 23rd.

We were told that we men of the Ivy Division fought with wonderful courage and devotion to duty. Our casualties had been heavy; this, a total loss in strength was 7,459 officers and men in the Ivy Division alone. The Division had traveled to a depth of over 8 miles over hills and though woods, capturing 2,731 prisoners, and taking 57 pieces of artillery, four minenwerfer, 228 machine guns, two tanks, and a vast quantity of ammunition of all types. Above all, the Ivy Division had remained in action for 26 days here in the Meuse-Argonne. Nine enemy divisions were against the Ivy men, one of them being the famous 28th Prussian Division.

During the night of October 19, after an all-too-brief respite, all units of the 4th Division were marched south to take up position in the vicinity of the Forêt de Hesse. These young men were now veterans, survivors who had entered the fray as green recruits and were ending as tried and tested warriors. Their fighting spirit and dogged determination had inspired all other divisions in their proximity and earned them the undying respect of all the other Allied armies.

The battle of the Argonne, or Meuse-Argonne offensive, that had started September 26 was a notable American victory achieved primarily by an overwhelming commitment of manpower. Nevertheless coordination between infantry and artillery was frequently inadequate and this problem was compounded by insufficient intelligence. Consequently some AEF attacks degenerated into bloodbaths and on some occasions the men advanced shoulder to shoulder in waves like so many before them and paid the ultimate price. Prior training proved to be both inadequate and inappropriate to the actual battlefield conditions they encountered. A glaring lack of coherent orders and innovative tactics were equally devastating to the men in the trenches and dugouts along the Western Front. Desertions reached such a serious level at one point that in a confidential letter to a division commander Pershing wrote, "Officers have to take all measures necessary, including the shooting of deserters, to put an end to that situation."

During the Meuse-Argonne offensive MPs arrested between 15 and 20 deserters a week. Although General Pershing had ordered officers to shoot deserters, this only happened on rare occasions. Nevertheless the AEF deployed more than 1.2 million for the Meuse-Argonne offensive and their total losses were estimated at around 120,000 men killed, wounded and prisoners, the German losses were about 100,000 men. The 4th Division had sacrificed more than their share toward this total.

Victory was now in sight for the Allies and the Ivy men had paid in full. During the fighting, although they had achieved many objectives, they had sustained some heavy losses. 45 officers and 120 men had been killed in action or had died later from their wounds, while a total of 188 officers and 6,048 men had been wounded, gassed, or noted as MIA. Two officers and 45 men had died from other causes, which added up to the loss of 7,459 officers and men and gave them approximately a 1 in 3 chance of survival. They had advanced 13 kilometers into German-held territory and taken 2,731 prisoners, 57 pieces of artillery, 228 machine guns and two tanks, along with a vast quantity of ammunition.

The most notable achievement was that the Ivy men had endured 26 consecutive days of combat against some of the best divisions the German army had to offer.

John Luebke, B Company, 47th Infantry Regiment, 7th Brigade

Honors: *General Pershing told us in many words what good soldiers we were and what this victory meant to the world. From the minute he first saw the regiment he was not slow to praise them. Finished with inspecting the Seventh Brigade where I served, General Pershing characterized it as the finest brigade he had seen in the AEF. The Fourth Division made the best showing. He complimented the Division on their magnificent appearance and thanked the officers and men for what they had done in France.*

General Pershing now began to focus on a new offensive scheduled to start on November 1. The attack commenced as scheduled and between November 1 and November 4 American troops advanced 19 kilometers, taking over 4,000 prisoners and more than 100 guns. By November 9 the front line ran roughly from Verdun to Sedan and the Germans were in full retreat. The battle of the Meuse-Argonne had lasted 47 days, penetrated the enemy lines to a depth of 55 kilometers, liberated 150 towns and villages and when the armistice was finally declared at the 11th hour of the 11th day of the 11th month in 1918, the Ivy Division had earned five battle honors. The Division's last casualties as the result of an enemy activity occurred at around 0200 hours on the day of the armistice when a heavy German shell wounded three men, and killed another outright. The victims were from the 1st Battalion 13th Field Artillery. They were also the last 4th Division regiment to fire a shot. Later that day the commander-in-chief issued the following statement:

The enemy has capitulated. It is fitting that I address myself in thanks directly to the officers and soldiers of the American Expeditionary Forces, who by their heroic efforts have made possible this glorious result. Our armies, hurriedly raised and hastily trained, met a veteran enemy and by courage, discipline, and skill always defeated him. Without complaint you have endured incessant toil, privation and danger. You have seen many of your comrades make the supreme sacrifice that freedom might live. I thank you for the patience and courage with which you have endured. I congratulate you upon the splendid fruits of victory which your heroism and the blood of our gallant dead are now presenting to our nation. Your deeds will live forever on the most glorious pages of America's history.

The war regarded as the war to end all wars was over. The Ivy then participated in the occupation of Germany. In recognition of their outstanding combat performance, General Pershing wrote to Major General Hersey was commanding the Fourth at that time:

AMERICAN EXPEDITIONARY FORCES
France, March 25th, 1919
OFFICE OF THE COMMANDER-IN-CHIEF

Major General Mark L. HERSEY, Commanding 4th Division, AEF Germany.
My Dear General HERSEY:

It was with deep gratification that I observed the excellent condition of the 4th Division on the occasion of my inspection on March 18th. On the morning of the 18th the field was covered with snow, which had partly melted at the hour set for the review, and the field was slushy and muddy. The day was cold and a strong wind in the faces of the men added to their discomfort. To make so well of an appearance under these conditions, called for a display of good will, discipline, and team work, that can come only from organizations that have been well trained and are imbued with the feeling that they have no superiors in the American Expeditionary Forces. The transportation and the artillery of the Division were in splendid shape and the general appearance of the men was equal to the highest standards. Throughout the inspection and review, the high morale existing in all ranks was evident.

Arriving in France in May, the 4th Division was first engaged in the Marne counter-offensive on July 18th as a part of the French VI Army. Detachments aided in the crossing of the Ourcq and on August 3rd/4th the Division advanced to the Vesle. In the reduction of the St. Mihiel salient, it carried its objectives with effectiveness and precision. For the opening attack of the Meuse-Argonne offensive, the 4th Division was put into the line as the center unit of the 3rd Corps and by its aggressiveness made a total advance of 13 kilometers despite continued and heavy resistance.

As a part of the 3rd Army, the Division participated in the march into Germany and the subsequent occupation of enemy territory. I am pleased to mention the excellent conduct of the men in these difficult circumstances, for which, as well as for their services in battle, they are due the gratitude of the nation.

I wish to express to each man my own appreciation of the splendid work that has been done and the assurance of my continued interest in his welfare.

Most sincerely yours,
John J. PERSHING

After successfully completing occupation duties in the Rhineland region of Germany the Ivy men returned to the United States on September 21, 1921. They were the last US division to leave Europe after World War I. The Division was inactivated at Camp Lewis, Washington in accordance with the Army Reorganization Act of 1920.

Order of Battle for the 4th (Ivy) Division in World War I

4th Division—Major General George H. Cameron, commanding; Lieutenant-Colonel Christian A. Bach, Chief of Staff; Major Jesse D. Elliott, Adjutant General.

- 7th Brigade Infantry—Brigadier General B. A. Poore
  - 39th Infantry Regiment
  - 47th Infantry Regiment
  - 11th Machine Gun Battalion

- 8th Brigade Infantry—Brigadier General E. E. Booth
  - 58th Infantry Regiment
  - 59th Infantry Regiment
  - 12th Machine Gun Battalion

- 4th Brigade Field Artillery—Brigadier General E. B. Babbitt
  - 13th Field Artillery Regiment
  - 16th Field Artillery Regiment
  - 77th Field Artillery Regiment
  - 4th Trench Mortar Battery

- Engineer Troops—8th Battalion

- Signal Troops—8th Battalion

- Division Units—4th Division Headquarters Troop; 10th Machine Gun Battalion

PART 2

WORLD WAR II

CHAPTER 7

"WE'LL START THE WAR FROM RIGHT HERE"

The 4th Division was effectively reactivated on June 1, 1940 at Fort Benning, Georgia, under the command of Major General Walter E. Prosser and sweeping changes were in the pipeline. The Division would be subject to quite drastic reorganization, transformed into a motorized division and assigned to the 1st Armored Corps. From July 11, 1941 the Ivy men would be formally recognized as the 4th Motorized Division.

The preceding 10 years had seen Europe once again descending into chaos as militaristic German expansionism threatened to engulf the whole continent in conflict for the second time in less than 40 years. The warning signs had been all too obvious as early as 1933 when Adolf Hitler was appointed chancellor of a coalition government. He made no secret of his ambitions and aspirations to expand the borders of the German Reich.

One of Hitler's primary goals was to amend the situation that had inflicted such hardship and deprivation on the German people during the Weimar republic of the 1920s and early 1930s. The last Weimar elections were held in March 1933. In spite of only receiving 44% of the national vote, with the support of nationalists and regional parties the Nazis used violence and intimidation to eliminate their opponents. Consequently, Chancellor Adolf Hitler managed to secure a legislative majority. The dictatorship moved swiftly to push the four-year "Enabling Act" permitting the government to decree laws without parliamentary approval. Social Democrats and Communist party members were quickly arrested and both parties were subsequently banned.

During the years that followed Hitler managed to annex all the territories that had been previously taken from Germany as a direct result of the inevitably flawed "Treaty of Versailles. By 1940 Japan had officially recognized the leadership of Germany and Italy in establishment of a new order in Europe by signing a document that was known as the "Three-Power Pact." The three countries agreed to co-operate and assist one another with all political, economic and available military means. December 7, 1941 all bets were off as Japan bombed Pearl Harbor and Germany declared war on America. It would soon be time to call on the Ivy men again.

Meanwhile in Washington DC it was generally acknowledged that reorganization within the US Army was long overdue. When Germany had invaded Poland in 1939 the US Army was ranked in strength only 17th in the world, marginally behind Romania. At that time there were only three effective divisions within the whole United States. It's remarkable to reflect that only six years later they would number over 6 million personnel.

Massive reorganization was imminent as the 4th Motorized Division was chosen as a prototypical unit to participate in what turned out to be a three-year-long experiment as military analysts scratched their heads and attributed due task and purpose to the Division. When the German Blitzkrieg had started in Europe, General George Patton, a vociferous advocate of mobile armor, had convinced Congress that the United States needed a more powerful armored striking force. This was effectively initiated in 1940, when Patton was transferred to the Second Armored Division at Fort Benning, Georgia. The initial purpose of the newly formed motorized divisions was to provide flank and rear support for armored divisions that would provide the spearhead for future combat missions. Originally conceived as a defensive unit, the 4th Motorized Division emerged from the experiment as a quintessential light armored division with distinct offensive capabilities. The 14,000-strong division would now comprise two infantry regiments and one mechanized regiment with over 2,600 vehicles at its disposal.

In preparation for eventual battles, the Division participated in rigorous maneuvers in the state of Louisiana that commenced in August 1940 and drew to a close in August 1943, whereupon they moved to the recently established Camp Gordon in Georgia and participated in further maneuvers. Their next move was to Fort Dix, New Jersey where US military commanders decided on a change of tack. They chose to completely ignore the previous motorized experiment and re-designate the Ivy men simply as the 4th Infantry Division.

In September 1943 they were transferred to Camp Gordon Johnston, Florida to undergo amphibious training. The purpose of this particular training wasn't initially apparent to the Ivy men at the time, but it would put them in good stead for the eventual assault on Adolf Hitler's Festung Europa "Fortress Europe." It was around late December 1943, when the Division was at Camp Kilmer, New Jersey, that they learned that plans had been made to ship them overseas, and on January 18, 1944 the 4th Infantry Division embarked their troop ship SS *George Washington* to travel from New York to Liverpool.

All GIs were issued with a small booklet titled *Instructions for American Servicemen in Britain 1942*. They usually received this while crossing the Atlantic. The 31-page booklet was intended to introduce them to the English people and their customs in the hope of avoiding any embarrassing incidents due to cultural misunderstandings.

The Atlantic crossing was desultory as seasick soldiers fought for space in overcrowded, malodorous conditions that tested even the most resilient. The Ivy men arrived at Liverpool docks on January 26, 1944. Before their last deuce and a half had departed the dockside, the Supreme Commander of the Allied Expeditionary Force, General Dwight D. Eisenhower, and his Deputy, Air Marshal Sir Arthur Tedder, paid them a visit. This was to be the first in a series of inspection visits by high-ranking British and American commanders.

Captain Walter E. Marchand, Battalion Surgeon, 4th Infantry Division

January 1944
    After 10-day Atlantic crossing sighted Ireland and England, and on this evening stood off to sea outside of Liverpool. Weather cloudy and rainy. Liverpool completely blacked out. Troops anxious to debark—great occasion as they noted a girl on a pier we were

passing on the way to our pier. Sick and wounded let off first. Chaplain Boice brings one of them—temperature 104 degrees, also a post-op appendectomy that Dr. Miller, Graf and I had operated on in mid-Atlantic with heavy seas. Gen. Barton had come down to visit him—the General extremely nervous in the hospital. Troops debarking steadily, others restless, watching from the deck side. Finally my group began to debark—at 10:00 at night. Walked about 1 mile to RR station in complete darkness. Red Cross girls met us at station—cigarettes, gum, donuts and coffee freely given. European RR cars a curiosity to all of us.

The ensuing months were spent at billets in the southwest of England around the picturesque Devonshire towns of Tiverton, Newton Abbot and Bishopsteignton, where the Division was preparing for the planned invasion of Europe. As early as May 1944 the Ivy men had been chosen to be the spearhead of the amphibious landing now being planned that would become known as Operation *Overlord*.

J. D. Salinger, author of the timeless classic *Catcher in the Rye* may have been inspired by the sights and sounds of Devon, because he was a staff sergeant in the 12th Infantry Regiment, 4th Infantry Division and he spent three months in Tiverton before participating in the D-Day landings.

While the finishing touches were being applied to the plans to assault Hitler's Atlantic Wall, civilian residents of the sleepy Devonshire village of Slapton Sands, along the south west coast were evacuated and their homes requisitioned. This was because, according to intelligence experts, the beach bore a close resemblance to the beaches in Normandy. It was to be the location of the full dress rehearsals complete with naval fire support, which would be known as "Exercise Beaver." It was there that the 4th ID incurred their first casualties when, during the final rehearsal and under cover of darkness, German E-boats struck with deadly accuracy.

During the early hours of April 28, Nazi forces at Cherbourg were alerted to heavy radio traffic in the vicinity of Lyme Bay on the English coast. In an attempt to discover the source of this disturbance they launched nine torpedo boats to investigate. It was sometime around 0200 hours when they sighted eight heavily loaded American LSTs (landing ship, tanks). Enemy torpedoes hit three of the LSTs. One made it to port while another burst into flames, and a third sank within six minutes. The official death toll incurred by this attack was 749 men, far more than were killed on the storming of Utah Beach on the real D-Day. It was the worst loss of life to befall American troops since Pearl Harbor but due to the secrecy and clandestine nature of this operation no details were disclosed to the press until long after the event.

During the final preparations the 4th ID took their first German prisoner. He was a Luftwaffe pilot who had bailed out of a plane shot down over their assembly area.

Prior to the planned invasion somewhere in the region of 3,200 reconnaissance missions had been undertaken to take photos of primary locations. Strict secrecy had been imposed for the duration of these rehearsals but once they were over orders for the final move arrived at 4th Infantry Division HQ during the third week of May. Contextually it wasn't really different from the orders made previously but as they arrived in the marshaling areas, units found the areas surrounded by high fences and barbed wire, and once inside the compounds, strict security measure were implemented, no-one was allowed to leave or have any contact whatsoever with the outside world. The Ivy men could feel that this was "game on" and that whatever ensued wasn't going to be another dress rehearsal.

By the end of May the 4th Infantry Division and other infantry divisions were preparing to embark the ships anchored at various British ports facing the English Channel. Two beaches were allocated to the US Army. Utah Beach was given to VII Corps and Omaha to V Corps. Due to the tidal surge along the Normandy coast it was decided that the 4th ID would be the first unit to go ashore. They had been thoroughly briefed on the task that lay ahead and each man knew what was expected of him. No stone was left unturned as models of the assault beaches were meticulously analyzed and scrutinized, gas-proof clothing was issued and as the troops loaded onto the ships they noticed that all vehicles had been waterproofed. Four ports were chosen to launch the armada.

The naval operation, codenamed Operation *Neptune*, to facilitate the D-Day landings involved 6,939 vessels including 4,126 landing craft.

It was destined to be the largest amphibious invasion that ever occurred in one single day. On June 5 the vessels assembled at a point indicated on Allied maps as "Piccadilly Circus," just off the Isle of Wight in the English Channel.

Captain Walter E. Marchand, Battalion Surgeon, HQ, 4th Infantry Division

June 5, 1944

A.M. still strong winds, but clear weather.

P.M. This is it, anchors aweigh!—we start out of the harbor—with strong convoy of Destroyers—will pick up Cruisers and battleships later. Captain makes announcement—giving plan: we are to sail eastward parallel to the English coast as far as the Isle of Wight, then turn south, then turn westward until we are 7 miles off the beach on the east coast of the Cherbourg peninsula. The convoy forms up—hundreds of boats of all sizes: the battleships Texas, Arkansas are right next to us, as are several large cruisers and many destroyers and mine sweepers. It is an Impressive sight, and in the PLAN for the landing, they are to help us by covering fire of large volume and also against possible air attack. Orders have been issued to the troops that no one will fire at any aircraft during D-Day—this makes it certain that we will have air superiority at all costs.

5 P.M. Isle of Wight sighted and passed and we change our course and veer south. Pulled a tooth of an infantryman who complained of a toothache. After supper which I ate rather nervously, I laid myself down to sleep—but couldn't, but I rested. Hyperkinesia is evident—all very talkative. All remains quiet on board and around us except the splash of water over the bow and the wind thru the masts. The captain of the ship reads a message from President Roosevelt, General Eisenhower. The Captain himself gives us a message of hope and a prayer of safety and he was followed by Lt. Col. Teague, our Battalion Commanding Officer, and the Chaplain. I gave a brief last minute message to the troops, telling them again of the various emergency First Aid measures to be taken if they became casualties. All then was quiet on board as midnight passed.

Eisenhower had initially selected June 5 as the date for the assault. However inclement weather conditions on June 4, were not conducive to launching landing craft, and low clouds would have prevented aircraft from providing support and finding their targets. On the morning of June 5 and on the advice of his expert team of meteorologists Eisenhower gave the green light for Operation *Overlord* to commence June 6, 1944. In an address to his troops he said:

"You are about to embark upon the Great Crusade, toward which we have striven these many months. The eyes of the world are upon you."

The beaches in Normandy constituted part of the German Atlantic Wall defenses that extended over 3,100 miles, from the North Cape in Norway all the way down to the Spanish/French border. The coastal defenses in Normandy were equipped with various obstacles such as hundreds of reinforced concrete pillboxes built on the beaches, or in close proximity to them. They were equipped with machine guns, antitank guns, and both light and heavy artillery. Land mines, antitank obstacles and Belgian gates (Cointets elements) had been planted on the beaches, along with various underwater obstacles and naval mines which had been placed in waters just offshore to cause maximum damage to ships and particularly landing craft.

B. P. "Hank" Henderson, Medic, 22nd Infantry Regiment

They had a large tent they called the "Blue Room" where they took us in small groups and briefed us on our mission for D-Day. The 3rd Battalion commander was LTC Arthur S. Teague, one of the finest officers in the army. On June 1, I loaded onto the supply ship for the 3rd Battalion. I was in charge of medical supplies for the assault battalion. My jeep driver, Dago Oliver and I were the only two 22nd Infantry medics on the ship. We spent five days on the English Channel, one of the roughest bodies of water in the world. The last three days I was so sick I hardly knew I was alive.

Meanwhile the "eyes of the world" were averted from the surging sea of OD green and khaki congregating well before daylight broke on the docksides of British harbors facing the English Channel. Young American, British and Canadian men talked, smoked and joked as they prepared to put their young lives on the line in the "Great Crusade" to rid Europe of the evils of Fascism. The exuberance of youth would have been somewhat suppressed though as the mighty ships sailed out into a windswept and rainy English Channel towards the beaches of Normandy. The 4th Infantry Division set out from Torquay harbor on the British ship HMS *Gauntlet* toward a very uncertain future. This was it! Now the stage was set and the Ivy men were going to war again.

Harry Bailey, Columbia, SC Company E, 2nd Battalion, 8th Infantry Regiment

Night of June 5, 1944

Early morning hours of June 6, 1944, found me on a troop ship with the rest of my company headed for the beaches of Normandy, France. I was a 20-year-old platoon sergeant trying to lead a platoon that had 38 men plus two medics. We had boarded a Coast Guard troop carrier, the APA Barnett, somewhere close to Plymouth, England. We set sail with thousands of other ships including big battle-wagons, cruisers, and hundreds of destroyers. The night of June 5, we moved all night getting into position at 0200 hours for the invasion. We had a breakfast of beans and bacon and got seasick pills. Then we prepared to go over the side of the ship on rope latticework, which was very hard to do with all the equipment we had to take, plus weapons, ammunition, K rations, and water. Some carried bangalore torpedoes to blow holes in the barbed wire.

The waves were about 10 feet high and the LCVPs were bouncing up and down. Some men got hurt getting into the assault boats. We got loaded and shoved off, joining many assault boats. We circled for about one hour, and then in a line we headed for the beach, which was about 12 miles away. At about 0545 hours we passed the rocket boats that were firing thousands of rockets on the beach that burst like artillery. Just then, the B-26 bombers bombed where we were heading. Our battalion, 2nd Battalion, 8th Infantry Regiment, was the first wave of seaborne troops to land on Utah Beach.

At 2200 hours, June 5, the first Allied bombs were dropped in the vicinity of the predesignated landing areas, targeting among other things, the German batteries just inland—the 4th Infantry Division would soon become very well acquainted with these locations. Commencing at 0115 hours on D-Day, June 6, 13,000 paratroopers from the 82nd and 101st US Airborne divisions were dropped behind enemy lines. Their mission was to neutralize German defenses, secure the landing areas, and counteract the arrival of enemy reinforcements.

Just past midnight on June 6, 1944, troop transports geared down until they were barely edging along behind the minesweepers, and at 0200 hours they dropped anchor off the French coast. The Allies had effectively crossed the Channel unopposed and up until that point the Germans had been blissfully unaware of their presence. Then at 0300 hours, 1,900 Allied bombers flew over Normandy. A staggering 7,000,000 lb of bombs were dropped that day and a total of 10,521 combat aircraft flew a total of 15,000 sorties.

Within moments of drawing to a halt the personnel and troops on the ships watched as heavy flak began to pierce the skies and grow in intensity as Germans looked up and traced the flights that were carrying in the troops for the airborne landings. Meanwhile out in the Channel, in pitch darkness, as orange bursts and thunderous explosions resonated from beyond the Normandy coastline, the first assault waves cautiously descended the widespread rope nets and clambered down the sides of their ships to get aboard the bobbing LCVPs (Landing Craft Vehicle Personnel).

Loading carried on until the first hesitant rays of dawn illuminated the windswept, spuming sea. Then suddenly as the first assault wave headed out an eardrum-shattering bellicose roar signaled the naval barrage delivered by the multitudinous battleships, cruisers, and destroyers anchored in the English Channel. The naval bombardment launched from seven battleships, 18 cruisers, and 43 destroyers began at 0500 hours and continued unabated until 0625 hours, a mere 5 minutes before H-Hour.

The destroyer USS *Corry* (DD-463) that had led this massive Allied assault force and was among the fleet assigned to provide artillery support to the 4th Infantry Division while they were hitting the beaches, was scuttled by a mine only 3 minutes after H-Hour. Some accounts claim that it was German artillery that inflicted the damage.

The 4th Division was part of VII Corps commanded by Lieutenant General Joseph Lawton Collins, known to his friends and contemporaries as "Lightning Joe." The planned assault led by the 4th Infantry Division on the east Cotentin peninsula would represent the furthest right flank of the greater Allied invasion. The initial plan for Operation *Overlord* made little or no reference to the eventual amphibious landings. The reason for this was that Allied HQ considered it more practical to focus on the beaches that lay between Grandcamp and Caen. However it was generally acknowledged that it would be tactically advantageous to be able to land on the beaches in the proximity of Carentan and actually hit east Cotentin head on. This would facilitate the eventual capture of the desirable port of Cherbourg. All previous strategic considerations had been directed to acquiring a suitable harbor.

Bernard Pelura, Company G, 2nd Battalion, 8th Infantry Regiment

> General Barton gave us a little talk and said that for the last two years, we pounded discipline up our rear ends. Then he said, "If you fellows ever want to get home, you have to be the meanest, dirtiest son-of-a-bitches the world has ever seen, or you'll never make it home."
>
> General Roosevelt said, "And, don't you ever think for one minute that they won't shoot to kill you." Then, about 2200 hours that night, the sky seemed to light up. A big arms and ammunition ship exploded, and it looked like a gigantic Fourth of July fireworks display.
>
> Around 0230 hours, they threw a big net over the side of the ship and we climbed over the side and down into small boats. There was one first lieutenant and 30 of us. I don't remember his name. We circled around, and at about 0620 hours, we headed for shore. It was hell trying to get to shore, and when we were about seventy-five or a hundred yards from it, the navy man started to lower the end gate. The lieutenant cursed the heck out of him and said, "Put that gate up and get us to shore." But it was down too far, he couldn't get it back up and the boat sank. We were lucky; the water only came up to our chests and we could walk to shore. There was a buddy of mine three or four feet from me. His last name was Walters and he was from Baltimore, Maryland. I said, "Walt, don't you get too far away from me. If I step in a hole, you pull me up." He didn't answer me, and I looked over and half his head was blown off.

Having being designated as the spearhead for Operation *Overlord*, the 4th Infantry Division was to assault Utah Beach at H–Hour, 0630 hours, reinforced by 359th IR, 90th Division, establish a beachhead, and then contact the Airborne units that had been given the mission of seizing the crossings and bridges over the Merderet and Douve Rivers. Together they would secure vital exits to causeways leading inland from the beach across the flooded areas, and assist in the expansion of the beachhead. Then the following day if all went well the 4th would drive toward the harbor at Cherbourg in conjunction with the 90th Division.

Harry Bailey, Columbia, SC, Company E, 2nd Battalion, 8th Infantry Regiment

> D-Day
>
> Everything happened very fast for this 20-year-old soldier who felt "like I was in a fog." Then the sailor on the assault boat dropped the ramp and we hit the water, which was about

waist deep, and headed for shore. Artillery and small-arms fire were all about the beach. My first scout, Douglas Mason, from Michigan, was the first to reach the sand dunes and I ran and dropped down beside him to look to see which way to go. He was immediately killed with a hit to the head by a sniper's bullet. I knew I had to move fast or I would be next so I ran forward as fast as I could go. The rest of the platoon followed. The lieutenant, who was platoon leader, when I last saw him, was pointing inland but would not go with us. He left my squad leaders and me to fend for ourselves. Colonel McNeely relieved him and sent him to another company. I was told he was killed on D+2.

We tried to move to where we thought the causeway was but got pinned down by machine-gun fire. We finally got moving and had to cross a minefield. I lost two or three men. My medic got his foot blown off. We made it to the causeway at a dead run and started to get fire from a "knee" mortar. A round hit close and I got shrapnel in my right leg. I didn't know I was hit until a medic saw blood. He gave me a shot and a band-aid.

E Company, 2nd Battalion, 8th Infantry Regiment kept attacking toward St. Marie du Mont. The tanks from the 70th Tank Battalion joined in the fight. One hit a mine and was knocked out. Airborne troopers took twelve prisoners from my company commander. They weren't playing any games. Airborne was called "Big Pockets." The Airborne was in St. Marie du Mont, but we didn't know it. We had the 70th Tank Battalion fire at a belfry, which was visible in the town. We moved into St. Marie du Mont and toward Ste. Mère Église where the Airborne were cut off by enemy forces.

Utah Beach is located directly east of Ste. Mère Église, it has shallow gradient and compact grey sand, which would make it the perfect place to hit, if the 4th could manage to hit to the right place of course. It's situated on the east coast of what is known as the Cotentin peninsula that borders a marshland area, 2,000 yards of which had been intentionally flooded by the Germans to provide an additional hindrance along with other low-lying river and estuarine areas along the coastal region. But as the Ivy men's landing craft approached this beach powerful currents drew them away south roughly a mile from their objective on Utah Beach, regardless of this as the ramps were lowered, at H-Hour the men of the 4th Infantry Division charged to the shore. There were only four accessible pathways that could be used to navigate this marshland beyond the beach and due to this obstacle German resistance in the area was lighter than expected.

Morris Austein, I/3-22 Regiment, 4th Infantry Division

It seemed as if you could walk from one boat to another, there were so many of them. The sky was so full of planes you couldn't see the sky anymore. Bombers were hitting the coast. We all had things on our mind like the enemy and what we would run in to. There were thousands of troops alongside each other going onto the beach. On the shoreline itself there were land mines. Germans put them down and if you stepped on one, you blew up. I lost 5 men that way. There was utter confusion on the beach and soldiers were crying for help.

We saw General Teddy Roosevelt Jr. He was riding along the beach in a jeep, yelling, "Move on! Move on!" Meaning get off the beach and keep moving forward. The beach was jamming up with men and equipment. He was afraid they would bomb the hell out of us.

My unit pushed forward off the beach. As we moved forward we could smell the stench of dead animals and dead German soldiers. We also found American paratroopers dying. They were hanging on the trees. They got caught in the trees when they came down and the Germans shot them while they were hanging there.

One of my men got a shell right in the middle of his back. He was sitting in a hole and a cannon shot from a mile away and hit him in the back. He never knew what hit him, he was killed instantly.

We spent the entire day just moving up the beach. We were moving steadily at a reasonable pace and we got about a mile up the beach. I didn't see a German until dusk. I was moving forward around the hedgerows. I looked at him and he looked at me and he turned sideways to walk away. He didn't know I was an American and I didn't know he was a German, it was too dark. But as he turned I recognized the helmet. It was in silhouette. It had a different shape from ours and in the excitement I raised my rifle. At that moment he realized I was an American and we both started shooting at each other. I thought I was shot for a second, but he missed me. I don't know if I hit him, because suddenly a heavy bombardment hit us. There were mortar shells and artillery rounds.

The fact that I shot alerted them that we were Americans. The artillery came in very heavy and everyone scattered trying to protect themselves. There were hedgerows all over and we didn't see anything at that time. I couldn't tell if anyone was being killed. We all ran behind hedgerows to protect ourselves and some ran into craters where bombs made big holes. We stayed there the rest of the night. We couldn't move because it was dark. If we moved, we would be shot. No talking even, no smoking and no noise. We covered ourselves to sleep and took our chances. That is how D-Day ended for us. It hurt very badly when you saw someone you know get hit. I lost many good friends … and it hurt.

After 21 days of straight combat, Austein was wounded on the outskirts of Cherbourg, France on June 27, 1944. He spent one year at Walter Reed Hospital in Washington, DC. and received an honorable discharge for medical disability.

Six hundred men of the 2nd Battalion, 8th Infantry Regiment were the first wave to inadvertently hit the beach at a very lightly defended area indicated on Allied maps as "Victor sector." The assistant division commander, 56-year-old Brigadier General Theodore Roosevelt Jr., who was with Company E, accompanied them. He was the oldest son of President Teddy Roosevelt. While other officers discussed the prospects of moving inland or making their way to the predesignated areas at Tare Green and Uncle Red sectors Roosevelt furrowed his brow and abruptly terminated their discussions. Then he insouciantly pointed his cane to the ground and said "We'll start the war from right here. Go inland any way you can, we'll worry about those bastards another day!" He volunteered to orchestrate the initial assault on the beach strongpoints until the arrival of Colonel Van Fleet the regimental commander. Despite landing at the wrong location Roosevelt personally made a reconnaissance of the area immediately to the rear of the beach to locate the causeways, which were to be used for the advance inland. He then returned to the point of landing, contacted the commanders of the two battalions, Lt. Col. Conrad C. Simmons and Lt. Col Carlton O. MacNeely, and coordinated the attack on the scant enemy positions confronting them.

Captain Walter E. Marchand, Battalion Surgeon, HQ, 4th Infantry Division

June 6, 1944

D-Day is here!—D-Day has begun, how will it end? We are now close to the German-held coast of France—all is unbelievably quiet, but it isn't for long. At about 1 A.M. I hear a low-sounding drone—I go on deck and here I see plane upon plane flying over our ship toward the hostile shore, towing gliders—these are the Paratroopers and Airborne Infantry—I wish them God's speed and wish them well, for as I am watching the first planes are over the Atlantic Wall I see tremendous flares go up and great quantity of anti-aircraft fire and flak. God what great numbers of planes there are, and all ours. To our right—toward the Barfleur Peninsula area our Bombers are wreaking havoc on some coastal installations, we can hear the detonations clearly. In the midst of this, the little Cavalry C.T. is preparing to debark and to take St. Marcouf island—this is at H-4 hours. At this time also, the C47s are returning from France—flying home after letting go of their gliders or human cargo.

Had very early breakfast—then lay on my bunk for a while—I couldn't sleep and I can't sleep—I keep thinking of my wife and my family—I love you my Corinne.

At 0400 the first wave of our Assault Battalion is called to stand-by to load into the boats—there is a great hum of activity throughout the ship. The Captain speaks— our LCM3s haven't come yet, but there is still plenty of time. We wait for 20, 40, 55 minutes. Then they come out of the dawn alongside—still enough time to make the H-Hour landing, for H-Hour has been upped because of the heavy seas. The LCM3s are having great difficulty tying up to the boat—they toss around like corks—but the landing nets are overside and the troops make their way down—but with great difficulty. Often large hausers, 2 inch thick, would snap like a thread and often the man climbing down would be thrown into the small boats. It was especially difficult to get the vehicles overboard into the small boats. "Man overboard" was heard once—a British sailor was knocked overboard but rescued.

First wave—Away, then the second, then the third, then it was my turn to get into my boat with 5 of my men and part of the Battalion Command section—it took too long, the boat crashed against the ship time and time again, bending the ramp, and tearing loose, snapping the hausers. Finally we are all in our boat with our equipment, and the men are getting seasick, and they huddle together toward the rear of the boat. I stay near the front of the boat, getting sprayed continuously and I look about me and see hundreds upon hundreds of boats, from the little LCVPs, LCMs, LCTs and LCIs, to the huge battleships and cruisers, and smoke is billowing from their deck guns, for this is H-40 min. and the naval barrage starts then, the fire directed against enemy shore installations. Our wave has now formed and we are heading toward shore 7 miles away through rough waters, while on the way in our Dive bombers get to work, pouring tons of bombs against the enemy fortresses.

We are getting close to shore and the boats of our wave go from a line in file to a line abreast formation and speed for shore. I can now hear cannon fire clearly as well as machine-gun fire. We all pray that our boat will not strike a mine or an underwater obstacle or get hit by a shell from a coastal battery. All sounds become closer, when about 50 yards from shore I see two splashes on our port bow—enemy fire. The boats streak for shore and hit the beach and we almost make a dry landing—we only have to wade knee deep thru about 20 yards of water. As we hit, the ramp goes down and we debark—wade in the water, then on hitting dry land start to run. I see dead Americans floating in the water—a ghastly sight. I get my men together and we run up across the beach to a concrete wall, faced with barbed wire and bearing signs.

There are many wounded lying about and we start to care for them, and carry some to the Naval Beach Party Aid Station which just landed after us. I try to orient myself, but we landed at a different place than was originally planned. Enemy fire is increasing, landing just to our left, from our right there is machine-gun fire. I have only 1 choice I lead the men thru a break in the barbed wire into the Mine Field and we go in about 50 yards—enemy fire increases, we dig in hurriedly to rest— we are all exhausted from the fear which we all know as shells come whistling overhead and landing close by. But we must get out of the Mine Field!—I find a path to the right and we start along it, seeing mines all around us—and then the path disappears and we turn back to our former spot—from there we find a small path to the left and we follow it—we see wounded about us and we care for them, carrying some along with us on litters, and the small path leads us to a road and we follow it to the first right turn and we follow it. Troops and vehicles are now storming ashore in great quantities—some vehicles are hit and burst into flames. We pass burning houses and many dead German and American soldiers. It is now noon—God the 5 hours passed like lightning. At 1300 we come to the "Old French Fort," now we are close to where originally we were supposed to land. I scout ahead and find my Battalion just 300 yards up the road, so I and Capt. Scott set up our Aid Station off the side of the road in a large hole and crater made by a 14-inch naval shell—12 feet by 5 feet and about 6 feet deep. By this time one of our Jeep ambulances has reached us and we are ready to function as an Aid station. We send out litter bearer groups into the minefields to pick up casualties. This is ticklish work, but the boys are excellent soldiers and go bravely although they have no paths to follow.

Our ambulance Jeep works up forward and brings back casualties—some are Paratroopers that are pretty well beaten up, having been wounded shortly after landing. We work from this spot for 2 hours and then we move forward to the Command Post which is along the side of a road near Fortress 74 which is still holding out. Shortly after arriving here, machine-gun fire becomes active and we have to duck low—pinned down here for 5 hours, could watch the attack on the fortress and the surrender of the Germans. Our boys are doing a splendid job and very few casualties so far. As the sun is setting we note hundreds of C47s again—more Airborne Infantry landing—they swoop inland and let go of their gliders, to come swooping back. Liason Sgt., from Co. C shot in the leg while lying on the road beside Capt. Scott.

Toward dark a few serious casualties encountered—difficulty of evacuating great—Plasma given right in open.

Difficulty in finding path thru minefield to farm house where we will stay for the night—had to cross tank traps filled with water and lined with mines—ticklish business in the dark.

Finally we got all of Aid station together—we were all exhausted—and were so tired that we just fell down and fell asleep—with artillery, mainly enemy, going overhead, most of it, fortunately for us being directed toward the beach. This is the end of D-Day—it was hectic from the start—but we had few casualties, and those mainly from mines, which were numerous. Heavy machine-gun fire heard all night.

At approximately 0745 hours (H+75 minutes) the 3rd Battalion, 22nd Infantry touched down on Utah Beach and moved north along the coast to reduce beach strongpoints. The 8th Infantry's 3rd Battalion landed in the same waves and moved inland. By 0800 hours four battalions of infantry had landed. Two more arrived at around 1000 hours. These were the 1st Battalion, 22nd Infantry, on the northern beach and the 2nd Battalion, 22nd Infantry, on the southern. According to plan these two battalions were to march inland through a location that had been designated as "Exit 4," which was one of the four exits to be used to broach the mainland.

Meanwhile directly in front of the 8th Infantry's 1st Battalion was a field fortification, and just south of the Exit 2 approximately 1,300 yards to the southeast facing their 2nd Battalion, was another. These fortifications were lightly manned and didn't present any serious obstacle to the 8th Infantry who took these positions without much trouble.

The original plan allocated Exit 2 and Exit 3 for vehicles. Due to the proximity of German positions, Exit 3 wasn't accessible and subsequently all vehicles tried to use Exit 2, which led to inevitable gridlocks. The tableau would have presented a fairly chaotic sight to the observer as causeways to the south of the landing area became seriously congested and because the eastern end of Exit 4 was still being subjected to sporadic enemy fire, some of the 22nd Infantry's units at "Tare Green Beach" were compelled to use alternative exits and wade inland almost 2 miles through the flooded areas. Due to these landing blunders further logistic problems were developing. Shortly after noon elements of the 12th Infantry had to face the same hindrance as the 22nd Infantry. Despite the water only being waist-deep, the area was full of inundated bomb craters along with irrigation ditches that French farmers had dug for their crops. Some of these were 7 foot deep and men frequently became completely submerged.

In the meantime Brigadier General Theodore Roosevelt remained imperturbable as he welcomed the men to the shore and sought to dilute their trepidation with jokes, one liners and anecdotes about his father. At one point he almost assumed the role of a traffic cop as he personally set about directing vehicles. Some years later General Omar Bradley was asked to name the single most heroic action he had ever seen in combat, he replied, "Ted Roosevelt on Utah Beach." For his efforts Brigadier General Theodore Roosevelt, Jr was awarded a Medal of Honor.

Brigadier General Theodore Roosevelt, Jr
Medal of Honor
Place and date: Normandy invasion, 6 June 1944
Citation date: 28 September 1944

For gallantry and intrepidity at the risk of his life above and beyond the call of duty on 6 June 1944, in France. After 2 verbal requests to accompany the leading assault elements in the Normandy invasion had been denied, Brig. Gen. Roosevelt's written request for this mission was approved and he landed with the first wave of the forces assaulting the enemy-held beaches. He repeatedly led groups from the beach, over the seawall and established them inland. His valor, courage, and presence in the very front of the attack and his complete unconcern at being under heavy fire inspired the troops to heights of enthusiasm and self-sacrifice. Although the enemy had the beach under constant direct fire, Brig. Gen. Roosevelt moved from one locality to another, rallying men around him, directed and personally led them against the enemy.

Under his seasoned, precise, calm, and unfaltering leadership, assault troops reduced beach strong points and rapidly moved inland with minimum casualties. He thus contributed substantially to the successful establishment of the beachhead in France.

Despite the successful landings it was becoming increasingly apparent that the German troops were rallying and resistance was intensifying, moreover the beachhead was still far from secure. Field Marshal Erwin Rommel was in personally charge of defending northern France against the expected Allied invasion but June 6 he was at home in Germany celebrating his wife's 50th birthday having been told the sea was too rough for a landing and Adolf Hitler was asleep when word of the invasion arrived. No one dared wake him, meaning that vital time was lost in dispatching German reinforcements to the area. German soldiers preparing to defend the beaches were unaware of heated controversies taking place in the German High Command over the best way to repel a potential Allied invasion. The German commander-in-chief in Western Europe, Field Marshal Gerd von Rundstedt, favored a mobile defense and vociferously disagreed with Field Marshal Erwin Rommel his most trusted subordinate. Rommel the "Desert Fox" commanded Army Group B and was therefore directly responsible for the defense of the northern coastlines of France. He favored a strong forward defense that would defeat the Allied invasion on the beaches. Adolf Hitler was aware of the disagreement between his western commanders, but failed to intervene to settle the dispute. Consequently, the Germans adopted neither the forward nor the mobile defense concepts as a distinct course of action.

Nevertheless with each hour that passed, the risk of a concerted German counterattack was becoming greater because some enemy positions in close proximity to the beach were still providing delaying actions. While engineers were preparing the beaches for the arrival of new troops, the 1st and 2nd Battalions of the 8th Infantry Regiment began moving forward inland to comply with their objectives. At that time the whole beach area was in uncomfortably close proximity to the 7th German Army defense zone. The 7th German Army comprised the 709th, 243rd and 91st Infantry Divisions and was commanded by experienced Nazi commander Col. Gen. Friedrich Dollmann.

Bill Parfitt had been appointed as Roosevelt's personal bodyguard and had first-hand knowledge of his boss's attitude and remarkable skill for leadership.

Bill Parfitt, 22nd Infantry Regiment HQ, 4th Infantry Division, Brigadier General Roosevelt's bodyguard

On this day in 1944 (June 6), I was puking over the side of a landing craft. One just big enough to have a jeep aboard. Getting more scared as I looked about at the tremendous number of boats involved in the landing, which I made about 6:30 the following morning. Can still recall a lot of it but time takes away some. The damned seasickness was most disruptive to all. I don't remember anyone that didn't get damned sick. We played poker on the hood of the jeep using the invasion money that was given to us... I can remember going over the side of the bigger craft and making it ok. It was so rough that we lost a couple of guys with broken legs trying to transfer.

I remember the general and colonels gathering in an area near the Limey soldier driving the landing craft. My memory jumps around as I try to account for the long times spent in line and then approaching the beach. I do remember that the rain had quit when we landed... The jumping off, the cold as hell water and the rush to the beaches is sorta blurry but I remember grabbing one of those welded pipe things (obstacles in the water) and reloading the rifle. Don't remember a bit about shooting though. I seem to remember reloading three times this way. The run to the sea wall was quick. Do remember the first meeting of the General with the Colonel behind the sea wall—the one used in the book (The Longest Day) for the first meeting. I remember Gen Teddy without his helmet. Also remember later on when Gen Hodges chewed his ass for not wearing it. Even then it ended up in the jeep. He detested the steel helmet.

While General Roosevelt and the battalion commanders were working on reducing the enemy strongpoints immediately confronting them so that their troops could proceed inland to their objectives, they noticed that the geographic error in the landings was actually proving to be quite fortuitous because the enemy shore defenses there were considerably less formidable than those on the intended landing beaches.

The 8th Infantry Regiment's men moved quickly inland and began arranging to meet up with the Airborne forces, which had landed during the twilight hours of June 6. Once the leading waves of the 12th Infantry were ashore they moved north along the coast, eliminating the remaining beach defenses. Then the 22nd Infantry landed and filled the gap between the two regiments. Fortunately the section of beach where the 4th landed was sparsely defended so opposition was negligible. The 8th Infantry managed to get some elements over to Les Forges crossroads while others infiltrated the Turqueville area. The Germans maintained a salient between these two locations and the 82nd Airborne units who were at Ste. Mère Église remained temporarily isolated. The 12th Infantry reached the Beuzeville au Plain area on the left flank of the 101st Airborne while the 22nd advanced along coast to general line Hamel de Cruttes–St. Germain de Varreville.

As successive waves advanced inland from the beach a move was undertaken to flank the German positions from the north and seal off the Cotentin peninsula while eradicating the coastal defenses. In the center of the 4th ID's thrust inland a vicious fight developed around the town of Emondeville which was one of the two strongpoints the Germans were desperately trying to maintain in a vain attempt to prevent the enlargement of the beachhead. North of these towns the enemy had dug in and formed a defensive line.

Although the 22nd and 12th Infantry regiments didn't fully accomplish their D-Day objectives, after wading through the flooded area, the 12th Infantry came up on the left of the 502nd Parachute Infantry, 101st Airborne south of Beuzeville au Plain, where they remained for the night. After being compelled to wade inland through the swamps the 1st and 2nd Battalions of the 22nd Infantry, had to spend about seven hours marooned there before they reached dry land in the vicinity of St. Martin de Varreville and then moved on to St. Germain de Varreville, where they bivouacked for the night. Meanwhile the 3rd Battalion, 22nd Infantry, was still preoccupied with the task of reducing enemy beach strongpoints. Eventually the battalion moved north past les Dunes de Varreville using Exit 4 and managed to reach the southern edge of Hamel de Cruttes by nightfall.

Due to the landings occurring south of their initial objectives certain logistical problems had materialized. Initially the four predesignated beach exits became congested preventing the continuous flow of men and vehicles away from the area. Despite this the whole 4th Infantry Division was ashore within those first 15 hours and by nightfall on June 6, 20,000 men and 1,700 vehicles were on Utah at a cost of 197 casualties.

On that same day units of the 82nd Airborne Division hit the beaches and followed the 3rd Battalion 8th Infantry. They're mission was to join the 82nd Airborne at Ste. Mère Église and clear out the area in order to clear the designated landing zone (LZ) where gliders were scheduled to land at 2100 hours.

Joseph Owen. HQ, 4th Infantry Division

> At about 1100 hours, General Barton sent me toward Ste. Mère Église to ascertain the exact location of the 8th Infantry Regiment. On my way, I was met by General Theodore Roosevelt Jr. who slowed down his jeep to yell out, "Hey boy, they're shooting up there," followed by a big "Haw Haw." At that, I proceeded to the 8th Infantry Regiment Command Post where Colonel Van Fleet instructed Captain Gilby to properly mark their exact front locations on my map for a quick return to General Barton on the beach.

The 8th Infantry Regiment performed brilliantly on D–Day and achieved its objectives. It had relieved some elements of the 101st Airborne Division in the Pouppeville area and by late afternoon it had linked up with the 82nd Airborne Division at Ste. Mère Église. It was now well placed to protect and propel the southwest flank of the rest of the 4th Division. The only serious problem they encountered after that emanated from a German pocket of resistance situated at the North of "Les Forges." This would be dealt with as soon as possible, and it would be in typical "Ivy men" style. The rapid progress of the 4th Division on D–Day greatly improved the initially tenuous situation of the two Airborne divisions, eventually allowing some of their units to provide further support to the 4th and others to be deployed elsewhere.

Private Jack Port, E Company, 12th Infantry Regiment, 4th Infantry Division

I landed at Utah Beach on June 6th. BT had taught recruits that if they had to run during combat, they should land on their elbows, with their rifle upright. I was so scared that I threw my rifle and it landed in the sand. I spent my first night in France in a foxhole. My unit had made its way to a village, St. Martin de Varreville. The town had been hit hard by Allied firepower. Without buildings to house the soldiers, we received orders to dig in. I teamed up with a New Yorker, Jim Rogers. Because he had difficulty pronouncing "Port," I called him "Jack Pert." A foxhole only needed to be twelve inches deep but we dug ours so deep that we could barely get out of it in the morning.

After-Action Report

Led by the 2nd Battalion, 8th Infantry Regiment, all three Infantry Regiments of the 4ID (8th, 22nd, 12th) were ashore by early afternoon. Although casualties on Utah Beach were light in comparison to the Airborne forces who had dropped in overnight. The carnage that the 1st Infantry and 29th Infantry Divisions experienced on Omaha Beach was far greater than that experienced by the 4th ID that incurred almost 200 casualties that day, including 60 men lost when their boat carrying Battery B, 29th Field Artillery hit a mine in the water.

Walter E. Marchand
Silver Star
Awarded for actions during the World War II
Walter E. Marchand, United States Army, is reported to have been awarded the Silver Star under the below-listed General Orders, for conspicuous gallantry and intrepidity in action against the enemy while serving with the 4th Infantry Division during World War II.
General Orders: Headquarters, 4th Infantry Division, General Orders No. 50 (1945)
Action Date: World War II
Service: Army
Division: 4th Infantry Division

CHAPTER 8

ARTILLERY FLYING ALL DIRECTIONS!

In the course of D–Day+1 over 10,000 men, along with 1,469 vehicles and 807 tons of supplies, were landed at Utah Beach. Although this was impressive it was actually less than expected. The 4th Infantry Division advanced inland from Utah Beach on predesignated routes, some of which had been initially secured by the Airborne units. The job now was to assault and capture other strategic objectives that needed to be taken before the planned assault on Cherbourg. In the small French village of Pouppeville the 2nd Battalion, 8th Infantry had established the first contact with paratroopers of the 101st Division at around 1200 hours on June 7. General Maxwell Taylor, commander of the 101st Airborne Division, was reliably informed that the 4th ID's progress had been rapid and that Utah had indeed been secured.

The 4th Infantry Division would now be given the daunting task of eradicating the remaining coastal batteries and capturing enemy positions in proximity to Utah Beach. They would have had relatively no idea of the magnitude of this assignment and what was expected of them.

The Germans had been initially quite lax in moving troops to secure the Cotentin peninsula but realizing the gravity of the situation now confronting them, they had managed to reassemble and reinforce vital positions in this area. Moreover many of these German troops were seasoned veterans while most of the VII US Corps men hadn't seen a great deal of action and were in some cases completely green, with the notable exception of the 70th Tank Battalion, which had seen action in

North Africa and Sicily. This would to some extent affect the engagements that ensued immediately after D-Day, but the Ivy men were as always quick to learn.

Darel Parker, Leipsic, OH, Company C, 1st Battalion, 12th Infantry Regiment, 4th Infantry Division

We traveled on without much trouble until well after dark—trouble came later. There was artillery flying all directions all night. I finally lay down in an open field (didn't even dig in) and tried to get some sleep, but it wasn't much.

Field Marshal Erwin Rommel had ominous forebodings about the Allied invasion and he already mentioned to some close associates that a successful landing in Normandy would inevitably lead to the downfall of Germany. About ten days before the invasion was due to take place, intelligence reported that there had been some changes in the enemy dispositions along with the appearance of a new unit on the intended VII Corps front. The German 91st Division had moved in between the 709th and the 243rd Divisions to increase the line of defense that ran from Valognes to Carentan on the Cotentin peninsula.

This change was the result of a difference of opinion between Rommel and his superior, Field Marshal Gerd Von Rundstedt, on the concept of defending the beaches. It was Rommel's considered opinion that any attempt at invasion should be decisively stopped at the beaches, or if possible before a landing could be made. Von Rundstedt wasn't convinced by this and preferred to have a covering force in place on the beach, with a close tactical reserve and a counterattacking force in the rear. As the result of a compromise, the 91st was moved as mentioned. If the intelligence was correct, the Germans were now estimated to have had the capacity to maintain a rigid defense of the beaches with at least four battalions on D-Day from the 709th and the 243rd Divisions and were capable of reinforcing the assault area at H-Hour with gradual counterattacks. Further counterattacks with armor would be possible on D-Day+2.

During the course of the day of the invasion, Rommel had returned to his command post at La Roche-Guyon. He immediately set to work committing reserves to the area but despite realizing the urgency and gravity of the situation now developing, he sensed it was already too late to deal with it effectively. Rommel was still subordinate to Field Marshal von Rundstedt, who reported directly to Hitler, who retained overall authority to commit the German armored reserve, a factor that severely restricted Rommel's capacity to respond to the Allied invasion of the mainland. Despite this Rommel, who was at that time in command of Army Group B, went ahead and ordered the 77th Division to move from Brittany to the area of St. Lô in Normandy.

On the night of June 7, the 4th Infantry Division's 12th Infantry Regiment received orders to take the high ground northeast of Montebourg while both the 8th and 12th Infantry prepared to attack this position from the northwest of the town. Forward observers noticed several enemy positions west of Montebourg, and on the basis of their information determined resistance was expected. The Germans had dug in along a low railway embankment between Montebourg and Montebourg station and were supported by artillery. The actual capture of the town of Montebourg was going to take considerably longer than expected. It wasn't a particularly sizeable place, numbering only 2,200 inhabitants, but it was strategically important to the Allies if they were going to press the advance to take the harbor at Cherbourg.

While the 12th Infantry advanced northwest towards the heights just beyond Ste. Mère Église in the direction of Montebourg, their 1st Battalion captured a fortified German position southwest of Beuzeville au Plain. At the same time the 2nd Battalion infiltrated the edge of Neuville au Plain, but didn't manage to occupy the village, that would be left for other units who would capture it later in the day. Sometime around mid-morning the two battalions had consolidated their current positions but by early afternoon, a further advance was brought to a shuddering halt on the slopes between Azeville and Bisson, where they stopped and regrouped for the night.

Meanwhile in front of the 8th Infantry at les Forges, a sizeable German force still held the ridge between Fauville and Turqueville preventing the Allies from using the important highway south of Ste. Mère Église.

By late morning the 1st Battalion's assault on Turqueville had succeeded in reducing at least part of this enemy salient.

The 2nd and 3rd Battalions of the 8th Infantry had attacked northward from their positions in the Les Forges area to link up with and relieve the 82nd Airborne Division at Ste. Mère Église and now they were jointly committed to eliminating the enemy positions in the vicinity, but it was going to be a hard fight. Lieutenant Colonel Carlton O. MacNeely, 2nd Battalion, 8th Infantry, and Colonel Vandervoort, 2nd Battalion, 505th Parachute Infantry, planned and executed the first coordinated attack. The 1st Battalion went in first while the 3rd Battalion advanced alongside the highway and the 2nd Battalion attacked toward Ecoqueneauville. As these two battalions came approached the enemy positions they were met with a hail of crushing machine-gun and artillery fire. What ensued was one of the toughest fights of those first long days after D-Day but by the close of the day the two battalions had killed or captured 300 Germans and dislodged them from their positions.

Captain Walter E. Marchand, Battalion Surgeon, HQ, 4th Infantry Division

June 7 D+1

We are aroused early—it is cold—casualties are brought in, several requiring plasma. One patient in shock we bring to the hot embers of a burnt house and so get him and keep him warm. Fortress 78 is holding out and giving much opposition. We move our Aid station away from the house we are at—to a field with a nearby road and we dig in. Also, we are in a large crater for our Aid Sta. Dead horse is nearby, not a very good sight, but this is the best we can do. The attack continues fiercely this A.M., Company K surrounds the fortress 78, but is in water and swamp 3 feet deep. Evacuation from such area is difficult. We use our litter Jeeps to go forward, but they are fired upon. I go forward myself to scout out a route, but unsuccessful and we get fired on—but no hits.

Late A.M.—Artillery barrage falls in vicinity of Aid Station—we make our holes in time and hear the fragments zip past—no one hurt. Routine evacuation going on most of day. Treating injured civilians also. Go out and try to find our 2nd Jeep—but no sign of it. Later it comes to our Aid Sa. We are all together now. Getting used to artillery and machine-gun fire. We stay low most of the time. Battalion Ammunition Dump set up 50 yards away from our Aid Sta.—but can't help this—everybody is crowded into small areas.

After supper Capt. Scott and the Chaplain and I were working on three casualties on the edge of a pit that was our Aid Station. Suddenly we heard planes overhead, then the death roar of six MGs we looked and instinctively dove for the Aid Station pit. Capt. Scott landed head first, the Chaplain and I got in at the same moment, and then a patient threw himself in—just in time for the bullets started zipping past. Then we heard the crash of bombs landing, and the earth shook—a bomb landed 24 yards away from us—then all was silent for a moment, then a loud crash, and another—God, the ammo. dump was going up in smoke—we trembled and prayed at the same time.

I looked over the edge of the pit to see that all was OK—the patients had found other holes to get into—I warned them to stay low, that the dump was on fire. And then things really began to happen as crate after crate of all size ammo. started to go off, forming geyser upon geyser of smoke and shells and dirt and rock. Tremendous detonations shook the ground violently and made our faces meet up with the ground. We were petrified with fear as things—grenades, shell fragments flew and whistled over our pit for minute after minute. At one time, something fell into our pit—it was a grenade—smoke—The Chaplain threw it out before it went off. We only hoped that no phosphorous shells were in the Dump, for if that went off we would all be casualties as a surety—some did go off, but only a little phosphorous flew around—some on my Aid pouch—it burned a hole in it.

After 2 hours, hours that were hell, the fire began to burn down—only small arms Ammo. going off now—and we get to work. Sgt. Hambly badly hit—two 50-caliber machinegun bullets get him—plasma given—1 quart.—then rapidly evacuate. Another man got phosphorous burns—serious—used water with wet blanket—many water cans which had been placed outside our Aid Sta. pit were empty—riddled by shell fragments. One of our trailers had caught fire, but no serious damage caused.

This strafing-bombing and setting off of Ammo. Dump proved an ordeal to our men, and they didn't get over it for some days to come—it was horrible namely in the length of time that fear gripped us—2 hours. We were completely exhausted by this. We were glad to see this day come to an end.

Now the 22nd Regiment was given the arduous task of reducing remaining enemy positions along the beaches and attacking fortified batteries, some of which were 2–3 miles inland. Two battalions of the 22nd now came up against two of these powerful coastal forts located at Azeville and Crisbecq. This was going to be one of the most difficult missions that the Ivy men were assigned to in those early days after D-Day.

On June 7 while Col. Hervey A. Tribolet, 22nd Infantry Regiment, launched the assault to eliminate these forts, the 2nd Battalion commanded by Maj. E. W. Edwards fought hard to take the town of Azeville that was defended by soldiers of the German 91st Air Landing Division.

The German artillery pieces at both locations were housed in reinforced concrete bunkers, protected by machine-gun nests, mines, infantry pillboxes, ditches and barbed wire. Each position consisted of four massive concrete bunkers complete with underground ammunition storage dumps in a line connected by trenches. During the preceding naval bombardments the German troops had sheltered in the underground tunnels that connected these two forts. Consequently these German troops had been relatively unaffected by the bombing.

The capture of these forts was imperative because the Crisbecq fort housed long-range 210mm guns that threatened the naval fleet out in the English Channel as well as the beaches. An arc of concrete sniper pillboxes partially circumnavigated the southern approaches to the Azeville fort. The 2nd Battalion opened the fighting by attempting to move forward against the Azeville position, but after a few hours and after sustaining heavy losses, a German counterattack drove it back to its line of departure. Meanwhile the 1st Battalion's fight to take the fort at Crisbecq was even more fiercely contested. They suffered heavy casualties from the still-operative Azeville batteries and were raked by small-arms fire as they crept along thickly hedged trails towards their objective. This was the 4th Division's introduction to what became known as "Bocage" or "Hedgerow" fighting. Suddenly, while the 1st Battalion was licking its wounds, the Germans launched another thunderous counterattack on their left flank causing them to retreat almost all the way back to the beach.

For countless centuries, Norman farmers had enclosed their arable land with these thick, almost impenetrable hedgerows known to the locals as *le Bocage*. In the US sector the bocage country began roughly 10 miles inland from the Normandy beaches and stretched from Caumont on the American left to the western coast of the Cotentin peninsula. The bocage consists of dense hedgerows and sturdy embankments. At their base, they resemble dirt parapets and are 1–4 feet thick and 3–15 feet high. Growing out of this earthen foundation is a hedge of various deciduous shrubbery and tangles of vines. This vegetation usually has a thickness of 1–3 feet and can vary in height, from 3 to 14 feet. Originally intended to serve as land boundaries, to keep in livestock, and prevent soil erosion caused by Channel winds, the hedgerows border every side of every field, which divides the terrain into innumerable walled enclosures. Because the fields aren't linear and small in size, about 200 by 400 yards, the hedgerows aren't assembled in logical patterns.

They provide excellent cover and concealment to the defender and can present a formidable obstacle to the attacker. Moreover the thick vegetation provides excellent camouflage and restricts the deployment of units along with restricting observation, which renders the effective use of heavy-caliber direct-fire weapons almost impossible and hampers artillery fire. Occupying a high place that afforded good fields of observation and a clear view of the surrounding countryside offered a distinct advantage. Many Allied units in Normandy had access to Piper Cub light aircraft that provided excellent intelligence to the attacking troops.

Clifford "Swede" Henley, Cannon Company, 22nd Infantry Regiment

> Crisbecq was one hell of a strongpoint but they took it about 1800 hours, and then the enemy counterattacked and drove them back south to St. Marcour. The 2nd Battalion, trying to take Azeville, was being pushed back. Cannon Company was called on for fire in front of the 2nd Battalion to stop the counterattack. We fired 800 rounds in about 90 minutes. Our ammunition nearly ran out, but the attack was halted and the Battalions reorganized for the night. Cannon Company had defensive barrages in front of the 1st and 2nd Battalions.
>
> Attacking the gun emplacements at Crisbeq and Azeville proved to be a laborious and costly operation for the 22nd Infantry and because their initial attempts failed, there was still work ahead. Just 24 hours previously the 3rd Battalion had managed to advance 2,000 yards inland and eliminate one fort completely, and on D+1 it pushed even further inland and captured two more but by the evening of June 7, fearing further counterattacks against the ravaged 1st and 2nd Battalions orders were received to relocate them and consign them as the 22nd Infantry's regimental reserve for the time being.

Due to the slow progress made by the 12th and 22nd Infantry Regiments on D-Day, Lt. Gen. Collins gave the order to the 4th Division to keep on pushing north and hit the line of coastal forts that stretched inland along a commanding high ridge from Montebourg all the way to Quinéville and formed a significant salient between the Merderet River and two of its tributaries. The responsibility for taking the area between Montebourg and Montebourg train station was now transferred to the 8th Infantry.

Meanwhile early on June 7, the 12th Infantry were instructed to seize a road junction about 3,000 yards inland from St. Martin de Varreville. Once this objective had been secured they were to make their north to Montebourg, which was to become the scene of one of the most desperate and violent clashes of those first days in Normandy. Just beyond this objective was a vital crossroads that would open the way to Cherbourg. Elements of a German Grenadier regiment belonging to the 91st Infantry Division, along with soldiers from the 709th Infantry Division, were well dug in at these positions. The Ivy men were going to have a hard fight. Nevertheless before they could proceed to seal off the Cotentin peninsula and advance on Cherbourg it was essential to enlarge the beachhead and eliminate all the German coastal batteries from the surrounding areas.

Jim Burnside, Company E, 2nd Battalion, 22nd Infantry Regiment

Working cautiously up the road towards Azeville, I became aware of some movement on the road ahead. Holding our fire, we waited to see what was coming. To our astonishment, it was an oxcart with an ox pulling a full load of straw. Astride the ox was a wounded paratrooper who had dropped in the night before D-Day. He had a bandage on one arm and a blood-soaked bandage on his forehead. In the cart were five or six of his wounded buddies. As they slowly passed us, looking for an aid station, the paratrooper raised his good arm, holding a Tommy gun. With a big grin he said, "Hi-Ho Silver, fellows." Thus, the gallantry and courage we were to see so often was always served so well by a keen sense of humor.

On a later date (I believe around Ste. Mère Église,) during a lull, Major Lum Edwards, our battalion commander, had cautiously worked his way to a shallow shell hole in the middle of a small field and squatted down to do his morning's duty. A shell landed in the same field. Lum squatted down a little deeper and pulled his helmet down a little further. Wham! Another shell hit a little closer. Lum—never rising up, holding his pants around his ankles in one hand and his helmet on with the other—did the most amazing duck waddle to safety in a nearby hedgerow, accompanied by our hysterical laughter.

On the morning of June 8, the 8th Infantry moved forward to take the western section of the Montebourg–Montebourg station objective. Supported on their left flank by the 82nd Airborne's 505th Parachute

Infantry regiment, the 8th Infantry attacked toward the main Ste. Mère Église–Montebourg highway and were promptly harassed by heavy German artillery from the offset. They didn't actually make physical contact with the Germans until they reached the village of Neuville au Plain, which despite repeated attempts was still in enemy hands. By mid-afternoon and after some vicious house-to-house, hand-to-hand fighting the Germans retreated leaving the immediate way ahead considerably less well defended for the time being.

The 8th Infantry pressed home the attack but was forced to lessen the pace when it approached Fresville and Grainville where they came under heavy enemy artillery, heavy machine-gun and sniper fire. At this juncture they decided to take cover and wait for tank support, which arrived promptly at 2000 hours. The arrival of the tanks added fresh impetus to the attack and it didn't take long before the Germans were recoiling from the onslaught and pulling back from this position allowing the 505th Parachute Infantry Regiment to move in and secure the village while the 8th Infantry's 3rd Battalion doggedly continued pushing north.

When the 3rd Battalion reached Magneville, Company I fought its way through the houses on the northern side of the town before contact with the enemy was established. The Ivy men quickly asserted that the Germans appeared to be firing from high ground directly in front of them. The 3rd Battalion soon figured out that they had inadvertently run into the main German line of resistance that ran parallel to the north bank of a tributary of the Merderet River. This well-defended German position forced the company to withdraw to the line established earlier on in the day. It was a restless and tormented night as terrifying barrages from German 88mms, mortars and the dreaded "screamin Meemie" Nebelwerfers pounded away incessantly at the 3rd Battalion's position.

The Germans were now gathering additional forces and making the first determined effort to establish and consolidate a serious line of defense. By June 9 they had reinforced the position with hurriedly assembled additional units, some of whom were from the Sturm (Assault) Battalion AOK 7 who actually rode down from Cherbourg on bicycles to join their men on the front.

On June 9 at around 0600 hours almost reminiscent of World War I, three battalions of US artillery launched a powerful preliminary barrage. This was the precursor to the attack by the 1st and 3rd Battalions, 8th Infantry, supported by paratroopers from the 2nd Battalion, 325th Glider Infantry, that commenced a half an hour later. The objective was the German line between the main highway and a tributary of the Merderet River. It wasn't long before withering German fire from across this creek brought the attack to a halt. The Airborne commander Colonel Ekman attempted various maneuvers to outflank the German positions but was eventually compelled to abandon the attack. The 8th Infantry didn't fare much better. In an attempt to try and assist the static 1st and 3rd Battalions, 8th Infantry, and salvage the situation Colonel Van Fleet decided to commit the 2nd Battalion in the center.

Despite repeated attacks the Germans managed to hold out at a well-prepared position all day, but by nightfall they decided to cut their losses and abandon the line. The previous 24 hours had been a grueling experience for the 8th Infantry and the attached Airborne units but although their dogged persistence yielded results, they expended a heavy price in casualties, and it was far from over.

On the same day June 9 the 3rd Battalion, 22nd Infantry, made substantial progress. Using revised tactics Lt. Col. John Dowdy organized further attacks on the Azeville batteries that were housed in four large concrete bunkers and this time it paid off. The 3rd Battalion assembled at 1100 hours roughly 1,000 yards southeast of Azeville and supported by artillery and tanks they moved out. By mid-afternoon a white flag was raised as the German commander surrendered all four bunkers along with a garrison of 169 men. It had been a tough fight that prompted General Collins to tell General Bradley that fighting in the bocage was as bad as anything he had encountered on Guadalcanal.

Francis W. Glaze Jr., HQ, 8th Infantry Regiment, Ammo Resupply

The time was probably about June 10 or 11, 1944, and we were holding just outside Montebourg in Normandy. The 90th Division had built up behind us and started across the Cotentin peninsula to seal it off before we started for Cherbourg. We were under pressure from the Germans all along our front and especially in the 2nd Battalion area. They did not want to be trapped on the peninsula, and we did not want them to break out.

During the day, I was sent forward from Regiment to determine the situation in front of the 2nd Battalion. My jeep was elsewhere, so I went forward with a commo man to visit Companies E and F. The commo man was looking for a wire break, as I remember. I couldn't find him when I was ready to go back, so I hitched a ride to the 8th Infantry Regiment CP.

Shortly after dark, the Germans attacked the 2nd Battalion sector. The line held, but the pressure built. Battalion said they could probably hold but that Company E was low on ammo. Captain "Squeak" Greenip, CO of Company E, told Regiment that I knew his location and asked that I bring as much ammo as a jeep and quarter-ton trailer could hold—by midnight! We loaded a good selection and took off for the "front," about 4 or 5 miles away. Time was short, so we used the main highway—a straight shot toward Montebourg. An 88 covered the road, but we felt that the dark gave us cover. About 200 yards short of where I planned to turn off to Company E, we found that the road had been mined. The Germans had not had time to dig in the mines; they just sat on top of the roadway. There were about 20 Teller antitank mines!

I decided that it was too dangerous to go off road around the mines so I walked in front, checked for trip wires, and guided Salvaggio, my driver, as he straddled the mines. We got through. The two "shotguns" rejoined us on "t'other" side. We continued for about 200 yards and turned left into a field, stopped against a hedgerow, and went looking for Company E. We finally found them. The firefight was about 100 yards to their front and slowing down a little. "Squeak" gave me a carrying party, and we went back to the jeep, picked up the ammo, and took it to the company.

About thirty minutes later we got back to the jeep, and Salvaggio was still there, but "as nervous as a whore in church." It seems that the Germans were digging in on the other side of the hedgerow to our front. They hadn't checked, and we didn't tell them. So, there we were—about 50 yards apart and separated only by darkness and a hedgerow!

It was after midnight. We shared Salvaggio's nervousness, so we pushed the jeep and trailer back to the road and down the road past the Teller mines.

It seemed like a good time to share our "nervousness" with the Germans, so we took two grenades apiece, and the four of us returned to the hedgerow. It was only about 100 feet long, so we spread out evenly and on my signal, we each threw one grenade long, and two or three seconds later, threw one grenade short, just over the hedgerow! By the time the first grenades went off, we were in high gear and running like a "Big A—Bird" for the jeep. The Germans were so busy shooting in all directions that we had no problems resuming our trip back.

It was very dark, and we were worried about our own sentries, so we made cautious haste. Suddenly we "sensed" a group of people in the roadway jumping into the ditches on each side of the road. The driver stopped about 50 yards from the group. We assumed it was an ambush about to take place and that we had appeared so suddenly that we had surprised them. We couldn't go back, so I decided to "run it" and throw two grenades in each ditch as we went by. I had just told Salvaggio to "gun it" and he had started the run when we heard *a baby cry. Luckily, I called out in time; only one man had to get the pin back in the grenade. We stopped and found about fifteen French women, children, and a grandfather who had slipped out of Montebourg before midnight and were trying to get to our lines before daylight.*

We spent a moment reassuring them, and then one of the men and I walked with them. The jeep led by a couple hundred yards to alert the sentries we might pass. The sentries were expecting us but not a gaggle of people walking down the road. About a mile later we arrived safely at an MP guarded road junction and turned our charges over to them. The French never knew the danger they were in, but we four were so thankful we heard the baby cry that we were downright maudlin.

After-Action Report: June 9, 1944

The 8th and 12th Regiments attacked at 05:30 toward the high ground east of Montebourg. Progress was continuous but slow at the cost of hard fighting and heavy losses (mainly around Ecausseville for the 8th, and at the Château de Dodainville near Joganville for the 12th). The 22nd launched a new assault on the four powerful forts of Azeville, abandoning the plan to take Crisbecq. Attacked to the rear, the position surrendered after the blowing of the ammunition caused by the flame thrower of Pvt Ralph G. Riley. In mid-afternoon, the 22nd formed with the 70th Tank Bn and 899th TD Bn, a special task force under command of Brigadier General Henry A. Barber with the mission of attacking in the direction of Château de Fontenay and Ozeville to capture Quinéville. The strong enemy position of Château de Fontenay pinned down the task force.

The weather was bad and no air support was available. For the first time, the distribution of rations for the infantry was initiated from the beach.

Not long after the Azeville batteries were silenced, assistant division commander Brig. Gen. Henry A. Barber, formed a task force comprising the 22nd Infantry, 899th Tank Destroyer Battalion and the 746th Tank Battalion. The purpose of this was to take the most easterly German positions at Quinéville and reach the high ground there. While a force of tank destroyers and infantry contained the Crisbecq position, the rest of the task force moved towards the Quinéville road but soon became pinned down by German fire. Their position remained static for almost three days. Persistent rains during June and July seriously hampered the efforts of the US Army and it was noted that the early summer of 1944 in Normandy was the wettest since 1900.

Unfavorable weather prevented Allied air support for the assault and the ferocity of the German defense exacerbated a bad situation even further. Eventually the 22nd Infantry was replaced by troops of the freshly arrived 39th Infantry Regiment, 9th Division, who managed to assist them in finally eradicating the Crisbecq position on June 12. Then the 22nd Infantry were ordered to clear the heights of German opposition and push north to continue their attempt, along with other US divisions, to seal off the Cotentin peninsula.

The way ahead was still not entirely clear and although the fringes of Montebourg had been secured, the 8th Infantry along with the 501st were still engaging the enemy all along their front. The 4th Division had been expected to relieve all Airborne units along the coastal region by this time but the town of Quinéville was still in German hands and the job was far from complete. The Germans' first line of resistance had been broken but they had fallen back on a new line and were tenaciously holding on to it with all they had.

Two battalions of the 22nd Infantry had been badly mauled in the previous assaults on the forts but the whole regiment was now called on again to capture the German gun emplacements at the town of Ozeville, which was the last remaining barrier before taking Quinéville. The German bunkers would be taken with hand grenades and bayonets. This freed up the 12th Infantry to proceed to the outskirts of Montebourg. It was here that General Barton exercised caution and ordered the two regiments not to go any further. This decision was prompted because of his recent assessment of the 4th Division's overall position at that stage of the invasion. He was justifiably wary of another German counterattack which, based on recent experience, he considered imminent. Moreover General Barton thought the 4th Division was far too thinly spread to manage and sustain further concerted enemy opposition. The daunting prospect of engaging his Ivy men in a house-to-house, hand-to-hand fight was too daunting at that time.

Although the 4th Division's position had been eased somewhat by the arrival of the 39th Infantry from the 9th Division they were still in a potentially precarious situation. On the strength of recent intelligence, which reported that Montebourg was only being lightly held, Barton informed Colonel Van Fleet that he would commit the 8th Infantry to taking the town only on the condition that it could be captured and occupied in one day. He would go back on this condition. This incited Van Fleet to organize a task force for this sole purpose. The task force was assembled in the course of the day and at nightfall, around 2100 hours, they moved out towards Montebourg. The task force comprised two rifle companies, each augmented with a platoon of engineers, heavy machine guns, antitank guns, 4.2-inch mortars and tank destroyers, and a cannon company. The 29th Field Artillery Battalion would provide direct support.

Before long they discovered that the approach roads to the town were well defended to such an extent that the task force was compelled to retire and resume the attack the following morning, June 13. General Barton defaulted on his previous condition and chose to opt for a different strategy on this occasion by placing the task force on the fringes of town and sending out patrols to probe the opposition. His trepidation was well grounded. While Montebourg remained occupied by Germans, a planned attack towards Quinéville by the 22nd Infantry and the 39th Infantry, 9th Division would render their left flank dangerously exposed and vulnerable. Unfortunately for the latter, June 13 didn't produce the expected results and by the close of the day despite repeated attempts to secure the ridges to the west of Quinéville neither the 22nd Infantry nor the 39th were able to make any substantial gains. A further attempt to capture these positions and move on Quinéville would be ordered the following day and on this occasion all three battalions of the 22nd Infantry would be engaged.

Bill Garvin, Company K, 3rd Battalion, 12th Infantry Regiment

I nervously peeked over the nearby hedgerow and discovered, shockingly, that a German patrol of six men was not more than 30 feet away creeping towards us. With no time to waste, I signaled to my buddies the danger we were in and then jumped up, John Wayne style, onto the hedgerow top. I leveled my carbine on the leader and yelled, "Achtung!" meaning, Attention! It was the only German word I knew that indicated to them that I meant business. The leader got the message and gave a command to his men to lay down their firearms and raise their hands. Motioning them to come forward, we took them prisoners.

There appears to have been a glaring lack of cohesion in the planning and execution of this attack. While the 22nd Infantry were advancing on the ridge, the 39th Infantry received express permission to hit Quinéville autonomously head on. The 39th discovered that the town was sparsely defended and managed to infiltrate the perimeter but were eventually forced back by heavy fire from the remaining German coastal fortifications. In the ensuing confusion supporting tanks from the 70th Battalion opened up a long-range barrage that hit tank destroyers of the 39th Infantry's 1st Battalion. The attack was temporarily halted while a reassessment of the situation was made.

A decision was made to neutralize the remaining German positions in proximity to the beach before resuming the attack. This proved to be the best course of action because although Lt. Gen. Heinz Hellmich, commanding the 243rd Division, augmented with elements of the 709th and 91st Divisions, had been ordered by Adolf Hitler to hold the Montebourg–Quinéville line at all costs, the attack by the 22nd and the 39th Infantry resulted in the capture of both Quinéville and the ridge on June 14. The Ivy Division was effectively held up for almost a week.

Donald Ellis, Company G, 2nd Battalion, 8th Infantry Regiment

Montebourg was the first big town we hit. After digging in for the night, Rip Colbath, some others and I, decided we would go into town to scout around. A common practice of the town folk was to hide in cellars of the bombed-out houses. When we came in contact with them, they would tell us whether the Germans had left or were hiding out. In checking out several houses, we entered a partially demolished large apartment building. Entering the cellar, we came upon a large group of French men, women, and children. We spent most of the night there trying to converse with our pidgin French and their poor English. They shared their meager food and wine, and we shared what rations we had with them. Just as it began to get light, we decided to go back to our lines. As we emerged into a large courtyard in a strung out line, a burst of machine-gun fire hit and killed one of the two guys ahead of me. My buddy, Rip Colbath, was stitched up. I picked up Rip and took him back to our line. Upon returning to our lines, we were met by a medic and Captain Haley. He radioed HQ that our patrol had discovered the town was very lightly defended. Having learned this information, it precluded a full-scale assault. As a result of this, we earned the Silver Star.

As we captured them, we would immediately separate officers from enlisted men because the privates wouldn't talk with the officers present. Breaking out of the hedgerows, we began to hit open country and thus made better progress. We would ride on the back of tanks and tracks, but when we hit resistance, we'd dismount and fight.

After-Action Report: June 21, 1944

Concrete and reinforced emplacements were successively occupied by the enemy as its units withdrew to stronger defensive positions around Cherbourg. All strong points along the eastern coast as far north as Quettehou (24th Cavalry Reconnaissance sector) were found free of enemy. The 8th continued the attack from positions in the vicinity of Ruffoses. The 12th attacked and progressed in the vicinity of Gallis until it was stopped by artillery, mortar and small-arms fire. The 22nd attacked at 16:00 from its positions in vicinity of Le Theil and captured the high ground. The advance was stopped at 22:00 by order.

Unaware that most of the German forces had withdrawn, the 8th and 12th Infantry Regiments now orchestrated a pincer movement on Montebourg, which already been pummeled by Allied air attacks, it was finally taken on June 19 with relative ease. It was the 3rd Battalion, 22nd Infantry that discovered that the Germans had cleared out.

James Drennan, HQ, 42nd Field Artillery Battalion

Walking into the city of Montebourg on or about June 14, 1944, I felt complete sadness imprinted on my mind. Dead mothers and fathers holding their dead children was a scene I was not ready to handle. Dead men from D-Day to the Battle of the Bulge have all but faded from my mind, but not the scene in the train or bus station. God, please forgive us.

As the 8th reached southeast of Valognes parallel to the 12th Infantry with the 24th Cavalry Squadron covering the right flank of 4th Infantry Division, the way was now clear to support the attack on Cherbourg that had commenced a few days earlier. The 4th, 9th and 79th Infantry Divisions began advancing north on a broad front toward Cherbourg, which was only 10 miles away. The Cotentin peninsula had been effectively cauterized but Cherbourg wouldn't be taken without a hard fight.

Stanley McKaig, Company C, 4th Engineer Battalion

The 4th Infantry Division troops handed all their German prisoners over to the paratroopers who had done their mission for the day and were heading back to the beach. From there on, we generally turned toward Cherbourg, and a few days later sealed off the peninsula.

Then, the real assault was on Cherbourg. As I remember, I didn't get to wash or shave for thirteen days as we continued through the hedgerows of Normandy. The first real hot meal we had was in Paris, on August 25, 1944, when the company cooks made fried chicken— nothing else but chicken, but it sure tasted good.

Bill Garvin, Company K, 3rd Battalion, 12th Infantry Regiment

A few days later, units of the 90th Infantry Division passed through our ranks heading south, to cut across the Cherbourg peninsula and seal off the German escape route with the eventual fall of Cherbourg. Capturing Cherbourg resulted in a bonanza of prisoners and a very important port that was not heavily damaged. The city was well fortified by dozens of huge concrete pillboxes and gun emplacements designed to repulse any Allied attempt from a frontal assault from across the Channel. Our attacking from the east, the opposite direction, fooled them completely.

Under the auspices of "Lightning" Joe Collins, the three US infantry divisions made their move and discovered that the commander of VII Corps wasn't nicknamed "Lightning" for nothing. The 9th struck from the west, with the 79th advancing from the south, and the 4th from the east. On June 22, the port city was hammered by 1,000 Allied aircraft and two days later Generalleutnant Karl-Wilhelm von Schlieben, in command of the German forces there, conceded that defeat was inevitable. After a bitter fight on June 25, Cherbourg was taken. It was the 12th Infantry who were given the honor of physically liberating the city. According to the 12th Infantry's official history, commanders of the 4th Division assigned the honor of taking Cherbourg to the 12th Infantry Regiment for its gallant struggle from the beaches. There would be five more days of fighting to effectively clear the whole area and several weeks before the Allies would be able to use the port. Cherbourg was in ruins and contrary to Allied expectations capturing the port didn't really help to resolve any supply problems.

The Ivy men had already paid a heavy toll since D-Day. It had been 24 days since they had landed at Utah and their fight to take the Cotentin peninsula had cost them over 5,450 casualties with 800 KIA. For some hitherto inexplicable reason all assault divisions were awarded the French Croix de Guerre except for the 4th Infantry Division.

After-Action Report: July 12, 1944

The 22nd Infantry launched its attack at 09:15 to capture the objectives east of Périers and encountered stiff enemy resistance. Enemy's strong resistance and extremely accurate artillery concentrations continued. The 8th Infantry supported the attack of the 22nd Infantry with all available firepower. The regiment remained in its former position and patrols were initiated across the Molerotte river. The 12th Infantry, in division reserve, assembled and moved to follow the advance of the 22nd Infantry and to protect the left flank and rear of the Division. At 21:45, the regiment started relieving the 22nd Infantry. Brigadier General Theodore Roosevelt, Jr. died of a heart attack.

CHAPTER 9

BREAKING HARD

The race was now on to take Cherbourg and open its harbor to Allied shipping. The floating British Mulberry harbors assembled off Omaha and Gold Beaches had performed well during the initial weeks of the invasion but recent bad weather had inflicted some damage and an impending bad storm had been predicted. Meanwhile both von Rundstedt and Rommel made a formal request to Adolf Hitler to withdraw their forces out of the range of naval gunfire. Hitler flatly refused permission. He wasn't in the mood to negotiate and ordered his commanders to hold their ground at all costs.

By June 18, the 82nd Airborne Division had reached the west coast of the Cotentin peninsula, completely isolating the northern section. Around 40,000 Germans from the 77th, 91st, 243rd and 709th Infantry Divisions were now completely trapped. Fortunately for the Allies they were all regular infantry but they would nonetheless put up a fight. The 4th Infantry Division continued following an axis in an easterly direction, starting out from Montebourg. On June 21, the 8th and the 12th Infantry attacked the primary defenses of Cherbourg from the northwest, including Hill 800 just northwest of Roudou wood where suspected V1 launch sites were located. The 8th Infantry were tasked with the mission of clearing the woods and, supported by a tank platoon, 8th Infantry eventually took the intersection at La Bourdonnerie, a vital crossroads. By the evening of June 21, VII US Corps was ready for the final assault against the fortress of Cherbourg. On this date other units from VII Corps attacked the perimeter around Cherbourg. General von Schlieben, the German officer charged with the defense of the city, was invited to surrender but refused the offer and issued strict orders to his men to thoroughly destroy all the port facilities. What was left of the German divisions resisted fiercely and fighting around the city's main fortification, the Fort du Roule, embedded in a cliff overlooking the harbor, was particularly intense.

By June 25, the 12th Infantry Regiment's three battalions had moved into Cherbourg from the east. The 2nd and 3rd Battalions encountered relatively little resistance and both of these battalions managed to reach Rue de la Bretonneniére in the center of the town, just 450 yards from the inner harbor. The 1st Battalion wasn't as fortunate, as daylight turned to twilight they encountered heavy opposition east of the "Fort des Flamands," which was largely destroyed by the German troops themselves. The 1st Battalion could not bring their attack to a close until the following day, when tanks arrived to provide support. The arrival of these Shermans was sufficient to encourage 350 Germans to surrender. One day later General von Schlieben and the Admiral Hennecke capitulated. When news of the surrender was given to Adolf Hitler he became incandescent with rage. Just a few weeks later he would survive an assassination attempt orchestrated by his own generals.

Operations against Cherbourg had taken longer than initially expected and when the city finally fell, the Allies discovered that the port had suffered such devastation it would be a while before the harbor facilities were usable.

After the capture of Cherbourg, the 4th Infantry Division spent about a week occupying the town and switching from one area to another. The attached artillery units were equally diligent in providing vital support for the 30th Division, 25 miles south of Cherbourg. With a new task looming for the Ivy men there was going to be no time wasted on much-needed rest and recuperation, and the time that they had was allocated to training up replacements to replace the numerous casualties incurred during those first tempestuous weeks of combat in Normandy.

Richard A. Sover, Company I, 3rd Battalion, 12th Infantry Regiment

On Sunday, June 25, we were nearing the city, according to the road signs. We proceeded cautiously. As we neared the English Channel, all hell broke loose. Artillery fire was hitting the road we were on. We spotted where the artillery was coming from. There was high ground to our left and we could see the flashes. I rolled off the road onto a ditch where someone had previously been digging. I slid into this ditch and stayed under cover until the firing stopped. Many Company I men were killed and injured on June 25, 1944. We made a direct attack on the enemy and secured Cherbourg around 0100 hours.

We reorganized and marched into Cherbourg and occupied many of the homes. The next morning, I took a patrol to see what damage we had done. We visited some of the concrete bunkers. The odor was awful. I did not stay in them very long. Our next visit was the "Atlantique Hotel," the General Headquarters of the enemy. Everyone was searching for souvenirs. I found an officer's trench knife with scabbard. It looked like a letter opener. I tied it under my left armpit.

We left Cherbourg on June 27, and headed toward St. Lô. On July 6, we were in a tough fight amongst the hedgerows. I had just dug a foxhole when the ammunition truck came by and dropped off some mortar shells. I got out of my foxhole to distribute the shells to my ammunition carriers. All of a sudden, enemy artillery was shelling us. One shell hit close to me. It lifted me off the ground and I did a 360-degree turn and was slammed into the hedgerow. I must have been knocked out for a few minutes, for when I came to, I heard my platoon sergeant, Prewitt, hollering, "If there are any walking wounded, head for the ambulance." I noticed that I could not see from my left eye. Blood was rolling down my cheek. My arms were bleeding from shrapnel. As I stood up, I noticed holes in my jacket and I was bleeding from my chest. I was able to walk, so I told the platoon sergeant that I was going to the ambulance.

As I approached the ambulance I started to vomit, but the medic said all wounded soldiers did the same thing. All this time, I thought I had lost my left eye. I got in the ambulance and we went to an Aid Station. Immediately, the nurses and medics started to check my wounds. The first thing they did was to check my left eye and then they gave me the good news. The piece of shrapnel had lodged in my left eyelid and had caused bleeding, making it difficult to see. In checking further, they also found a piece of shrapnel in my right eyebrow, shrapnel in both arms, and across my chest.

The Germans had been forced to surrender Cherbourg under pressure, and now after four long years occupying France they were determined to raise the stakes. On July 3, rain set in and it continued for days saturating every GI to the skin and depriving any offensive actions of vital air cover. Then on July 6, on the orders of General Collins, some units of the 4th moved into position near the 83rd Division, which was holding a narrow promontory in the Carentan sector. Collins was hedging his bets and being somewhat overoptimistic by sending in the 4th Division in the hope that the 83rd Division would strike forward and reach Sainteny in one day and rejoin VII Corps in launching an attack through the bocage country that lay to the west of Carentan.

On July 7, the US Army went on the offensive and made an initial effort west of the Viré River. The purpose of this was to capture the high ground that lay to the east of St. Lô. If this could be achieved then the Allies would have a tactical advantage because numerous roads converged at St. Lô. Some of these roads were being used as supply lines for the German army who were now in the process of gathering their forces.

Francis W. Glaze Jr., HQ, 8th Infantry Regiment

Teddy (General Roosevelt) escaped from the Division Command Post and was reviewing the situation with Colonel Van Fleet, our Regimental Commander, when a tremendous German barrage started. For once, it wasn't for us. It was landing 3 or 4 miles to our rear and obviously aimed at our Division CP. Teddy was enthralled. He got up on a hedgerow, hooting and hollering. "Give it to them—that will make those bastards back at division get off their asses and down in the foxholes," he said. He was cheering the Germans on at a great rate.

The last time I saw Teddy was one morning after we had taken Cherbourg, when we were starting the attack out of the bocage country toward the St. Lô–Periers Road. The attack was the first of nine days attacking on a regimental front against the German 6th Parachute Regiment. The 8th Infantry Regiment started the attack, but each regiment got in its three days' worth. The 6th was well dug in and we only made 200–300 yards a day. After nine days we reached our objective south of the St. Lô Road. The German 6th made us pay dearly at a three to one casualty rate, but they no longer existed as a unit.

My driver and I had been up with the assault battalion for the jump-off at 0400 hours and then reported back to the Regimental CO. My driver was very proud of his brand-new jeep. It replaced the old one that died after three and a half weeks of combat. The new jeep was three days old and did not have a scratch on it. It was about 0700 hours. I was tired, so I crawled into the sack to catch a few winks. About an hour later, my dog-robber wakened me to report to the CP "ASAP!" Colonel Van Fleet and Teddy needed a guide to the battalion HQ, and I was volunteered.

I went looking for my jeep and driver but found only the jeep, so I drove myself back to the CP. The other two jeeps fell in behind, and we took off. The attack battalion CP was on a forward slope, so we stopped about 100 yards behind the ridgeline and went forward on foot. At the CP the Battalion CO joined us by the side of the road and discussed the situation with Teddy and Van Fleet.

About then some enemy shells came moaning in, just cleared the ridgeline, and exploded yonder. Since I was just a captain, I felt more vulnerable than the high-paid help, so I lay down in the ditch by the side of the road. Their discussion seemed to speed up, and then Teddy looked down at me and said, "You are probably smarter than we are. Why don't you lead us back and out of here? We've been brave and stupid long enough."

We quickly went back to the jeeps, and I noticed the new shell crater about 10 feet to the left of my new jeep. The side was a sieve, the muffler was no more. The windshield, cover, and half the steering wheel were gone, and the spare tire was history. It sounded like a tank, but the four wheels were round and the motor "moted." I led my little entourage back to the 8th Infantry Regiment CP and then I went back to my Company CP. There my driver was waiting with folded arms. He fell on me from a great height, berating me for going without him. He had believed me to be dead and buried, and he held me fully accountable for breaking his new jeep. It is difficult to watch a grown man cry, but he insisted that I go along to the Service Company Motor Pool and explain why he needed a new jeep after only four days. He got a new one, so I was back in his good graces again.

The 4th Infantry Division advanced down the eastern coast of Carentan to cross the Periers road and begin attacking the 7th German Army but soon realized to their consternation that this part of Normandy was not really conducive to the type of mobile warfare that Collins and other Allied commanders wanted to conduct. For a start there was the centuries-old bocage bordering almost every field and giving excellent defensive cover to the Germans, and then there were large areas of marshland that were devoid of navigable road systems. The outcome of the first day of the big drive south was entirely predictable as the 4th only managed to advance 400 yards and over one week later they had only moved 4 miles. Inclement weather conditions restricted the use of covering Allied air support so the 4th were compelled to run the gauntlet through terrifying narrow corridors of hedgerows against expertly arranged enemy positions.

All the advantages were with the Germans in those first days and the advance proved to be painstakingly difficult as 4th Division casualties mounted hourly. Allied commanders agreed collectively that the cost in human lives for the areas gained was becoming reminiscent of World War I battles, and this costly attrition style of warfare had to be altered.

A decisive blow had to be struck against the German army that would shatter their current resolve.

By July 10 the German units in the vicinity of the Ivy men were gradually beginning to fracture and dissolve under the strain of constant attacks. They managed to organize a counterattack but when the 4th decisively repelled this they began to fall back. Having fought its way to a point near Periers, the 4th was now pulled out of the line and moved to an assembly area further east in order to make preparations for the great drive south that would for all accounts and purposes end the current stalemate. The Allies had the ground forces in place along with adequate supplies and vastly superior air power. Now all they needed was a good plan to finally demolish German resistance in Normandy.

John C. Clark, HQ, 29th Field Artillery Battalion

I will never forget our landing on Utah Red Beach on June 6, 1944. The smell of everything was unforgettable. I remember the difficulty in breathing as a result of all the burned powder from the bombing and the shelling. As impressive as that was, I remember more about our St. Lô experiences on the morning of July 25. Maybe I was too high strung to really appreciate what was happening on the beach.

We 29th Field Artillery forward observers were on point with Company B of the 8th Infantry Regiment that morning. Our objective was to lay a line of smoke shells along the St. Lô–Periers road as a marker to guide the planes on their bombing run. If memory serves me, it was a little after 0900 hours that we called for the smoke shells, and it was just a few minutes until we heard the sound of incoming planes.

There must have been several hundred fighter bombers that hit the smoke line from every direction for about a half hour. It looked as if they did a good job, but we wondered if this was all we were getting to soften up the line for the break out. Then we heard what sounded like a swarm of bees, but as the sound became louder, we realized it was hundreds of planes. It was one group of planes after another; they stretched as far as we could see. I had never seen so many planes at one time.

As the first bombers flew over us, the German 88s started to shoot at them and they got two or three before the Piper Cubs could report where they saw the gun flashes. After our artillery opened up, the 88s became quiet. I have no way of knowing how many planes were up there that day but it was an impressive sight.

As we watched them coming, we began to hear the bombing getting louder. Then we realized it was getting closer. The wind had come from the south and was blowing the smoke back over us. The planes were dropping their bombs on our positions. My driver, Jones, and

I crawled under a tank and hoped we didn't get a direct hit. The bombs were so loud that all we could think to do was wrap our field jackets around our heads to help stop the noise. We put our arms up over our ears and found it helped to open our mouths when we heard some close ones coming in. We were in as safe a place as we could find so all we could do was sweat it out and hope they missed us. The bombing lasted maybe a half hour, but it seemed like forever.

After the bombing stopped, Jones and I came out from under the tank into an eerie quiet. The ground was covered with craters. The raw earth was everywhere. As we started to regroup, we were very fortunate to find our jeep would run, but the radios were out.

When we looked around for our squad, we found that our two new replacements, McGrady and McLeroy, had completely lost it. We tied their shoelaces together, wrapped their gun belts around their arms, and took them back to the command post. As for Jones and me, it was several days before we could even talk in a normal voice, rather than shouting at each other.

After we picked up some radios, we went back up to B Company, which was regrouping. A lot of them were wounded or in shock, so it was not a good situation. We heard later that we had over six hundred "friendly fire" casualties, including General McNair. As I look back over my war years, St. Lô stands out as the worst incident among many traumatic occurrences.

The previous weeks of fighting in the bocage country had cost the 4th Infantry Division dearly. The three regiments had incurred 2,300 casualties and among them were three battalion commanders and nine rifle company commanders. As a testament to the ferocity of the fighting that they had endured, only five of the original rifle company commanders that had participated in the D-Day landings still remained, and the 4th Division had been compelled to augment their depleted ranks with 4,400 replacements. Nevertheless they had played a key role in the southward advance and now they were going to be an important component in the next major offensive. They were moved into Avranches on July 30, which would effectively situate them nicely to participate in the offensive that would become known as Operation Cobra.

General Omar Bradley was becoming increasingly frustrated with the Allied failure to effectively reduce the German defenses in Normandy. The whole premise of a tactical warfare of movement was degenerating into a punishing war of attrition that Bradley feared could become "trench war" if left unattended. The stalemate had endured too long and it was time to make a decisive thrust to break whatever resolve the Germans still had.

The 9th and 30th Divisions were nearing exhaustion from their battles in the Taute and Vire region so Collins requested and received the 4th Division and assigned to it a role in the initial infantry assault. General Bradley had initially planned to retain the 4th as army reserve, but he acquiesced to Collins' request in order to insure a quick follow-up to the planned air bombardment. It was time to call on the Ivy men again.

Captain Walter E. Marchand, Battalion Surgeon, HQ, 4th Infantry Division

July 5–17

Days become confused, all mixed together, and I lost ability to account for each day. Not that I can't remember what happened, it's that the sequence of events was lost sight of.

It was in this period that we really got Artillery—as heavy as any so far since D-Day and the country was tough to fight over yes we advanced after bitter fighting only some days we attacked and attacked with great loss of life and we took only a few hedgerows.

And Jerry planes started coming over more and more frequently—strafing in the daytime, and bombing at night and dropping occasional paratroopers, which caused confusion always and made us form a different defense.

The Germans had a stubborn defense and used Tiger tanks freely but by piecemeal commitment the terrain did not allow them to use them in Company strength or larger as is their method this is not tank country definitely but it is excellent for mortar and the Germans used plenty of them as we also did.

General Collins' VII Corps attack would be coordinated through two distinct phases. Using the Periers–St. Lô road as a starting point, the first task following a heavy Allied air bombardment was to send in his infantry divisions to puncture German defenses, and capture crucial road junctions. The 83rd and 9th Infantry Divisions would head in from the west, while the 4th Infantry Division covered the center, and the 30th Infantry Division in the east would seal the flanks of the penetration and then secure the shoulders, which would effectively establish a corridor to allow necessary mechanized reserves to be brought up. In the second phase these mechanized reserves would be expected to take critical advantage of the breakthrough. It looked good on paper.

Darel Parker, Company C, 1st Battalion, 12th Infantry Regiment

I joined the 4th Infantry Division at Camp Gordon Johnston in Florida. We moved from there to South Carolina, then to New Jersey and then to England. From England, we went to France, and then to Normandy on D-Day. The water was rough, but we made it and went on to cross the flooded areas. Some of the water there was 6–7 feet deep, and with all the equipment we were carrying, it wasn't very easy. We then attacked on to Cherbourg and through the hedgerows. Then we went to Bloody Mortain, St. Lô, and on to Paris, which was a story in itself.

On July 25 the Ivy men, along with the US 2nd Armored Division, were chosen to spearhead Operation *Cobra*. The 2nd Armored Division would be augmented with the attachment of the 4th Infantry Division's 22nd Regimental Combat Team.

Between July 18 and 20, poor weather delayed the start of Operation *Cobra*. When the offensive was given the green light, around 1,600 bombers and six groups of fighter-bombers of the 9th TAC (Tactical Air Combat) took to the skies over Normandy and began saturation bombing along a narrow corridor located 3 miles northwest of St. Lô. Low cloud and poor visibility caused almost 500 of these bombers to abort. Then, during the night of July 23/24, US forces located in the area were ordered to withdraw to a distance of 1,000 yards to the northeast to avoid collateral damage but this didn't prevent the accidental bombing of the 30th Infantry Division. Twenty-five US soldiers were killed and 131 were wounded. Dozens of soldiers were buried alive under tons of earth thrown up by the bombs. General Bradley was extremely distraught at the reports of the friendly bombing incident but decided to push on with Operation *Cobra* regardless.

After-Action Report: July 24, 1944

> Enemy started defensive fires using mortars, machine guns and interdictory artillery barrages. The 8th Infantry (with other units among which were the 70th Tank Bn and the 634th TD Bn) attacked at 1300 in columns of battalions. The 2nd Battalion succeeded in advancing against heavy artillery and mortar fire to a line north of St. Lô–Périers highway. Upon division order, the battalion withdrew to streamline and consolidated positions. The 12th Infantry and 4th Reconnaissance Troop remained in reserve and were prepared to follow the advance of the 8th Infantry. The divisional Artillery and attached units supported the advance, 29th FA and 42nd FA in direct support, the 20th in general support with harassing and interdiction missions.

War correspondent Ernie Pyle summarized the events of the following day when he wrote "The great Allied breakthrough on July 25, spearheaded by three infantry divisions with the Fourth Division in the center of the thrust, will go down as one of the great historical dates of World War II."

One the biggest bombardments occurred the following day, Tuesday July 25, when 1,500 B-17s and B-24s bombed an area northwest of

St. Lô and dropped around 3,300 tons of bombs. On this occasion collateral damage resulted in the deaths of 111 and nearly 500 wounded GIs. Lieutenant General Lesley J. McNair was counted among them. He was the highest-ranking American soldier killed in action in the European theater. Ground forces followed up the air strike with a thunderous artillery barrage delivered by 1,100 guns.

Even though the collateral damage incurred by US forces was hugely distressing, the Germans suffered a much greater toll. They lost a substantial amount of their armor support along with innumerable soldiers and vehicles. The Panzer Lehr was reduced to having to make do with only seven operable tanks. The combined Allied air and land bombardments didn't only cause significant damage to the German forces; they were so devastating that in some places they even altered the geography, which actually hindered US Army progress and made some villages in certain areas completely inaccessible.

The Americans launched their ground attacks with six divisions located between Montreuil and Hebecrevon. They were up against the battle-hardened 2nd and 17th SS Panzer Divisions along with the 352nd Infantry Division and the 2nd Parachute Regiment. The 4th Infantry Division progressed to Canisy. The 2nd Armored Division, strengthened by the attachment of the 4th Infantry Division's 22nd Regimental Combat Team, attacked St. Gilles while the 30th Infantry Division on their left flank headed south below St. Lô. By the evening of July 25, the front line had only extended roughly 1.5 miles. The limited progress caused some consternation among US commanders. Many of the German POWs taken were still in shock caused by the Allied bombardments. On the basis of this, the following day US forces decided to up the pressure on the enemy and increase the shelling.

South of Caen on the same day, the British launched their supporting Operation *Spring* offensive, which prevented the Germans from sending reinforcements to fight against the American offensive. At the center of this thrust the 4th Division's 8th Infantry achieved initial success by advancing with two battalions abreast covering an area of 2 miles. They captured the completely demolished village of La Chapelle en Juger early on in the day and by dusk they had advanced around 7 miles. In the process they overran part of the German 353rd Division and completely outflanked both the Panzer Lehr artillery along with their remaining 275th Division reserves at Marigny.

By August 2, some incursions had been made into the German lines and General Patton had joined the fray with his Third Army which, along with elements of the First Army, was making a dash for the town of Avranches, where a corridor had been formed with the sea on one side and 4th Infantry Division on the other. Maintaining this corridor was of vital importance to the offensive and it the Ivy men contributed greatly by ensuring that the corridor remained open and accessible allowing other US forces to pour through.

German forces to the east of the corridor posed the greatest threat at the time because they had every intention of remaining in place and severing this opening. Recognizing the magnitude of this potential problem, the 4th Infantry Division launched its entire strength to neutralize any German attempts to accomplish this. One of the most pressing problems the 4th encountered was due to the fact that the Germans still held the high ground and a commanding 360° view of the whole terrain. This fact impeded their progress, moreover the Germans were more inclined to fight during daylight hours and use the cover of night to withdraw to strategically important high ground. This is precisely what they did when they fell back onto a long line of hills that ran east parallel to the road from Villedieu to St. Pois. It became an imperative to remove them from these hills. They were eventually dislodged by the 4th. The summit of these hills offered perfect observation of the retreating German columns and the 4th was able to bring mortars and artillery to bear on them with deadly accuracy.

Conrad "Frenchy" Adams, Company E, 2nd Battalion, 8th Infantry Regiment

Before I start, let me tell you that I am very proud that there were six of the Adams brothers who served in World War II, and, thanks to the good Lord above, we all made it home alive. And second, let me tell you that I believe in miracles. I have highlighted the miracles that happened to me in my story below.

July 25 came and while we were in the foxholes, we saw around five thousand bombers dropping bombs. This was St. Lô. People wondered why Americans were killed by our own bombers. The reason was when the smoke bombs were dropped, the good Lord above had the wind change, and the bombers didn't know, so they dropped the bombs short. They hit us just outside of our foxholes. Only my buddy Bell, did not survive. He died of a concussion, leaving me and the others to go on fighting the Germans. And boy what a feeling. (And that's another miracle.) Then as the joke goes, someone hollered, "Get some Greyhound busses to catch up with the Germans!"

I turned nineteen, and our objective was a railroad depot. That was early in the afternoon. The 4th Infantry Division wasn't satisfied, so we kept on pushing and passed a well-camouflaged German tank. We went into position, not knowing we had passed a tank.

As you know, the riflemen guarded one flank and the BAR man and his assistant, along with the machine gunner and those assistants, guarded the other flank.

The camouflaged German tank came from our rear and started firing at us. Then the riflemen jumped over the hedgerow and we had to cross the field to the other side. The machine gunner ran across and we heard him holler. We figured he had been shot. After one assistant gunner tried to go across, we heard him holler. I told my buddies, the BAR man and his assistant, that we should back up and jump the hedgerow around the back. One jumped, then the other jumped, and then it was my turn. By then, the German tanks had seen us and as I jumped over the hedgerow, my helmet came off and a bullet creased my head. Just a quarter of an inch lower and I would not have been able to write this. (Again, that's another miracle.)

As we jumped over the hedgerows, we jumped into the German hands. They had captured the BAR team of Brown, from California; Clarence, of Fort Wayne, Indiana; and me. The first thing the Germans asked us was if we had American cigarettes, but none of us smoked. Then they questioned us about our Army and how many, etc. But they seemed to know more than we did.

I put a bandage on my head. I was weak from the loss of blood. The bandage was white and green. They started taking us to the rear and marching us to a Stalag. Eventually, the American airplanes must have seen my bandage and started spraying us, not knowing that some of us were Americans. We were not hit. (That's a miracle.)

On the third or fourth day of captivity (I said I was weak from loss of blood), I dug into the pockets of my jacket and found two hand grenades. I'm glad no one said anything because the Germans could have killed me then. (I say again, another miracle.)

We started to march at night and hide in the day. A week passed and we were stopped along a hedgerow. When they heard the walking and heard American soldiers, the German lieutenant pulled out his Luger pistol from his holster, pointed it at my head, and told me if the soldiers opened fire that I would be the first to die. No one opened fire. (Another miracle.) By the way, that lieutenant could speak better English than I could.

When we heard machine-gun fire, we would hit the hedgerows, and then some of the Germans would pass me up. I don't know what happened to the lieutenant. I guess it was everyone for themselves so I lay down and let the Germans pass me up. I waited ten minutes or so then started to walk back the way we came from. I would walk at night and hide in the daytime.

One morning, I ran across a field to a barn and must have walked in a circle, because when I went into the barn, I walked right into the same Germans. (Another miracle.) This time they, too, were tired and hungry. They had hidden their weapons under the hay.

I heard the American tanks coming. I asked "Luxembourg," who was dressed in a German uniform, if he could understand French, and he said he could. I told him I was going outside and stop the tanks. I stopped the first tank, and all full of blood, not shaved, and dirty, the tank man pointed the .50 caliber machine gun at me, but he decided not to shoot me. (Again, a miracle). When I got on the tank, I told the captain there were German soldiers in the barn. He asked me if I was an American and I told him I was, but had no tags on me. Then he saw my ODs under my fatigues. They picked up three truckloads full of German prisoners and made a pile of weapons 4 feet high and 15 feet long. That was the 2nd Armored Tank Division that saved me.

They took me to G-2, in the rear and I was questioned a lot. I told them what happened and that the Germans were out of fuel, food, communications, and transportation. I know because they made me carry two 88 shells. The information I gave them helped Patton and Montgomery to close in that pocket much sooner. The captain said I would be awarded the Purple Heart, Silver Star (which I never received), and the Bronze Star.

Then I was brought further on with G-2 to a radio station. I was to make a speech that would be broadcast by a New Orleans radio station, telling on the radio just how I had escaped and so on. After the speech, they said I was like Superman, and then they asked the American people to buy more American war bonds. I refused to make the broadcast. I am sure the Germans would have picked up that radio broadcast, and I figured the next American to be captured would not be as lucky as me. I thanked God for what he had done for me. They told me to go back to America for a 30-day furlough. Then I would be transferred to the Pacific theater. Having the experience of combat, I chose to stay in the European theater and not go home.

By August 6 the 4th Infantry Division had reached an area north of the See River and on the night of August 6 a concerted German counterattack got under way. US forces reacted quickly and decisively and by the following day they had all but repelled this attack. The Ivy men were in close proximity to the action occurring around the town of Mortain and their artillery slowed the main German thrust along with helping to contain the counterattack. While the enemy threat from the east was beginning to dissipate, the vital corridor had been maintained and even extended. As elements of the First Army drove through to Mortain, Domfront, and other towns southeast of Avranches, Patton's Third Army headed to the Brest Peninsula. Then on August 6, somewhat unexpectedly, in a vain attempt to address the imbalance the Germans launched a further series of desperate counterattacks.

Now that six American divisions had already struck south through the breakout zone General Omar Bradley was faced with two stark choices. He could recall one or more of these divisions and commit them to stem the counterattack or he could take a calculated risk that the units guarding the Avranches corridor could handle the situation, repel the counterattack and keep the route open. He went for the latter option.

During the small hours of August 7, the Germans advanced westward with a sizeable force of infantry and tanks on the south bank of the See River. Adolf Hitler personally planned the massive counterattack at Mortain. Four German tank divisions were to move from Mortain to Avranches, attacking first the 30th Infantry Division. It was going to be the last opportunity Hitler's forces had to divide the Allied armies in northwestern France. The 4th Infantry Division was tasked with zeroing its artillery on the enemy's forward positions and checking the advance.

Meanwhile simultaneously one of the 4th Division's combat teams was dispatched to the 30th Division to assist them in salvaging their hold on Mortain, and rescuing its besieged battalion there. In four days of constant engagements with the enemy, the 12th Infantry suffered 1,150 casualties. By August 13 Mortain had been secured, the combat team taken out of the line and the German counteroffensive had been totally routed.

Despite the initial problems caused by the air bombardment, Operation *Cobra* had been a resounding success. In one short month the Allies had successfully engaged four German armies and thrown them out of western Prance. However contrary to what the media was reporting, these victories did not completely annihilate German forces in the West.

The 4th Infantry Division had played a critical role in the Normandy campaign. Wide smiles spread across the faces of infantrymen when they were reliably informed that they would soon be pulled out of the line and sent to a rest area. After almost two weeks of bitter, continuous fighting they would now finally have a chance to recuperate before the next move. This would be the first time since the landing at Utah Beach that Ivy men would be able to kick back a little and relax, finally they could look forward to the prospect of hot showers, fresh uniforms, movies, USO shows, and even visits from the Red Cross "donut girls" but it would be over all too soon.

Unit Citation – Presidential Unit Citation – St. Lô Breakout

The 22nd Infantry Regiment is cited for extraordinary heroism and outstanding performance of duty in action in Normandy, France, during the period 26 July to 1 August 1944. The 22nd Infantry Regiment was the infantry element of an armored-infantry combat command (66th Armor Regiment was Armor unit) which successfully effected a breakthrough of the German line of resistance west of St. Lô, forming the St. Gillis-Marigny gap through which the armored-infantry column surged deep into German-held territory. Operating against hardened infantry, artillery, and panzer units, this Regiment, often riding its accompanying tanks, met and overcame the stiffest German resistance in desperate engagements at St. Gillis, Canisy, le Mesnil Herman, Villebaudon, Moyen, Percy, and Tessy-sur-Vire.

The 22nd Infantry Regiment, in its first action with an armored division, after a short period of indoctrination, assumed the role of armored infantry with unparalleled success. Throughout the swiftly moving, seven-day operation, the infantry teams kept pace with the tanks, only resting briefly at night relentlessly to press the attack at dawn. Rear echelons fought with enemy groups bypassed in the assault. There was little protection from the heavy artillery which the Germans brought to bear on the American armor. Enemy bombers continually harassed the American troops at night, but in an outstanding performance of duty, the 22nd Infantry Regiment perfected an infantry-tank team which, by the power of its determined fighting spirit, became an irresistible force on the battlefield.

NO BOCHE IN THE BUILDING!

The prospect of leave was extremely enticing indeed to these young men who had spent the most of the previous six weeks watching their friends being killed or blown to smithereens, dodging enemy bullets, bombs and shells. So far France had meant fear, anxiety, rain and perilous hedgerows. Ah Paris! The name alone took on great significance for many Allied troops and evoked images of beautiful, exotic ladies, good wine, good food and if the rumors were true, much more than just that. Most of these men were virgins with rifles and many hailed from close-knit, religious communities where people did things the right way. They hadn't been exposed to the heady world of Paris nightlife and its time-honored bohemian allures. What would it be like? Most GIs were convinced that there were hundreds if not thousands of willing young ladies just waiting to be liberated. Would they be grateful to their liberators? How grateful? They would soon find out, or not as the case may be.

The Ivy men may have been preparing to go to Paris but the fighting in France wasn't over just yet. A free French unit, the 2nd French Armored Division commanded by Maj. Gen. Jacques Philippe Leclerc would spearhead the drive into the "city of love." Leclerc had been requesting permission to the point of nagging for the opportunity to be the first Allied unit to get to Paris. Eisenhower and Bradley kept him waiting a while but eventually complied with the request. In accordance with the V Corps plan, the French would go into Paris from the west, while the American 4th Infantry Division attacked from the south.

On August 18, Colonel Rol-Tanguy the commander of the French Resistance in the Paris region called for a general mobilization. Almost a week before the arrival of Allied troops, Rol-Tanguy was so hungry for personal glory and fired by his own ego that he acted autonomously and completely ignored the instructions of de Gaulle's local representatives in Paris. Consequently administration buildings, newspaper offices, the police headquarters and City Hall were attacked. Rol Tanguy led the insurrection in the capital that allowed General de Gaulle to unashamedly disseminate the blatant lie that Paris, and in fact France, had liberated herself from Nazi tyranny without the assistance of the Allies. This myth would be perpetuated among the French for years to come.

The 2nd French Armored Division ascended their vehicles and on the morning of August 23 they set off toward Paris. Along the roads leading into the capital the remaining Germans were fighting hard, and it was universally noted by the US troops that there were many delays caused by crowds of French people who lined the roads bestowing flowers, kisses, and wine on their liberators. Unaware of the real extent of German opposition, the American generals remarked that Le Clerc's division was "dancing its way into Paris," and on the basis of this, Bradley directed General Hodges and General Gerow to give the incentive to the 4th Infantry Division to get on with the job and move faster.

On August 22 the Ivy men drove through Chartres then advanced to the Arpajon-Corbeil area, south of Paris. The general situation in and around Paris was unclear at the time and the Allied High Command felt the need to take a more powerful stance. Finally, on August 25, the 4th Infantry Division and the 2nd French Armored Division were ordered to move on Paris.

At 0600 hours the 12th Infantry were transported from their assembly areas to Longjumeau-Villejuif, whereupon they entered Paris at 1220 hours and arrived at the Town Hall at 1315. There was hardly any opposition and on the way they only had to contend with a few scattered snipers in the southeast of the city.

Early in the evening of August 25 on the outskirts of the city the 1st Battalion, 8th Infantry secured bridges and established a bridgehead on the east bank of the Seine river, while later that evening the 2nd Battalion established positions west and northwest of Longjumeau to protect that flank against pockets of enemy resistance, and the 3rd Battalion took control of the airports.

The 22nd Infantry were trucked out to the vicinity of Corbeil to establish a bridgehead across the Seine River and protect the construction of a Treadway bridge there. At 0900 hours, Company L attempted a crossing but was forced to turn back after losing two boats and 15 men. While attempting to secure the location for the Treadway bridge, Company G came under heavy 20mm and 40mm flak emanating from woods on east bank of the Seine River. The 2nd Battalion responded with mortars and small arms while relaying the coordinates of the German positions to heavy supporting artillery units.

At 1030 hours, 2nd Battalion sent foot patrols along the Seine toward Company G. Later that afternoon a diminutive German force surrendered and at 1520 hours the 2nd Battalion and Company G crossed the Seine in rubber dinghies. The 1st Battalion followed on at 1800 hours when they established a bridgehead on the far bank to enable the completion of the Treadway Bridge.

Sporadic small-arms fire had initially caused some minor delays but by noon some units of the 4th Infantry Division had already reached the heart of the city. The main obstacle to the rapid advance was the frenzied zeal of the Parisians but finally after four long depressing years of Nazi oppression Paris had been liberated thanks to the Allies, and particularly the 4th Infantry Division.

Carlton Stauffer, Company G, 2nd Battalion, 12th Infantry Regiment

At 1900 hours, August 23, 1944, our 12th Regimental Combat Team consisting of the 12th Infantry Regiment, the 38th Cavalry Reconnaissance Squadron, the 42nd Field Artillery Battalion, Company B of the 634th Tank Destroyer Battalion, and Companies B and D of the 70th Tank Battalion, started a motor march, which was to be the most exciting experience I would have during my army career. The mission of our combat team was to seize and hold the bridges over the Seine River in the vicinity of Corbeil, which is approximately 25 miles southeast of Paris.

As it seemed to be in our usual pattern of things, the weather was dark and stormy. It was another night of skidding off the road into ditches with the usual few Nazi planes overhead. This motor march was in 6x6 trucks with as many fellows as could possibly fit into the cargo area jammed in. There were fold-down seats along each side, but most of us sat on the floor. To say we were miserable is a gross understatement, with the rain coming down in buckets all night long.

Every few hours we stopped to let the men stretch their legs and make the necessary nature calls. I remember one guy in the front part of the cargo space who had very little control and had to relieve himself several times during the night. Naturally, he used his helmet, the all-purpose accessory of the infantryman. As we were moving forward, he had to pass it back to have someone in the rear empty it so as not to blow into the side of the truck body. By morning, all of us were losing patience with the guy and about the only thing to relieve the tension was to curse at him.

As dawn appeared, matters became more tolerable. The rain finally subsided and we saw a new world—gently rolling terrain—the kind we felt would be tank country. Gone were the hedgerows of Normandy. War had moved quickly over this terrain, and there was less evidence of its devastation. As we passed through the small French towns, the townspeople lined the streets and greeted us with enthusiasm, holding flowers and wine up to us. It was only a taste of the celebration that awaited us in Paris.

We stopped at a little town named Orphin at about 1030 hours on the morning of August 24. We let ourselves dry out as we stretched our legs and got some rations. The vehicles were gassed up. We got the word that it would be the honor of the 12th Regimental Combat Team to be the first US troops to enter Paris. We were to support the 2nd French Armored Division, which was given the political role of liberating Paris. To insure that nothing went awry, the Supreme Headquarters, Allied Expeditionary Forces assigned the responsibility to the 12th Infantry to insure a smooth liberation. We resumed our motor march some time during the afternoon of the 24th, and since we were in the suburbs of Paris, the celebrating was getting into high gear even then. Madly cheering French people wanted our convoy to slow down to give their hands, their flowers, their wine, and their sincere thanks to their liberators.

About 0800 hours on the morning of August 25, we began to move into the city of Paris. The details of an acceptable surrender with the Nazis are a matter of history, but we in our six-by-sixs knew nothing of the plans. We all felt an exhilaration that would not be surpassed in the lives of any of us infantrymen. As we entered the Rue d'Itale, our tactical motor march became a huge victory parade, and our vehicles became covered with flowers. The pent-up emotions of four bitter years under the Nazi yoke suddenly burst into wild celebration, and the great French citizens made us feel that each of us was personally responsible for the liberation of these grateful people. We felt wonderful!

The men, women, and children surged against our trucks on all sides, making a four-mile travel to our positions hours long. There were cries of, "Merci! Merci! S'ank you,

S'ank you Vive la Amerique!" Hands reached out just to touch the hands of an American soldier. Babies were held up to be kissed. Young girls were everywhere hugging and kissing the GIs. Old French men saluted. Young men vigorously shook hands and patted the GIs on the back.

Finally, late in the afternoon we took up our position for the night. I had the good fortune to be assigned to a chemistry building at a university on the west side of the Seine. We walked into the building and were met by a lady who was determined to make life just wonderful for us.

Captain Tallie Crocker, who was our company commander at that time, spread his blanket on the floor. Being an infantryman, he was always getting as close to the ground as possible. The lady immediately took his blankets and spread them out on a sort of couch that looked like an operating table. It was easier to let her do that than to explain anything. When she left, Captain Crocker put his blanket on the floor. At about this same time, we all heard loud machine-gun fire outside the building. I went out with the captain to see what all of the noise was about. In the courtyard outside our building, a Frenchman of their 2nd Armored Division was in a jeep with a .50caliber machine gun firing away at the corner of a building in the court. Captain Crocker approached the Frenchman and asked what he was firing at. The Frenchman told him there were "Boche" in the building. Captain Crocker tried to convince him there were no Boche in the building. There was no meeting of minds. Finally, the Captain took the Frenchman on a "Boche hunt" through the building, proving once and for all—no Boche. Situation resolved! The girls came back to the jeep and we did more wild riding around Paris. When we went back into the chemistry building, Captain Crocker's blanket was back on the table. That evening some of us went for a walk around town, hitting a few places for a celebration drink. The best part of the evening was to return to our chemistry building with its indoor plumbing.

At 0930 hours on the morning of August 26, Father Fries, our regimental chaplain, held Mass in the famous Notre Dame Cathedral, the first mass said after the liberation. Joe Dailey and I attended. It was a strange sight for Notre Dame to see us doughboys sitting at Mass with our rifles and battle gear. The problem confronting us at Mass and afterwards was to keep civilians away. There were ten civilians to one soldier. At last, the company commanders told the crowds that the soldiers were tired and needed sleep. Immediately, and with apologies, the civilians left our positions. That evening we were abruptly brought back to the reality of war when at 2330 hours, the Germans launched a heavy aerial bombing. Fortunately, all we encountered were the flashes and the booms—someone else at the distant part of Paris took it all.

French men, women and children turned out in droves to enthusiastically applaud and greet the US troops. They lined the streets and crowded in front of the Notre Dame Cathedral and Town Hall, to greet the Ivy men with hugs and kisses in that inimitable French way. Flowers were thrown, copious amounts of wine were consumed and the bonhomie would take a considerable while to dissolve. This was all somewhat overpowering for those men in the 12th Infantry but while their faces were being plastered with lipstick, other men from their division were fighting their way across the Seine River and encountering varied responses—in some places there was serious resistance and in others the Germans couldn't get the white flags out fast enough.

Robert Gast, Companies B and C, 1st Battalion, 12th Infantry Regiment

Stories of our entry and stay in Paris are plentiful. I still have a hard time convincing people that women brought their babies to me—a 21-year-old second lieutenant—to be blessed and kissed. There are four things that I remember the most about Paris: One, the children watching us eat, and we were not allowed to feed them. Two, the rumor that the 4th Infantry Division would stay in Paris and guard the bridges. Three, the day they bombed Paris I was officer of the day and riding about in a jeep.

When the siren sounded, the driver headed into a tunnel. It turned out to be a command post for the Free French Army. It was quite an experience. Four, the day we left Paris on foot. All of my men had stashed bottles of wine, loaves of bread, and jars of jam under their shirts. It was a very hot and humid day. The farther we walked, the hotter it got, and the more bread, jam, and wine ended up on the road.

The "Victory parade" in honor of the liberation of Paris would be for other Allied units following in the path of the 4th Infantry Division there were other matters to attend to. The whole 7th German Army was effectively on the run and the Allies were in hot pursuit. With each new day that dawned the objectives were extended to cover the vast distances required to stay on the tail of the retreating Germans.

Ever since the vicious fights at St. Lô Falaise pocket there had been a prearranged Allied plan to round up the whole 7th German Army. This entailed the 1st US Army sweeping north to the Belgian border town of Mons in a wide arc with the purpose of mopping up the remaining German units or doing what General Troy Middleton would later describe as "Disinfecting the place of krauts." Well there was still a lot of disinfecting to do but Paris and Normandy were now Allied territory.

It was September 1, Paris was completely liberated and the Germans were now retreating with such speed that it was nigh impossible for the European Theater of Operations to establish coherent front lines. The 4th Infantry Division remained focused on their drive to the northeast of France and the 8th Infantry were sent up to clear the woods along the Morienbal–Berneuil sur Aisne road and seize crossings over the Aisne River. The last time the 4th had been in the vicinity of the Aisne River had been during World War I and back then it had been an entirely different story. This time the 4th Reconnaissance Troop, supported by two task forces, only encountered sporadic, feeble resistance when they took the crossroads just south of the town of Chauny. The main column was delayed by two hours as a result of these minor engagements. At 1530 hours, 1st Battalion, 22nd Infantry eliminated the resistance and continued on their original route. Shortly after this time the crossings of the Aisne River were secured and the 4th could continue its rapid advance.

By September 3, the Ivy men had reached St. Quentin, capturing or killing many German soldiers en route who were inadvertently heading in the same direction. Some of the retreating Germans had made meager attempts at setting up roadblocks but on the whole these had been regarded more of an annoyance rather than a determined attempt to prevent the advance. September 4, 5, and 6, saw the Division turn eastward in a final drive across the mighty Meuse River and the Belgian border. Some enemy resistance was encountered as they closed in on the Belgian border and this increased as they crossed the frontier. They were not going to be in Belgium for long.

The 4th Infantry Division was one of the many new divisions formed to fight in Europe during World War I. The 'Doughboys' were from all over the United States and they were able to help fill the gaps in the British and French lines. *National Archives*

According to his Medal of Honor citation, Sergeant Shemin left cover and crossed open space, repeatedly exposing himself to heavy machine-gun and rifle fire, to rescue wounded. After Officers and Senior Noncommissioned Officers had become casualties, Sergeant Shemin took command of the platoon and displayed great initiative under fire until wounded on August 9.

Medical Specialists from the 4th Infantry Division attached to 28th Field Hospital pose in front of their hospital in Bad Bertrich, Germany. The medical specialists were needed for complex surgeries or treating diseases which were caught while fighting in the trenches. *National Archives*

Enlisted personnel from the 28th Field Hospital, 4th Infantry Division, pose in front of their hospital in Bad Bertrich, Germany. Enlisted personnel were used as medics and stretcher-bearers who would help bring the wounded behind the lines to aid stations and field hospitals. *National Archives*

Staff Officers of the 28th Field Hospital, 4th Infantry Division, pose in front of their hospital in Bad Bertrich, Germany. *National Archives*

The hours leading up to the D-Day invasion were tense and being on landing craft made it even worse for members of the Ivy Division. Here infantrymen and paratroopers mingle as they prepare for the invasion. *National Archives*

Members of the 4th Infantry Division landed on Utah Beach on D-Day, June 6, 1944. They did not face a difficult fight to establish a beachhead, but the fight off the beach was much more difficult. *National Archives*

Members of the 4th Infantry Division wade onto Utah Beach on D-Day from landing craft. Although the 4th did not face the difficult fight as the 1st and 29th dealt with on Omaha Beach, it was still difficult getting onto the beach due to the Atlantic Wall. *National Archives*

Two medics administer plasma to a wounded medic on Utah Beach as the 4th Infantry Division establishes a beachhead on D–Day. Medics became crucial to keeping soldiers moving onto the beach and any wounded medics needed to be treated quickly. *National Archives*

Two infantrymen carry a wounded soldier from the water's edge during the invasion of Utah Beach. The 4th Infantry Division landed 21,000 infantrymen onto Utah Beach with 197 casualties. *National Archives*

After the 82nd Airborne fought to take St. Mere Eglise in France, the Fourth relieved the paratroopers in the town during their push towards the important French port city of Cherbourg. *National Archives*

Members of the 4th U.S. Infantry Division look at the Eiffel Tower in Paris, after the French capital had been liberated on August 25, 1944. *National Archives*

Col. Lanham, Commanding Officer of the 22nd Infantry Regiment, 4th Infantry Division talks with Major Gen. Raymond O. Barton, Commanding Officer of the 4th Infantry. They were both part of the first Army unit entering Germany on September 14, 1944. *National Archives*

Although known for his coming of age book, *The Catcher in the Rye*, author J.D. Salinger served in the 12th Infantry Regiment of Fourth and was assigned to a counter-intelligence division. *Associated Press*

As a war correspondent, author and World War I veteran Ernest Hemingway, pictured here with Colonel Charles 'Buck' Lanham, joined the Fourth Infantry when they entered Paris. *National Archives*

Several infantrymen of the 4th ID take a moment to rest while fighting in the Hurtgen Forest in late 1944. The difficult terrain in Hurtgen Forest along with the lack of air and armored support made this battle another tough fight for the 4th Infantry. *National Archives*

A Fourth infantryman interrogates a bearded German POW outside of Jungersdorf in the Hurtgen Forest. The German soldier's face illustrates the difficulty of the battle of the Hurtgen Forest for both American and German sides. *National Archives*

With freezing temperatures and snow overtaking Luxembourg during the Battle of the Bulge, members of the Fourth supplemented their meager rations with local deer and rabbits. *National Archives*

Spread out on the thin line in Luxembourg when the Battle of the Bulge began, the men of 4th Infantry were able to hold off the German advance before the arrival of reinforcements from General Patton's 3rd Army. *National Archives*

Soldiers of the 4th Division's 8th Infantry Regiment going into a day of rest at Moestroff, Luxembourg on January 20, 1945 after the successful Sauer river crossing on January 18, 1945. *Roland Gaul*

Members of the 4th Division's 8th Infantry Regiment clearing of the north shore part of the village of Moestroff, Luxembourg on January 20, 1945. *Roland Gaul*

4th Division Infantrymen help displaced Luxembourger civilians who were keeping warm with small fires during the Battle of the Bulge. *National Archives*

Below and following page: Fourth Infantrymen fighting through the ruins of Prum, Germany in February 1945 illustrated how dangerous the push into Germany would be for the Allied forces. *National Archives*

Soldiers of the 4th Division walk through the ruins of Crailsheim, Germany in late April 1945 as they pushed their way deeper into the country. *National Archives*

Members of the 4th Infantry Division pose for a photograph on a troop ship on their way home after the end of World War II. The 4th Division's ivy patch is clearly painted on the ship above the troops. *National Archives*

An Army helicopter lands with supplies for the members of Charlie Company 22nd Infantry Regiment, 4th Infantry Division in Vietnam. With the 4th Infantry spread out in various positions, helicopters were the critical in providing supplies and ammunition. *CharlieCompany.org*

A 4th Infantry Division Huey Medivac helicopter prepares to liftoff in Vietnam. Medical helicopters were vital to helping bring wounded troops out of remote areas during the Vietnam War. *CharlieCompany.org*

U.S. soldiers of the 3rd Brigade, 4th Infantry Division, look on a mass grave of enemy combatants after a day-long battle against the Viet Cong 272nd Regiment, about 60 miles northwest of Saigon, in March of 1967. U.S. military command reported 423 Communist forces dead, with American losses at 30 dead, 109 wounded, and three missing. *National Archives*

Members of the 4th Infantry Division Artillery load one of their 105mm artillery pieces in Vietnam. Although air power was a major part of the Vietnam War, artillery was valuable when fighting in remote areas of the country. *CharlieCompany.org*

Above left: A group of 4th Infantry Division soldiers pose on a military vehicle during a brief respite during fighting in Vietnam. *Robert Babcock*

Above right: This is Bob Babcock, 3rd platoon leader of Bravo Company, 1st Battalion, 22nd Infantry Regiment, 2nd Brigade, 4th Infantry Division during Operation Paul Revere IV in the jungles of the Central Highlands of Vietnam, along the Cambodian border, in early December 1966. *Robert Babcock*

Master Sgt. Pablo Jimenez, 4th Infantry Division, keeps watch as part of security outside of Kandahar Airfield, Afghanistan on October 15, 2013. *Defense Video and Imagery Distribution System*

Right: 1st Battlion, 6th Infantry Regiment, 4th Infantry Division soldiers keep watch in Baghdad while the Division Commander Maj. Gen. Jeffrey W. Hammond walks through the area on August 22, 2008. *Defense Video and Imagery Distribution System*

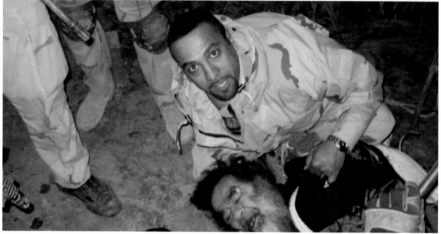

Samir, a 34-year-old Iraqi-American military interpreter, is pulling former Iraqi Dictator, Saddam Hussein out of his hideout in Ad-Dwar, near Tikrit, Iraq, who helped find Saddam with the 1st Brigade Combat Team of the 4th Infantry Division. *Associated Press*

Left: Steve Russell, who commanded 1st Battalion, 22nd Infantry Battalion, 4th Infantry Division, communicates via radio on a mission during the 4th ID's tour in the Sunni Triangle. *Defense Video and Imagery Distribution System*

Lt. Antonio Salinas takes a break and poses in front of a mountain range in Forward Operating Base Blessing, Afghanistan. *Antonio Salinas*

Lt Antonio Salinas and Lt Florent Groberg (a recent Medal of Honor recipient) conduct a key leader engagement in the village of Semetan, Afghanistan. *Antonio Salinas*

This monument by Iraqi sculptor Khalid Alussy was placed in the entranceway of the 4th Infantry's headquarters in Tikrit and later flown to the unit's home base in Ft. Hood, Texas. He was provided with bronze from two statues of Saddam Hussein, which the 4th Division blew up and melted down. *Defense Video and Imagery Distribution System*

This 4th Infantry Division Monument is located the Combined Arms Center, Home of the Infantry and Armor on the 'Walk of Honor' site at National Infantry Museum at Ft. Benning, Georgia and it was dedicated on July 18, 2013. *Robert Babcock*

CHAPTER II

MAINTAINING CONTACT

Most of those early days in September were dedicated to going after the Germans who fought various delaying actions on the rugged terrain in the south of Belgium. Supreme Allied Commander Eisenhower took over complete control of the ground forces on September 1 and on September 5 Montgomery repeated his objections to Eisenhower's "Broad front strategy." Despite the resounding Allied successes of the previous weeks, and despite the media claiming that the Germans were broken, Eisenhower was far from convinced that he had sufficient resources at his disposal to finish the job. General Patton, almost intoxicated by paroxysms of military fervor, was racing across northern France. He moved with such speed and enthusiasm that his forward combat units were experiencing logistic problems. Eisenhower recognized these problems and, induced by this and other considerations, declared a pause in offensive operations so that he could set about rebuilding the strength of the ETO's armies. Following the capture of Paris Eisenhower said

> "In long term estimate we were weeks ahead of our schedule, but in the important matter of our supply capacity we were badly behind. Because almost the entire area had been captured in the swift movements subsequent to August 1, the roads, military lines, depots, repair shops, and basic installations required for the maintenance of continuous forward movement were still far to the rear of front lines."

Although buoyed by the pace of the Allied advance, "Ike" was still being cautious. His first consideration was for the men in the field who would discover the importance of good logistics all too soon. At the same time he was convinced that he needed to exploit recent successes and breach the Siegfried Line. This would allow the Allies to advance on the industrial areas of Germany and destroy their capacity to manufacture weapons and military hardware. Monty was incandescent with rage at this proposed strategy and had strongly objected to its implementation from the offset but he would have to toe the line for now.

Eisenhower wrote a private memorandum dated September 5 and outlined his position:

> *"For some days it has been obvious that our military forces can advance almost at will, subject only to the requirement for maintenance . . . The defeat of the German armies is complete, and the only thing now needed to realize the whole conception is speed. Our rapidity of movement will depend upon maintenance, in which we are now stretched to the limit . . . I now deem it important, while supporting the advance eastward through Belgium, to get Patton moving once again so that we may be fully prepared to carry out the original conception for the final stage of the campaign."*

By "campaign" he meant the "broad front." He was making far too many assumptions that weren't conclusively supported by available intelligence. There was indeed a reason for optimism but that optimism had to be tempered with hard facts.

Hitler hadn't given permission to release some of his infantry divisions to fight to fight in the Normandy campaign, because he remained convinced in his delusional, irrational mind that despite overwhelming evidence to the contrary, Normandy wasn't the "real" invasion. He was still convinced that it would still occur at the Pas de Calais, which was still being defended by the 15th Army, which consisted of relatively well-provisioned infantry divisions who would later provide troops for the defense of the Reich.

The 4th Infantry Division noticed that the closer they got to the German border the harder the fighting became as the enemy attempted but failed to hold back the surge of Allied power now rushing towards their domestic borders. On September 11, 1944, the 4th Infantry Division was the first Allied force to breach the infamous Siegfried Line and physically take the fight into Germany.

Poolaw, Pascal Cleatus (KIA)
Silver Star (First Award)

> The President of the United States takes pleasure in presenting the Silver Star Medal to Pascal Cleatus Poolaw (18131087), Staff Sergeant, US Army, for gallantry in action against the enemy while serving with Company M, 8th Infantry Regiment, 4th Infantry Division, near Recogne, Belgium, on 8 September 1944. While attacking in support of a rifle company, Sergeant Poolaw displaced his machine gun squad forward across an open field under heavy mortar and small-arms fire in such a manner as to effect a minimum number of casualties among his squad. After reaching his new position, Sergeant Poolaw saw the enemy advance in a strong counterattack. Standing unflinchingly in the face of withering machine-gun fire for five minutes, he hurled hand grenades until the enemy force sustained numerous casualties and was dispersed. Due to Sergeant Poolaw's actions, many of his comrades' lives were saved and the company was able to continue the attack and capture strongly defended enemy positions. Sergeant Poolaw's display of courage, aggressive spirit and complete disregard for personal safety are in keeping with the highest traditions of the military service.

After-Action Report: September 11, 1944

> The enemy continued its determined defense. A 22nd Infantry patrol crossed the German border, vicinity of Elcherath at 2120 and procured among other things, a package of German soil, prior to returning. The 8th Infantry with same attachments as before, resumed the attack at 0900 and by 1200, reached the intermediate objective. The Combat Team (motorized) moved out at 1320 to its final objective south of Bovigny and reached it by 1800. The 2nd Bn moved to the high ground to protect the right flank of the Division and at the end of the day, was still en-route. The 12th Infantry with its same attachments continued the advance and at 0900, removing unmanned roadblock en-route, had encountered the enemy. By 2000, all battalions were forcing crossings of the Salm river against enemy opposition. The 22nd Infantry continued its advance at 0900 and by 1800, the entire Combat Team had closed in its assigned area after having overcome the enemy but still maintaining contact with it by dispatching patrols to the German border.

The Ivy men passed through the historic town of Bastogne and eventually found themselves in the Belgian town of Sankt Vith. This place was a peculiar anomaly because although the inhabitants were Belgian nationals they all spoke German. Their legacy was that this town along with a considerable swathe of land from the surrounding area had been given to the Belgian people in 1919 in observation of the Treaty of Versailles. Consequently many of the residents in this area had fathers, sons, uncles and brothers fighting in the German army so it was safely assumed that, unlike the French and particularly the Parisians, they would be quite reluctant to welcome the US Army. Most of the locals in this area saw the Americans as an army of occupation, not liberation.

Just a few miles to the east of Sankt Vith is the German border and the area known as North Rhine Westphalia. The picturesque countryside that lays along this frontier, complete with rolling hills, farm pastures and chocolate box little villages, is called the Schnee Eifel. A patrol from the 22nd Infantry crossed the Our River that traverses the border near the village of Hemmeres. They interacted with local civilians, and to prove to their commanding officer that they had crossed the border, they managed to procure a German army cap along with some Nazi issue Deutschmarks and peculiarly enough a packet of soil.

The 4th Infantry Division, a component of V Corps since August 22, was attached to the First Army, 12th Army Group and given the job of clearing the way forward through this Schnee Eifel area. It extends around 15 miles from Ormont to the vicinity of the village of Brandscheid where it develops into a high, relatively open plateau. The 4th Infantry Division was ordered to seize the crest of the Schnee Eifel to facilitate advance of the 28th Pennsylvania National Guard Division across the plateau. The objective ran straight through the Siegfried Line and it was generally accepted that this defensive position, known as the "West Wall" to the Germans, would be a serious obstacle to their progress.

Robert Gast, Companies B and C, 1st Battalion, 12th Infantry Regiment

My platoon was the second platoon from our battalion to enter the Siegfried Line. I was to contact the first platoon that had gone earlier and had not been heard from. We were very fortunate and stumbled onto a bunch of German soldiers that were caught completely by surprise. They surrendered without a shot being fired. This gave us the wrong idea as to what to expect from the enemy. One very unusual thing happened. We were dug in and tied down and here comes another battalion attacking through us. I thought, my God, what are they doing? It wasn't long before they came running back to us. Another strategic withdrawal. A young lieutenant jumped into my hole with me. It was Bud Reed, a guy I knew at Indiana University and a good friend of my sister and brother-in-law.

On September 12, the 4th Infantry Division decided to organize some reconnaissance of the area and initial findings were encouraging. It wasn't until the following day that they began to notice a considerable increase in the amount of enemy artillery being brought to bear on the combat patrols from behind enemy troops occupying hastily assembled positions. By nightfall the next day both the 12th and the 22nd Infantry had crossed the border and moved into assembly areas in the shadow of the Schnee Eifel. On the north flank the 12th Infantry gathered at the village of Radscheid while the 22nd Infantry settled nearby at village of Bleialf. General Barton was so impressed by the lack of enemy opposition that he immediately ordered both regiments to organize further reconnaissance patrols. Although he remained convinced that the Germans were not capable of providing any serious obstruction to his division's progress, at the same time he deferred any real attempt to make a move on the Siegfried Line.

The patrols returned with information that an indeterminate number of Germans were occupying a series of bunkers and pillboxes to the east. While the 8th Infantry remained in reserve Barton ordered the two infantry regiments in the field to go on the offensive and attack abreast of one another toward an elevated plateau just beyond the Prüm River. The Prüm River is named after the German town of Prüm, which at that time had a population of around 30,000.

The 4th Infantry Division would have had scant indication what actually broaching the Siegfried Line would entail. They were now in danger of waking the Teutonic dragon in its well-prepared lair. It was noted that on September 13 there was a considerable increase in the size and amount of incoming German artillery and that Messerschmitts were flying random sorties over the 4th Infantry Division sector. To provide for this the 8th Infantry reserve were ordered to move forward behind the 12th and 22nd Infantry as they approached the heights of the Schnee Eifel plateau. At 0800 hours, the 12th Infantry sent out a few patrols first to reconnoiter the area and their main body followed on at 1000 hours. Throughout the afternoon the advance continued against light resistance and by 1800 hours the first objectives had been reached. The 22nd Infantry followed roughly the same route and having encountered only light sporadic opposition before dusk set in they had secured and consolidated their objectives.

The Germans had managed to dig in just west of the Siegfried Line and the following day, they offeredmore concentrated resistance from their reinforced concrete bunkers and pillboxes.. They opened up on the Ivy men with everything that they had at their disposal but despite this fierce opposition the 4th still managed to breach the Siegfried Line at a number of places. By this time the road network and dense stretches of woodland in the area were becoming a real hindrance to the progress of the 4th Infantry Division's vehicles, but this was just a precursor of the difficulties they would encounter later on as they came face to face with the Waffen SS.

John Dowdy, CO, 1st Battalion, 22nd Infantry

John Dowdy was one of the most aggressive, yet charismatic, commanders that 1st Battalion and the 22nd Infantry Regiment has ever seen. He led his men always from the front, never expecting them to do anything he was not prepared to do himself. He inspired courage in his Battalion, motivating his soldiers to continue pressing on in the face of extreme hardships, regrouping them after costly setbacks from the enemy, and instilling in them the dedication to ultimate victory which was the essence of his fighting spirit.

In 38 total days of combat, John Dowdy received the Distinguished Service Cross, two Silver Star Medals, two Purple Heart medals and the Combat Infantryman's Badge.

Colonel Charles "Buck" T Lanham 1st Battalion 22nd Infantry

When this fight was over I gave John back his battalion (1st Battalion) which had suffered heavily in his absence. Within 24 hours it was like a new outfit. John was everywhere and his courage, his strength, his spirit, and his personality ran like flame through the command. I think he was the greatest leader of men that I have ever seen, and I have spent a lifetime in the Army. And certainly no man has ever been more deeply loved by those he led and by those who had the high privilege of serving with him as fellow officers. John was with us when we broke the Siegfried line on (Sept) 14th. The blow that he and his battalion struck that day will never be forgotten by our enemy. We ruptured the line on September 14th and on September 15th we continued the attack to widen the breach and to improve our positions. The fighting was bitter and the enemy was fanatical. The troops that opposed us were largely SS formations, the elite of the German Army, with orders from Hitler in person to fight to the death. And in large measure this is what they did.

On September 16th John and his battalion again took their objective a critical hill in our zone. The enemy reaction was violent. He made repeated efforts to throw John from his hard-won position, but these were beaten off. He then resorted to violent artillery and mortar fire—this was probably the heaviest series of concentrations we have ever received. John ordered his battalion to dig in on the high ground for the night. He then began circulating among his troops; adjusting their positions, correcting their dispositions, placing his weapons in the most advantageous locations, joking with the men, reassuring them, seeing to their safety. He walked through the storm of shellfire as if he were walking down a street in his home town calm, cool, completely composed, and without the slightest trace of hurry or excitement. He was a fountain of strength at which all-men might drink.

He made two complete circuits of his position, and still not satisfied that his men were adequately cared for, he began a third trip. He was perhaps halfway through when the fatal shell landed. He was killed instantly, and though it might well have been otherwise, his body was not mutilated. Only a fragment of the shell did the deadly work. For his leadership and bravery under fire, at the cost of his life on that September day, John Dowdy was awarded his second Silver Star and second Purple Heart. He was 26 years old when he died.

As the Ivy men attempted to exploit their gains, they discovered that these Waffen SS soldiers were not easy targets. They would fight till the last man and refuse to surrender. Among the units in contact were the 12th SS Division "Hitler Jugend," 2nd SS Division "Das Reich" and the 9th SS Division "Hohenstaufen." All of these divisions had earned fearsome reputations during World War II and many of the soldiers serving in them were seasoned veterans. Some of these units had been transferred from the Eastern Front and many were laboring under the delusion that the GIs were going to be easy targets.

Hans Baumann, Unterscharführer, Jagd Panzer IV 12th SS Panzer Division "Hitler Jugend"

I hadn't been with the 12th SS all that long when we first encountered some Americans near Prüm. I'm not sure which division they were but someone told me afterwards they were probably 4th Division. I couldn't say for sure. I remember there was a lot of artillery falling on our unit at the time fired by the Amis (American troops). I wasn't there for more than a few hours before my vehicle broke down and I had to abandon it out on the Schnee Eifel. It was recovered later but I didn't see another American until just before I got hit in Rochrath.

As the 4th ebbed and flowed in proximity to the Belgian/German border, plans were being made to further extend their drive into German territory. The maps indicated a densely forested area above Prüm to the north of the Schnee Eifel that hadn't been approached yet by the Allies.

To the north Montgomery had executed his daring, but controversial Operation *Market Garden* plan and despite evidence to the contrary he was still claiming it had been a 90% success. Meanwhile probing attacks and patrols along the Belgian/German border increased as plans were made to continue the drive east into the heart of the Reich. There was still some disparity at ETO concerning the way forward. Eisenhower continued to pursue his "Broad Front" strategy despite vociferous objections from Monty while Patton remained in the Alsace region of France with his Third Army where he continued hammering away at Metz.

The area below Aachen was the location of various dams that provided hydroelectric power for Germany's industrial region of the Ruhr. Many of these were still intact despite intensive Allied bombing.

The Allies had liberated the harbor of Antwerp in early September but the estuary that connected it to the North Sea was still the scene of fierce fighting and as long as that continued Allied shipping couldn't land valuable supplies for the northern European offensives. This would greatly affect the momentum and direction of the on-going campaigns. The first American cargo ship, the *James B. Weaver*, wouldn't land there until November 28.

John Worthman, Medic, 22nd Infantry Regiment

On September 13 we were in Germany near Urb and Groslangerfeld. We were low on gasoline and had to stop even though there was no organized resistance. Trucks and planes delivered what they could. We thought the 3rd Army tanks were getting the fuel while running around down south, and we were in Germany and otherwise ready to continue. Later we learned that they too, were in very short supply of gasoline.

On the way we passed some WWI trenches already well eroded and grass covered. In Belgium there was cheering and waving from the civilians. In Germany there were looks of concern and disbelief and white flags from the windows. They didn't seem angry, just amazed. We were now at the Siegfried Line. It was formidable in appearance with essentially four lines of defense and up to 35 miles deep. Bunkers were well camouflaged, well fortified, and connected to each other by tunnels. Ditches, barbed wire in concertina rolls and concrete dragon's teeth tended to deflect the assault to places where the bunker-mounted guns could crossfire. This was hard fighting again, but we were much more familiar with fortifications after Normandy. Now we concentrated on a bunker.

First, we used heavy small-arms fire at all embrasures while flamethrowers and "pole-charge" men moved up. The flamethrowers then heated an embrasure. If it went well, the metal and cement exploded on the heated embrasure. If successful, the metal and cement yielded, and the bunker was breached. Then we pushed explosive charges through the breach to finish the bunker. As a result, bunkers lateral to it were exposed to flank fire and fell easily. We did this for three weeks and breached nearly the whole line. We felt certain we could have done so with adequate supplies.

We were limited again by lack of supply. We were too far from the supply areas in Normandy. We were also competing for supplies with the 3rd Army, which consumed fuel and ammunition faster than we did, particularly gasoline. On October 4 the 22nd Infantry was moved to a location near Bullingen. From then until mid-November we did some fighting, did a lot of patrolling to find German resistance pockets, had a wonderful opportunity to eat hot meals, got new clothing, and trained the regiment to its peak. It was cold at night and cool in the day. For a three-day period, we were near a small fast stream where I bathed daily. I never felt so clean. I had all my personal gear mud-free, and the aid stations were supplied fully. On November 16, we moved to the Hürtgen Forest.

In Normandy the zealous novelist Ernest Hemingway, who was working as a correspondent, observer, and scout, had accompanied the 4th Infantry Division. He was often in the front lines and shortly after the liberation of Paris Hemingway traveled to the north of France to join his friend Col. Buck Lanham who was with the 22nd Infantry as the 4th pushed toward Germany. Hemingway spent a whole month with Lanham, long enough to observe American forces crossing over into Germany and long enough to see some of the bloodiest fighting of the war. Some of what he witnessed was obliquely recorded in his novel *Across the River and into the Trees* which was published in 1950.

September had been a wet month and as temperatures dipped and tempers frayed, October wasn't faring any better. As early as September 18 American troops in Germany had carved a serious path through the

Siegfried Line that extended 18 miles between the east and southeast of Aachen. The first heavy German counterattacks since First Army commander Lt. Gen. Courtney Hodges penetrated the line were decisively repelled in this area, but to the north of the 4th Infantry Division positions there was still heavy fighting around the town of Stolberg near Aachen. The advance through a forest southeast of Aachen continued and the enemy reluctantly admitted the loss of some fortified positions in this area but refrained from being too specific.

Throughout October, the 4th Infantry Division participated in numerous combat missions in the proximity of the Belgian/German border. They established positions in bunkers along the Siegfried Line and continued sending out patrols. Some periods were allocated to care, cleaning of equipment, rest and recreation, cleanliness of personnel and clothing, and training. Patrols maintained almost constant contact with the Germans until early November when the Ivy men were alerted to move to the Hürtgen Forest just to the south of Aachen. It was a place that most of the men had never heard of but in time they would get to know it well and those who served there would have a tough time forgetting about it.

As early as September 12, US troops from the 1st Infantry Division and 3rd Armored Division had reached the German western frontier border at the small town of Roetgen and skimmed the fringes of an area known in German as the Hürtgenwald (Hürtgen Forest). Overstretched supply lines prevented any serious advances at the time but the name of the Hürtgen Forest was gradually filtering down through the Allied ranks and it wasn't being described in comforting terms.

CHAPTER 12

THE HÜRTGEN FOREST: INTO THE "MEAT GRINDER"

During briefings on the developing military situation after the Normandy campaigns, General "Lightning" Joe Collins, the commander of VII Corps, would often insist to his fellow officers and subordinates that terrain was all-important in any offensive or battle, but sadly he would neglect his own advice when he sent VII Corps into the Hürtgen Forest. This beautiful forest that extends almost to the German/Belgian border is a hikers' paradise but in the fall of 1944 it turned into a military nightmare for the US forces that were sent in there. They became inextricably embroiled in one of the bitterest struggles of World War II, and although it was largely overshadowed by the Battle of the Bulge that followed, everyone who survived the Hürtgen would carry those daunting memories for the rest of their natural lives.

A combat command consisting of elements from the 3rd Armored Division entered the fringes of the Hürtgen in early September 1944. By September 19 the 9th Infantry Division had taken up positions in the forest supported by the 3rd Armored Division but successive attacks failed mainly due to intensifying German resistance and excessive underestimation of the area. These initial engagements were a precursor for the abject slaughter that became synonymous with the Hürtgen Forest.

The Germans would have the upper hand from the offset. This inhospitable terrain, in the region known as the North Eifel, would effectively deprive the US Army of all previous tactical advantages and defy all military logic. American soldiers were neither trained nor equipped to deal with the steep hills and dense pine forests. Use of heavy vehicles was superfluous and initially air cover was almost non-existent. The Siegfried Line may have been breached at various locations, but not in the Hürtgen where two fortified lines ran parallel through almost the whole length of the forested area.

This was a dank, terrifying world where the sun was reduced to meager splinters of foreboding, caliginous twilight that barely managed to filter through the dense canopy of tall pines onto spongy brown needles and decaying foliage below. A sniper's paradise propagated with minefields and booby traps and punctuated throughout by reinforced concrete bunkers and pillboxes. Mines were arranged in overlapping layers so that clearing one layer was no assurance that the area was safe. Continued use of a particular road or trail would soon cut deep enough into the all-consuming mud to activate the next layer. In addition there were the dreaded effects caused by "tree burst" when shells exploded in the canopy. A company could be reduced to a platoon and a platoon could be reduced to a squad in a matter of days. This expression is often inaccurately applied, but this really was "hell on earth."

"Hug a tree" had been the advice of 28th Division soldiers who became entangled in this terrible life and death struggle early on, where gains were measured in feet and yards rather than miles. In the course of the fighting in the Hürtgen their numbers were decimated and the whole division was damaged almost beyond repair.

Since being assigned to V Corps, the 4th Infantry Division had occupied positions in the line south and east of the picturesque little German town of Monschau, on the corps' southern flank. This was where General Courtney Hodges, commander of the First Army, had set up his HQ. There had already been significant activity in this sector but now the 1st US Army was planning a major coordinated attack timed to begin around November 11. The purpose of this was to eventually facilitate crossings over the Roer River and allow the movement of 1st US Army in preparation for the eventual assault on Cologne. Generals Hodges and Collins had mutually agreed early on during the campaign that the Hürtgen Forest was too big an obstacle to be bypassed. The problem was that Hodges was resolute in his insistence that the forest had to be taken and appeared oblivious to the protestations of his subordinates—this would have inevitable consequences that would be suffered by the GIs as a result of intransigent, uninspired military strategies.

Unbeknown to the Americans at the start of the campaign, on the southern perimeter of the Hürtgen Forest near the town of Schmidt, lay the Schwammenauel Dam, one of two major dams on the Roer River that provided power for the adjacent industrial areas, one of the places that provided power for the Nazi war machine.

In early November the 4th Infantry Division was transferred back to General Collins' VII Corps to reinforce the corps' strength in preparation for a new drive east. Hodges was aware that they were taking on difficult terrain but despite reports he had little idea of precisely how difficult it would be. One of the main problems was that the maps distributed at HQ and to the troops at the time did not accurately represent the area. Some of the roads that were clearly indicated on maps turned out to be nothing more than dirt trails and country paths. Moreover the topographic information failed to indicate one-in-three gradients—hills that were so steep no vehicle, tracked or wheeled, could navigate them. The soil in the Hürtgen Forest has a high clay content, which when wet transforms into a slimy mud that coated everything it touched. It was completely demoralizing for soldiers burdened with heavy equipment, drenched to the bones, cold and exhausted to attempt ascending hills under fire and then find themselves irrevocably sliding back down the steep slopes.

Tallie Crocker HQ, 2nd Battalion, 12th Infantry Regiment, 4th Infantry Division

On November 6, 1944, the 12th Infantry Regiment was attached to the 28th Infantry Division, which was having a rough time in the Hürtgen Forest. The Germans had driven a salient in their lines and had essentially split their defense in half. The 12th Infantry left for this assignment at 1745 hours for the 45-mile motor march to the location of the 28th Infantry Division. The weather was miserable with a cold rain falling. The original plan was for the regiment to go into a bivouac area and wait until morning for the relief of the 28th.

Colonel Luckett, the Regimental Commander, and his staff, along with Lieutenant Colonel Montelbano and the staff of the 2nd Battalion of the 12th Infantry, went ahead to meet with the staff of the 28th to get more information on the relief. I was S-3 (Operations Officer) of the 2nd Battalion. When we reached the headquarters of the 28th, we were informed that the relief was to take place immediately, rather than the next morning, so there was no time for reconnaissance. Since we were operating with radios silenced, a messenger was sent to inform the columns that they were not to go into bivouac. At 0400 on November 7, the relief began in pouring rain, total darkness and was not completed until mid-morning.

The positions that were occupied by the 109th Infantry Regiment were along a salient that the Germans had driven into the 28th's lines and were not always in the best place for fighting. The positions that were occupied by the 2nd Battalion of the 12th were along a firebreak and not passable by vehicles, so everything had to be hand carried.

There were dead bodies of the 109th all over the area. Since we had replacements who had not done any fighting, we had some of our troops who had combat experience move the frozen dead bodies, pile them in several spots, and hide them with boughs broken from the trees by artillery fire.

On November 10, there was a 500-yard gap between Company E and Companies F and G. The plan was for the 1st Battalion to attack at the deepest part of the German salient; Company E was to attack the edge of the salient, and Companies F and G were to attack their fronts. Shortly after the attacks began, the Germans stopped them and got behind F and G Companies. With Companies F and G were the Battalion CO, the S-3 (me), and an artillery observer with his radio operator. When we tried to send wounded people out, we discovered that we were surrounded by the Germans.

Every day we were subjected to an attack by the Germans. After each attack, we took stock of the .30 caliber ammo on hand for the machine guns, as well as for rifles. If we felt that we didn't have enough machine-gun ammo for the next attack, we took ammo from the M-1 eight-round clips and hand inserted it into the wet cloth machine gun belts or vice versa. We withstood an attack each day, with two attacks on one day.

On one occasion the Germans brought tanks within 100 yards of our positions and yelled for us to surrender since they had us surrounded. The men yelled back, "F–k you," and we requested the artillery forward observer to request artillery fire, high-explosive as well as white phosphorus in the area of the tanks. The artillery officer at the guns requested a repeat of the coordinates because of the nearness to our troops. I took the handset from the observer, told the officer to fire, and assured him that we knew what we were doing. When those tanks saw the white phosphorus, they left the area in a hurry.

The lack of food was quite a problem. We searched the packs of the dead 28th Infantry Division troops for food, and retrieved from the ground the "dog biscuits" and cheese that had been discarded by the troops. Our first-aid station, which was in large, log-covered holes, had a number of casualties to handle. We had a medic sergeant and aid men manning the aid station, and they really did an excellent job.

By the morning of the third day, November 12, only two of our radios had batteries with a little life left. Fortunately, the artillery radio worked until noon. We were finally left with our battalion radio, which couldn't reach our Battalion HQ. I knew that the 1st Battalion was closer to us than our Battalion CP. I remembered the channel number of their radio net because of a firefight we had taken part in with them in the Siegfried Line. When in a stagnant or offensive operation, we used call signs of Red, White, and Blue for the battalions. Also, when in a defensive situation, we used a three-day prearranged code. That code expired on our first day of isolation. I switched our radio to the 1st Battalion's channel and called, "Red from White," twice, with no response. I then called, "Red from White, come in Chuck." (Chuck Jackson, the 1st Battalion CO, and my brother-in-law.)

His reply was, "Love from ___," (I don't remember his code name now). But I still remember ours. His message was, "Bring all your loves to me." We interpreted that to mean, "withdraw," but we wanted to make certain, so I replied, "I think I know what you mean, but want to be certain."

His reply was, "What do you do when you meet a girl with more than you have?" I later told Chuck that the reply should have been, "Attack!"

There was very little daylight left, so we assembled the two company commanders and discussed a withdrawal plan. We decided to withdraw to the location of the 3rd Battalion since it was a shorter distance (about 600 yards). We also prayed for a foggy morning, but while we slept it snowed all night. When we got up it was to a bright sunny morning. For some reason the Germans had left during the night, and we lost only two men to mines during our withdrawal. When Chuck Jackson greeted me, he said, "I'm so glad to see you—I wondered what Mary would say if she found out that we were so close, and you didn't make it."

When we reached our Battalion Headquarters, Major General R. O. Barton, Division Commander, was standing outside to welcome us and to inform us that we were again in the 4th Infantry Division.

When I returned to the CP, I learned that I had trench foot and was evacuated two days later. I didn't return to the 12th Infantry Regiment until early February 1945, so I missed the German breakthrough. We had been told nothing about trench foot or its prevention, but when more casualties were being sustained from that problem than from the Germans, prevention was really enforced. Trench foot was encountered in WWI also—guess that's where the word "trench" came from.

Most officers at VII Corps HQ had scant idea what it was really like in that forest, and nothing above the rank of Captain ever went to look.

It was going to be another slogging match, a battle of attrition that would see divisions such as the 28th decimated and whole companies reduced to just a few men. This would indeed be, as Hemingway accurately described, reminiscent of the World War I battle of Passchendaele with initially neither side making any substantial gains. Another comparison to the famous WWI battle was the dreadful weather conditions. Soldiers in the Hürtgen Forest had to contend with incessant deluges of freezing rain that turned all trails and roads into impassable quagmires and rendered vehicles immobile.

One night, during a brief hiatus from the fighting, two American writers met up. Ernest Hemingway was briefly stationed just a mile from J. D. Salinger's encampment. Hemingway was a correspondent with the 22nd Infantry while Salinger was still with the 12th Infantry and a few months previous they had met during the liberation of Paris. Salinger turned to a fellow soldier and suggested visiting Hemingway. The two men made their way through the dense forest to Hemingway's quarters, a comfortable small cabin lit by its own generator. For two or three hours they yarned together and drank champagne from canteen cups. Neither Hemingway nor Salinger would ever forget their experiences in the unforgiving Hürtgen.

Matthias Hutmacher Sturmgeschutzbrigade 341, 116th Panzer "Windhund" (Greyhound) Division, LXXIV Corps, 5th Panzer Army, Army Group B

I was 17 and half when I joined the German army. I was born in Schmidt. When we started our counterattack in the Hürtgen Forest I was 20 years old. I knew this forest very well indeed because I had grown up there. The battle raged for several days from dawn until dusk. At first I thought that this was just another battle because I fought almost everywhere in Russia and in Normandy with my unit. I had operated my Pak 88mm from the Caucasus in the Crimea to the steppes of Vitebsk and at the Battle of Kursk. At the start of every battle I was always almost rigid with fear but you overcome this and do your duty with your comrades. From Vitebsk we were sent to the vicinity of the Ruhr River to defend our homeland. The battle of Hürtgen was the most terrible slaughter that I ever witnessed. There were dead bodies from both sides lying everywhere. Our officers told us that the Americans were going to be easy but this was not the case because they fought valiantly. Early in November my unit drove to Kreuzau, and from there to Brandenberg. We had been told that we should attack Vossenack. I remember the Americans firing at us with bazookas and causing serious damage. We didn't have enough good infantry to fight back with but we caused many American casualties. There were many futile attacks in that forest but eventually the Americans were too strong for us. The weather was bad in these days of November. Rain and snow most of the time but we had been on the Russian front and so this wasn't so bad for us. The Americans fought very well and they kept their positions despite everything we threw at them. It was a terrible battle and I will never forget it.

At 2245 hours on November 15, the 4th Division's infantry regiments were notified that an attack would commence November 16. By this time the fighting in the Hürtgen Forest had reached new terrifying heights. The first few weeks of November had seen a fresh attack by the 28th Infantry Division along a path known as the "Kall Trail" toward the town of Schmidt that had culminated in a well-prepared ambush and inevitable disaster for the US troops. The badly mauled 9th Division had also experienced more than its fair share and was in such a poor state that it had been withdrawn from its positions and was now replaced by the 4th Division.

The most disquieting aspect of the battles in the Hürtgen so far was that, despite incurring hundreds of casualties, the American plans hadn't been changed or adapted to suit the environment. The method of sending out widely separated columns through such inhospitable terrain was a recipe for catastrophe, as had been effectively demonstrated by the 9th Infantry Division as early as mid-September. At this juncture another comparison with World War I battles emerges because during October, the 9th had attempted the same strategy and had been followed by the 28th Infantry Division who repeated these mistakes and paid dearly for this military failure to work with rather than against the terrain. Unfortunately the 4th Infantry Division did not learn from the mistakes of their predecessors and prepared to pursue the same tragic pattern.

Private Isaac C. Phillips, 1st Battalion, 22nd Infantry

We had been in Aachen for a couple of days and then we began attacking the Siegfried Line in the Hürtgen. There were two rows then there was a space in between. In that space there was bunkers and machine guns. The German fired all night long to the left and to the right but they didn't fire in the middle where I was. I told my officer that it was a dangerous thing to attack straight down the middle but he didn't listen to me. We started going up a hill and as we neared the crest the Germans started raining artillery in front of us and behind us and it closed on us. I heard an 88 firing so I hit the ground and I couldn't find my rifle anywhere it was gone. While I was looking around they fired off some more rounds. The Germans didn't shoot at the Americans, they shot at the trees and the big pieces of wood fell down on us. I must have got hit because I woke up in Paris one month and a half later. I don't know how I got from the Hürtgen Forest to Paris. I don't know what happened. Where I was and where they found me was 25 yards farther down. They don't know how I got there but I probably had concussion. Another soldier in my company of 250 men said that he and I were the only ones left alive the rest of them was dead.

The 4th Infantry Division would begin a series of heavily fought battles that would eventually culminate in the capture of the town of Grosshau on the eastern perimeter of the forest but it would be a grueling fight. They would suffer the same hardships and make the same mistakes as previous US divisions but that wouldn't prevent or discourage General Hodges from sending even more divisions into the place that by November had ominously become known to the GIs as "the meat grinder."

On November 16, the 4th Infantry Division began a coordinated attack that would involve all three regiments. Reinforced by CCR of the 5th Armored Division, they attacked on a broad front between Schevenhütte and the village of Hürtgen in the direction of the city of Düren northeast of the Hürtgen Forest. In doing so, and in an effort to break the stalemate they covered ground that had been ravaged by earlier battles. Some of the forest had already been decimated and trees reduced to matchwood from the constant shelling. It had already been discovered on the information of German POWs that their troops in the forest were not of the best quality, but they were so well dug in and protected by reinforced concrete that at the time it didn't really matter.

The starting time was 1245 hours, when lead elements of the 22nd Infantry's 2nd Battalion began moving out and were quickly followed by soldiers of the 1st and 3rd Battalions and with three regimental combat teams moving forward simultaneously they initially managed to advance around 2 miles.

Making the main effort on the left in order to support the 1st Infantry Division, elements of 8th Infantry and the 22nd Infantry made extremely slow progress against well-organized positions within the forest. The 12th Infantry remained virtually immobile on a small plateau that lay just to the southwest of the forest.

Patrick L. O'Dea, Company F, 2nd Battalion, 22nd Infantry Regiment

The afternoon was rather mild, and I took the opportunity to clean my rifle since it was getting downright rusty in lots of places, and I began to doubt if it would work when I needed it. After I got it a little cleaner and oiled it, I felt more like a soldier. I was making plans to get a good night's rest with the blankets when the word was passed down that we were going to attack that night. This was really bad news since I hated the thought of fighting in the dark of night. So, we ate our evening meal with a great deal of somber thoughts about what might come later.

At dusk, we gathered into squads and prepared for the advance to our objective. I was in the third squad, and I remember the company commander flying into a rage and whispering furious curses, calling for the third squad. Actually, we were in the right place all the time, but Dan, the squad leader, had not spoken up when the CO called for him. There were only six or seven of us in each squad so we looked more like a couple of squads than a platoon. No wonder the CO got confused. He was in a vile humor when we started out. Incidentally, that was the first time I ever saw him. I never did learn his name.

We started out walking in a single file, following the perimeter of the forest religiously. It was a grueling march. The ground was soft and thick with mud. I had a pair of galoshes on, and these made walking difficult, and with my bad feet I was in no shape for easy walking, much less this kind of hike. We were supposed to keep 5 yards distance between us, and this was not easy. When we walked through patches of the forest it was impossible to keep 5 yards and still maintain contact with the man in front of you. And, if there was one thing I didn't want to do, it was to lose contact with the man in front of me. I had horrible visions of doing this and thus leading the scores of troops who followed me into some kind of a terrible trap or ambush.

To say that this march was tiring would be a miracle of understatement. It was a march through forest and bush, up slimy hills where roots and low brush tripped your feet and sent you crashing to the ground. It meant walking through forests, straining your eyes to see the man you were following, only to have a pine bough set in motion by the man in front come springing back to lash you across the eyes or in the mouth. It meant having strong branches reach out and try to knock the rifle from your shoulders. It meant plodding along gullies and stream bottoms where the soft mud allowed your feet to sink 6 or 8 inches, and then closed over them like an earthen vise from which you struggled, cursing, to release your foot with a squishing gurgle. Every now and then, we would come to a flat area where, to our right, a large plain lay quiet and foreboding in the soft light of the newly risen moon. Occasionally we would stumble over a body. I hoped they were all Germans.

At one time we were moving along the side of a hill with as much stealth as possible when a young, clear, American voice rang out from higher on the hill, "Who's that walking along there?"

We were startled to hear the voice from what I thought was a "no man's island." No one answered. The voice came again, more insistent.

"Are you guys GIs?"

Still no one answered him, and I glanced around impatiently to see if the sergeant was nearby and whether he was going to answer. I didn't want to answer myself, but I was scared that the young soldier might start firing at us. I told the man behind me what I thought, and I could hear whispers along the line. The boy's voice came again, and I could still hear whispers. The boy's voice called once more, this time almost pleading, "If you guys don't answer me, I'm going to open up with this machine gun."

That was the final straw. Since the sergeant didn't seem to know what to say, a whole chorus of voices went up telling him, "Shut up—we're GIs."

I don't know how long we walked, but it was something more than an hour, maybe an hour and a half. We stopped once for a rest and then moved out again.

The second time that we stopped, I sat on the muddy ground, pretty well exhausted. After a few minutes I revived a little and started looking around.

I was surprised to see a house about 100 yards away, faintly outlined in the moonlight. A few seconds later I heard the sound of many approaching footsteps. A group of German prisoners appeared, being herded by some GIs on their way to the rear. I realized then that we must be near our objective. This was the first time all evening that I had any idea of what we were supposed to do that night. Since there were no sounds of a battle nearby, I guessed that there was a village close by that some other company had already taken and that we would be used as reinforcements to hold the village. Sure enough, the sergeant came back soon and told us we were lucky because the village had been taken, and we wouldn't have to do any fighting that night. This news made me a bit happier, for I was very tired and my feet pained me considerably.

At a signal from the sergeant we started out again, and in a short time we emerged from the forest into a small village that had been destroyed by the war. All the houses had been severely damaged: some were burned-out shells; others had huge holes in them. It was a typical German village, the first I had ever seen. None of the houses was more than three stories, and most of them appeared to be well built. A couple of the houses were still burning, and we ran past them as fast as possible because our silhouettes made fine targets against a background of flame. I saw a number of GIs throughout the village, but not one German civilian. I assumed that they all had fled the area long before the battle started. Other groups of German soldiers were being returned to our rear. Most of them looked dirty and exhausted.

We continued through the village and were ordered to take up positions on the outskirts, at a point from which we had a clear view of several hundred yards of bare ground. It was a good place to set up a line against possible German counterattack. At this point, the sergeant learned that several of our platoon had become separated and he got mad and went back through the town yelling for them.

Having found most of them, he came back and started assigning us spots to dig in. We were still tired from our hike, and none of us wanted to spend three hours or so digging a foxhole. But the thought of a possible German attack in the morning made up my mind for me. Our platoon started digging in about 15 yards from a road that separated us from the village, which was probably called Grosshau. After we had been digging about twenty minutes, I realized that a tree only a few feet away might be a source of danger, because a shell hitting it would send a deadly shower of shrapnel into our hole. I remarked about this to Steve, my 21-year-old foxhole buddy. We were halfheartedly considering digging in at some less dangerous place, but I hated to have all that work on the present hole go to waste. The dilemma was solved from an unexpected quarter when the sergeant came over and ordered the whole platoon to fall back about 40 yards to the other side of the road and dig in there instead. There was the usual grumbling, but I was willing enough. The area was pockmarked with shell holes, and most pairs of men selected a shell hole for conversion to a foxhole because it meant less digging. The hole that my partner and I got was sort of deceiving because we had to do a lot more digging than I estimated. The ground was rocky and our entrenching tools would only go an inch before they hit a rock. We both dug silently for a while. It was only about 2030 hours, and we had been in Grosshau for less than an hour.

I suppose it took the enemy a little time to dispatch messages to his rear echelon informing them of his withdrawal from Grosshau. They, in turn, would instruct their artillery to blast the town before we had a chance to dig in. The German artillery did just that, and soon the first salvo of 88s came screaming in. We dived for our half-completed holes and huddled in terror as the great shells exploded near us. In a few minutes the barrage was over and we jumped up and resumed digging with increased fervor. I wondered anxiously when the next barrage would be hurled at us. The time between barrages would be a good index of how frequently we would be blasted for the rest of the night.

As daylight came, it was time for the attack. To my surprise about a dozen GIs lined up on the road and headed as a skirmish line toward the enemy. I supposed they were another platoon of our company. One fell wounded before they had advanced a dozen yards. Our sergeant gave the order to move out and we followed about 50 yards behind the other platoon. Enemy shells began to fall and small-arms fire began. Two German soldiers jumped up and surrendered about 40 yards in front of us; they were manning a machine gun. I was amazed that the enemy had been that close to us all night. In a few minutes the enemy shells had disrupted our formation so that we and the other platoon were all mixed up together. Our own heavy weapons platoon observers were with us, and they passed back orders to raise or lower our mortar fire. It seemed to me that their orders were being garbled, as they were being passed back orally, and I expected our own mortars to fall on us. I don't know whether they did, but we were brought to a halt just a few hundred yards from the town. The artillery shells and mortars fell on us in such numbers that the men hugged the ground for safety. Most of us were able to find shell holes that were shallow and dish like, but they did afford some protection. Small-arms fire would frequently come our way, but it was not as dangerous as the shellfire.

At one point during a heavy shelling, I noticed large lumps of what I thought were clods of dirt falling around me. A few of them hit me although they did not hurt me. One that fell looked like a potato, but on closer inspection, it turned out to be a turnip. I must have been lying in somebody's turnip field. It occurred to me that the army might have to send my mother a telegram saying, "Your son was killed by a large turnip." I still had my sense of humor.

Our platoon became more and more scattered. We were mixed in with people from other platoons. It was hard for our sergeant to pass orders along to his platoon. During a short lull, after we had endured a long artillery bombardment, the sergeant crawled over to me and some of the other platoon members and said he wanted us to move forward about 150 yards because the enemy seemed to have his guns zeroed in on this spot. A few minutes later the sergeant yelled out the command to get started. Several of us jumped up and followed him, dodging shell holes and changing direction every few steps to prevent a sniper from getting a bead on us. When artillery shells exploded near us, we would hit the ground. Some people say it's too late to hit the ground when you hear the shell explode, but that's what we did. I was able to keep the sergeant in view and tried to follow him closely. In a few more minutes, it seemed to me, the sergeant and I were the only men who were moving forward. The others seemed to be lost. Finally, the sergeant stopped running, hit the ground, and motioned me to join him.

"Stay here," he said, "I'm going back to get the other men. I'll be back in a few minutes." All I could say was "OK," but I wasn't happy about it because it seemed to me that the sergeant and I had made the deepest penetration of the German lines in that sector. I could imagine a squad of Germans rushing up to me, blasting away with their burp guns. I fired at where I thought the Germans were likely to be dug in, but I could see no action there.

Sure enough, the sergeant returned in a little while with other men from our platoon. My foxhole buddy from the night before, Steve, dropped into a shell hole not far from mine, close enough so that we could talk. After each nearby, heavy shelling, we would rise up to see if the other had been hit. The shelling continued to be heavy, and I was convinced that the Germans had us under direct observation. Surprisingly, I did not see any of our tanks. I thought that this terrain would be excellent for tank support of an infantry advance. The tanks could smash machine gun emplacements and even bunkers that were holding us up. Off in the distance, to the north, I thought I could see GIs from other companies also trying to advance in the face of withering artillery.

Finally, during a severe bombardment by 88mm shells, I felt a sharp blow on my arm as if someone had hit me with his fist. I was lying in a shallow shell hole holding my helmet on with my hands when it happened. As usual, I was praying for protection from the shells. I was pretty sure that a shell fragment had hit me. I could still wiggle my fingers and move my arm, so I thought I was not in immediate danger from the wound. After a while, I could feel blood running down my arm and I stuck my other hand inside my shirt. I raised my head and asked my buddy if he had been hit. Sure enough, he had. The shelling continued, and I decided it was too dangerous to try to go back to the village and look for a medic. My buddy agreed, so we remained.

Our attack was probably part of a general advance by a battalion or two in our sector, but it seemed clear that our attack had stalled. None of the men near me were trying to advance. We were all pinned down by artillery. Small-arms fire swept over us at times, but the artillery was causing the casualties. As far as I could see, no American units were making any progress as the afternoon dragged on. The last time I saw the sergeant, he was about 20 yards to my left in a shell hole. I debated whether to wait until dark and then try to return to the village or whether it would be smarter to start back right away. But the artillery shells bursting around us made me postpone any attempt to go back to the village.

The hours dragged by. I felt sure that the wound was not bad and that I would not bleed to death. As evening approached my buddy and I agreed that we should start back for the village and try to stick together. We waited for a lull in the shelling and then jumped up and headed for the village. It was a long run. We would hit the ground every hundred feet or so and sooner, if shells fell nearby. It was hard to maintain contact with each other. I left my rifle in a shell hole. While running, I noticed that my web belt with an entrenching tool hanging on it and a canteen and several clips of ammunition was slowing me down. I had already discarded my bandoleers of ammo. At one point, I jumped up and looked for my buddy to do the same, but I couldn't see him. I hesitated for a few seconds and resumed running toward the village. I met a GI who was lying on the ground, badly wounded and promised to get a medic for him. As I reached the village edge, a mortar shell seemed to explode a few yards away from me. I was running at the time and couldn't believe that I wasn't wounded. I saw a red cross and headed for it. The officer in charge, a doctor I suppose, made me take off my jacket and open my shirt so that he could see the wound. He then told me to wait for transportation back. I told him about the wounded man out on the field. Here in the village, there was a semblance of normality; jeeps and trucks came and went and men walked around ... but carefully.

After a while, a jeep drove up to the aid station, and I was sent back to another aid station about a quarter mile back. The medic examined me, and since my wound was not life threatening he offered me a cup of coffee and told me to sit down and wait for the truck going back to the next aid station. The coffee was hot and revived my spirit. Eventually a truck drove up. By now it was dark, and several wounded men were helped into the truck. We drove in the darkness for what seemed to be a long time and were taken, finally, to a building where our names and other information was taken. We were given more coffee and some doughnuts, I think. Then we took another truck ride in the darkness and ended up in town, probably in Belgium, and were taken to a field hospital. About one hundred wounded men were there waiting for some kind of treatment. Most were American, but a few were German. One German soldier sat on a chair with his chest bare and a neat bullet hole where his heart was supposed to be. A lot of us wondered how he could still be alive. He sat up straight and never whimpered. Before long, he was taken by a medic to the operating room.

My feet were hurting, and I thought the warmth of the building had something to do with it. At least I knew that sooner or later somebody would treat my feet as well as my wound. Eventually my name was called, and I was led to an operating room. I got to see my wound in the bright light. A shell fragment had entered my right arm near the shoulder. It missed the bone and had partly exited on the other side of the arm. I could see the metal fragment sticking out of the arm. The doctor told me that he would put me to sleep and would remove the shell fragment and dress the wound. He and his helpers gave me sodium pentothal, and I drifted to sleep almost immediately.

I woke up the following morning in a ward with about two dozen other GI patients. Someone was shaking me and telling me to wake up. Someone else was handing me a cup of coffee telling me that it would wake me up. Someone was holding me in a sitting position, but I kept going back to sleep. They kept talking to me and asking me questions and trying to make me wake up. One nurse was being helped by the GI patients from nearby beds who were trying to awaken me. After I was wide awake, they asked me my name, where I was from, and what outfit I was with. One man, who I later found out was a sergeant from the 29th Division, asked me where I was when I was wounded. All I could say was that I was in "the woods."

He then told me that it was the Hürtgen Forest, and that it was a major German defensive point that protected Cologne.

So, for the first time, I learned where my adventure had taken place. I was very dirty, and a ward man brought me a towel, soap, and water. I cleaned myself as best I could and felt a lot better. Shaving was next, and that turned out to be a painful process. My face had been caked with mud for ten days, and it had been ground into the skin. The razor was army issue and not very sharp to begin with. The ward man helped me all he could, and after a painful hour, my face looked a lot better. That ten-day growth of beard was tougher than I had ever dreamed it could be.

At the commencement of the attack Major General Barton had dispatched the 12th Regiment on the left flank. Two days later the 22nd Regiment was committed in the center, then the 8th Regiment on the right. The Germans responded by raining artillery and mortar shells the like of which had not been experienced by combat troops on the Western Front since WWI. The approaches to all the bunkers and pillboxes were strewn with mines and in some places up to three or more rows of barbed wire. The excellent field of fire from these positions allowed the Germans to deliver instant death and mutilation on any approaching potential assailants.

As the month of November dragged on and the objectives moved gradually further east the 4th became ever deeper embroiled in the fighting. Beset by problems of inadequate supply, desperately bad weather conditions and mounting casualties they battled on. All advances on Grosshau were vigorously contested and the enemy continued to offer stoic resistance at every juncture, but eventually they began to fall back slowly, moving from one line of well-prepared positions to the next. These mainly fruitless attacks persisted against well-defended positions throughout November. Every single yard gained was paid for in blood and misery. The Hürtgen had no precedent and almost every other campaign to date on the Western Front to date paled by comparison.

First Lieutenant Bernard J. Ray, Company F, 8th Infantry set out alone to blast a path through a German concertina entanglement that blocked his unit's advance. He stuffed blasting caps in his pockets, wrapped primer cord around his body, and grabbed several Bangalore torpedoes. He made it to the wire but was severely wounded while he was setting his charges. Realizing his wounds would disable him before he could complete his task, Ray connected a Bangalore to the caps in his pocket and the primer cord around his body and detonated the explosion. For this heroic act he was awarded a Medal of Honor. Later the barracks at the Friedberg/Giessen Depot in Germany the barracks were named for him.

First Lieutenant Bernard J. Ray
Medal of Honor

He was platoon leader with Company F, 8th Infantry, on November 17, 1944, during the drive through the Hürtgen Forest near Schevenhutte, Germany. The American forces attacked in wet, bitterly cold weather over rough, wooded terrain, meeting brutal resistance from positions spaced throughout the forest behind minefields and wire obstacles. Small arms, machinegun, mortar, and artillery fire caused heavy casualties in the ranks when Company F was halted by a concertina-type wire barrier. Under heavy fire, 1st Lt. Ray reorganized his men and prepared to blow a path through the entanglement, a task which appeared impossible of accomplishment and from which others tried to dissuade him. With implacable determination to clear the way, he placed explosive caps in his pockets, obtained several bangalore torpedoes, and then wrapped a length of highly explosive primer cord about his body. He dashed forward under direct fire, reached the barbed wire and prepared his demolition charge as mortar shells, which were being aimed at him alone, came steadily nearer his completely exposed position. He had placed a torpedo under the wire and was connecting it to a charge he carried when he was severely wounded by a bursting mortar shell. Apparently realizing that he would fail in his self-imposed mission unless he completed it in a few moments he made a supremely gallant decision. With the primer cord still wound about his body and the explosive caps in his pocket, he completed a hasty wiring system and unhesitatingly thrust down on the handle of the charger, destroying himself with the wire barricade in the resulting blast. By the deliberate sacrifice of his life, 1st Lt. Ray enabled his company to continue its attack, resumption of which was of positive significance in gaining the approaches to the Cologne Plain.

As the attack continued the 12th Regiment's F and G Companies tenuously edged their way up a forested slope and somehow, despite powerful opposition, managed to carve a wedge into the German lines. In response the Germans released an intense barrage of mortar shells above the GIs' heads that exploded in the treetops and showered everything in proximity with deadly jagged fragments of metal and wood. Then the deadly splutter of German machine guns and tracers ripped the murkiness as the Germans attempted to rectify the situation and take advantage of their defenses.

On November 17, 1st Battalion, 22nd Infantry attacked again in an effort to secure the high ground that dominated the area. Fighter planes of IX TAC supported and the advance was preceded by a 30-minute artillery preparation. The Germans responded accordingly with intense concentrations of artillery shells and bullets. Extensive minefields impeded the progress of 1st Battalion and 2nd Battalion was ordered to push to the east toward high ground but enemy infiltration to the rear of the battalion position and stiff resistance in front made the going tough. Despite this, by 1630 hours both battalions had reached their prearranged objectives.

A platoon of light tanks used to support the 1st Battalion was eliminated by mines, and the remaining vehicles were unable to make any progress due to dense woods and heavily mined firebreaks. Engineers were brought up to help clear some of the minefields but they also came under heavy fire and were unable to operate effectively. The advance of the assaulting battalions continued but torrential rain had flooded supply routes to such an extent that the one engineer platoon available in support of the regiment wasn't capable of dealing with the problem alone. Not one single vehicle could negotiate the roads and get up to the front lines to provide supporting armor.

As the situation developed the Germans managed to surreptitiously creep into a ravine and threaten the meager supply line to 22nd Infantry's F and G Company. Then for two days and nights the Germans poured mortar and artillery shells into the area as the GIs fought back to back to repel constant counterattacks. Owing to the nature of the terrain in the Hurtgen it was often difficult to determine the source and direction of incoming fire. F and G Companies became isolated and assumed that they were surrounded. Within the claustrophobic confines of this dense forest and under a canopy that excluded almost all light the Ivy men scrambled in the ankle-deep mud to dig foxholes and offer themselves some kind of protection from the shells and the unforgiving elements. In this green, foreboding place temperatures dipped below freezing and incessant drizzle soaked everything, and if things weren't bad enough, that rain soon turned to snow. Two additional engineer platoons were brought up but in three days of heavy, sustained combat the regiment only managed to advance approximately 2,000 yards at a cost of 300 enlisted and 24 officer casualties.

The emotional toll on the soldiers was extremely high and in addition to the thousands of wounded and killed, a significant percentage of ordinary soldiers and officers succumbed to the constant stress and became "battle fatigue" casualties. In forward positions, isolated groups of soldiers spent as much as two weeks under continuous enemy fire, in muddy foxholes, deprived of hot food or medical assistance. Whole areas of once lush pine forest were reduced to matchwood and the scars were so prolific that they can still be seen today.

Major Erwin Kressmann, Heavy Panzer Brigade 519 (Knight's Cross)

The attack began in the morning it was still dark. My company had 12 Jagdpanthers. We saw Americans fighting our infantry and destroying them in Kommerscheidt. When we approached the front line we received artillery support from our positions in Vossenack. After several attempts I got my Jagdpanther out into some open ground and took out two Sherman tanks. Some Americans showed a white flag and surrendered. They had occupied the place with a full battalion. I remember that one day we were ordered to continue the attack towards Kommerscheidt. I could not believe my ears because we were being ordered to engage the Americans in broad daylight in full view of enemy fighter bombers and to make things worse the Americans had more artillery. A tank battle developed in Kommerscheidt and we were not able to take the town. Many of our vehicles broke down and could not be repaired. One evening as I sat on my tent sheet on a patch of grass on the slope of the hill north of Schmidt in the evening sun, our commander appeared. He told me that our attack had missed its objective. This was pretty much as I had feared it, I told him that my company was no longer operational due to the breakdowns. He ignored this information completely and ordered that I should kindly get into my Jagdpanther and get those vehicles repaired. After dark using a tractor I managed to recover six Jagdpanthers.

We received reports that American tanks had been seen in Kommerscheidt so another attack was ordered against the town with all the armored forces combined to form a task force. My company was on point because we had the heaviest vehicles. I was planning the positions of my unit like I had done in Russia but this time we attacked without infantry support.

There was a forest hut near me that had clay walls as I drove I pushed the muzzler of my cannon against the wall and it collapsed. The same thing happened with a second house then I was among the trees. The strongest part of a tree is the base so I drove slowly against it. Because of the soft ground, it was easily uprooted. This was not a good place for tanks and heavy vehicles and too much time was wasted attempting to maneuver around them.

F and G Company realized that there was only one small but useable foot-path for bringing up ammunition and it was subject to constant enemy fire, preventing food supplies from being delivered and wounded men from being evacuated. Rain continued to shower through the gloom, seeping into foxholes, saturating winter clothing and reducing the already limited visibility to just a few yards. What medical supplies they had were completely insufficient to provide any care for injured men whose gaping wounds festered under blood- and rain-drenched bandages.

E Company was in closest proximity to the besieged companies and made repeated attempts to relieve them. On the third day, A and C Companies moved up under the cover of darkness and nervously waited for the first suffused rays of daylight to launch an attack. Casualties mounted on both sides but the Germans, caught between the isolated companies and their relief, were annihilated, and F and G Companies were rescued to fight another day.

Then, eventually in late November, as the 4th Infantry Division prepared to attack in the direction of Grosshau again, pale brown streams already swelled by rain increased in size even further as the rain turned to snow that clung to the branches of tall pine trees, decking foxholes and shell craters. The suffering of the GIs in Hürtgen was further compounded when the few still navigable roads became impassable quagmires that pulled down tanks, supply trucks and jeeps struggling to reach the front.

Billy Cater, OH Service Company, 22nd Infantry Regiment

During the Hürtgen Forest campaign, I was Services Company commander. The HQ company commander was killed, and I was assigned as Headquarters CO. The personnel wanted to take a patrol to recover his body. I did not approve it and so was not in very good with the troops.

The cooks were trying to prepare turkeys for Thanksgiving dinner. We were under artillery fire from the Krauts—they carved our turkey. The last available men from our Regiment (I think about 135 cooks, clerks, and truck drivers) were assembled, and we were assigned a sector of the front line with me in charge. We established a line of defense in previously dug foxholes. I was checking positions toward a concrete pillbox with a door, where my company clerk (probably seventeen years old) and a recently decorated truck driver (who was still badly shook up from moving a truck load of ammo that was on fire from a congested area) were standing. The pillbox and our sector came under a heavy shelling with a direct hit. Both men were standing in the door; the company clerk in front was critically wounded and died in the hospital.

Apart from supply issues, one of the main problems encountered by the 4th Infantry Division and many other US divisions in the Hürtgen was the requisition and delivery of replacements to the regiments. The fighting was so intense and deadly that necessary daily supplies were simply not delivered.

The forest had been divided into sections with concrete markers indicating the section numbers at each trail intersection. The pine trees in the planted areas of the forest were arranged in neat rows that were between 10 and 15 feet apart, which provided a dense canopy and in some places limited visibility to just a few yards. Those areas not planted were almost impenetrable due to dense undergrowth. East of the forest roads led out towards the Roer plain and in the villages of Grosshau and Gey, the two primary targets selected for the Ivy men, a 630-feet-deep ravine stretched 2,000 yards separating these two vital villages. One of the roads connecting the two villages snaked along a twisted route and was flanked with an almost 60-foot sheer drop on one side. Such features frequently deprived the infantryman of supporting armor and artillery. Poor roads and the sheerness of the hillside gradients prevented and restricted the use of armor until paths to open terrain were cleared.

US Army artillery observers were often hindered by limited visibility, which impeded the effective deployment and use of long-range artillery.

Air support was also rendered superfluous on occasion, and a combination of these elements virtually negated the almost 5-to-1 numerical advantage held by American forces at the time.

The system of resupply could not provide adequate numbers of fresh troops, with the result that the strength of all three regiments decreased steadily. By end of November they were all well below fighting capacity. This was attrition at its most malicious and fatal, causing disproportionately high battle and non-battle casualties on both sides. Cases of trench foot verged on epidemic proportions due to the fact that US Army issue boots were inadequate for constant use on wet ground and the majority of replacements were not issued with overshoes. The latter problem wasn't addressed until the end of November.

During those first five days of combat, the 4th Infantry Division suffered disproportionately heavy casualties. Every new enemy line was as tough as the last and every time they went on the offensive the same procedure had to be repeated. Meanwhile the Germans, who were considerably more familiar with the area, managed to bring up fresh regiments and counterattack almost daily. That said, the quality and fortitude of these troops was often abysmally below par and their leadership also left a lot to be desired.

On the US side, companies were often caught before they had a chance to dig in. Taking Grosshau proved to be considerably more difficult than initially expected and it would mean even more fiercely contested battles to throw back the stubborn Germans. After every advance, the Ivy men spent hours digging new foxholes and sawing logs to cover them. This was frequently done while under bombardment.

After a day and night of vicious fighting, by November 27 the 22nd Infantry finally managed to reach Grosshau, eliminating all opposition on the way before clearing the last strip of the forest that lay just beyond the town. Not far behind, the 8th and 12th struggled forward to get in place for the final assault on the town of Düren, but first there was three more days of intense combat before the 4th Infantry Division broke through the last German line of defense and emerged on the east perimeter of the forest.

The drive on Grosshau had demanded coherent leadership and individual courage of the highest order under the most adverse conditions. The fact that the 4th Infantry Division finally overcame the many obstacles in their path and drove the enemy from the dominating hills overlooking the Roer River is a tribute to the skill, determination and fighting spirit of all ranks.

Nevertheless, battle casualties were exceedingly high due to the great number of mines, booby traps and tree bursts from German artillery and mortar fire. The shrapnel from enemy rounds was highly effective against attacking soldiers in the open, but US artillery was often redundant when the targets were defending soldiers dug in with overhead cover.

No one was spared. It was often the case that a good soldier might begin an attack as a rifleman but by the time the objective was taken he could find himself acting squad leader. In an attempt to maintain cohesion he might move about among his men—risking becoming a casualty himself. The highest percentage of casualties incurred was among the officers and platoon leaders of US Army units. The hell of the Hürtgen Forest indelibly scarred the 4th Infantry Division but they would fight on. More than 70 years after the conclusion of the battle, the mortal remains of US and German soldiers are still being found in the Hürtgen Forest.

On December 3, the seriously depleted 22nd were pulled out of the line and moved to Luxembourg followed by the 12th four days later and the 8th on December 13. The troops were exhausted, battle weary and in dire need of replacements but just a few days later they would find themselves in yet another bitter life and death struggle as the Battle of the Bulge erupted along a thinly held 87-mile front.

John E. Kunkel, Company L, 3rd Battalion, 22nd Infantry Regiment

I would like to relate something that took place a day or two after we were relieved in the Hürtgen and pulled back to what I recall was an old German training camp. A short time after we got there, we were all given a bunk and a gray German army blanket. Well, about midnight it happened—we all started to itch all over. My buddy said he felt something crawling on his neck. I took my pen flashlight out and, sure enough, there they were—body lice. Now the problem was getting rid of the lice. About daylight we found an old kerosene lantern. We poured the kerosene into a steel helmet and with an old dirty sock, we all took a sponge bath. It was hard on the skin, but we got rid of the lice. It was some time until we could take a real bath with good old water. We started to smell to the point we all smelled like Billy goats—it got to where we could not live with one another.

Key US officers involved in the battle were General Omar Bradley, Twelfth Army Group Command; General Courtney Hodges, First Army Command; General J. Lawton Collins, VII Corps Command; and Major General Barton, 4th Infantry Division Command. Eight US infantry and two US armored divisions fought the battle of Hürtgen Forest. In addition to the thousands of wounded and killed, a notable percentage of ordinary soldiers and officers succumbed to the constant stress and became "battle fatigue" casualties. The emotional toll on the soldiers was exceedingly high. A staggering casualty rate of more than 25% implies that more than 24,000 American soldiers were battle casualties with another 9,000 victims of disease or combat fatigue. Over 120,000 Allied troops fought in the Hürtgen Forest, in organized units and replacements numbered in their thousands.

They were resisted by around 80,000 Germans—six full divisions, along with units from other divisions. In addition to the protection they got from the dense forest, the Germans also had pillboxes and dug-in positions to protect them from US fire. Enemy soldiers were often barricaded inside buildings and used small towns for cover. The cover and concealment used by the Germans limited the effectiveness of US indirect fire, as well as aerial bombardment when it was available. The dense undergrowth and large trees made armor movement almost impossible, except along well-established roads. The marshy ground also hindered any mechanized cross-country movement. The Germans had multiplied the effectiveness of the natural obstacles many times over through the effective use of wire, booby traps, and minefields. The wire was well protected by small-arms and machine-gun fire, making it difficult for advancing troops to advance more than a few feet or yards at a time.

The fighting in the Hürtgen Forest, combined with the Battle of the Bulge, bought the Germans a little time and inevitably delayed the Allied thrust through Germany. When the Allies finally took the Hürtgen Forest, many high-ranking ETO officers realized that the area was of little strategic value, and there was little to show for the horrific price paid in human lives. Military historians all over the world still hotly debate whether the capture of the Roer River dams could have been achieved without the Hürtgen Forest battle.

One of the main problems encountered by the 4th Infantry Division was a major underestimation of the Germans' capacity to defend this area and an overestimation of the US Army's capacity to maintain the momentum and advantage that had kept them going since the successes in the Normandy campaign. Moreover the offensive action that was undertaken by the Ivy men covered a front that was far too wide for them to be effective. This resulted in them having to reduce the area and frequently forced them to bypass objectives and on occasion become completely surrounded.

German forces may have been severely depleted in Normandy but they still had reserves and ammunition at their disposal and, contrary to popular belief at ETO, they were not on the verge of total collapse. The divisions sent into the Hürtgen Forest discovered that the fighting there had no precedent or comparison in their previous battles. Here in the Hürtgen Forest the Germans had the advantage of being able to contain most assaults from their well-defended and entrenched positions.

Hundreds of US casualties were sustained because of excessive exposure to front-line conditions that resulted in battle fatigue and debilitating weather-related ailments such as trench foot and hypothermia. Replacements were often inexperienced and unprepared for the horrors that confronted them in the Hürtgen. This often resulted in a terrible waste of dearly needed men and equipment.

Grosshau was only taken after a murderous frontal assault that in retrospect contributed little to the overall mission. Nevertheless the plan of attack was approved and authorized by Division HQ and, despite their intelligence regarding German defenses, the attack went ahead on

November 29. The fact that the mission was accomplished was largely due to the skill and guidance of respected regimental commanders such as 22nd Infantry's Colonel Charles T. Lanham, who displayed calm and thoughtful leadership throughout.

The Germans had the high ground and took full advantage of their position to hamper and impede that attack by zeroing in artillery and mortar barrages with deadly accuracy. The enemy shells were augmented by rigorous small-arms support from earthen emplacements. All approaches to the German positions were heavily protected by rows of barbed wire, the ubiquitous booby traps and minefields.

General Collins paid tribute once again to the Ivy men when he said,

> *"The drive required a continuous display of top-notch leadership and the highest order of individual courage under the most adverse conditions. The fact that the 4th Division overcame these many difficulties and drove the enemy from the dominating hills overlooking the Roer River is a tribute to the skill, determination and aggressiveness of all ranks."*

Russell J. York, combat medic, 4th Engineer Battalion, 4th Infantry Division

Silver Star

> *For gallantry in action in Germany, November 20, 1944, Technician Medical Fourth Grade York accompanied an engineer squad on a mission of building a two-span trestle bridge. The bridge site [The Weiser Weh near Grosshau] and a nearby crossroads were under direct enemy observation and subject to mortar and artillery fire. While the work was in progress, the enemy delivered a concentration of heavy caliber artillery fire. As the squad dispersed, several members became casualties. Although the shelling continued, Technician Medical Fourth Grade York went from one man to another administering first aid. While one casualty lay in an exposed position, directly on the crossroads, he bandaged his wounds and assisted in removing him to a vehicle. As the shelling continued, York repeatedly entered the zone of fire to administer to the casualties, regardless of personal risk involved. Many shells burst close by, but he persisted in work until all wounded were evacuated … York's spirit of courageous self-sacrifice resulted in saving many lives.*

During the incident York ran out of tourniquets and went to Major General Barton, his commander, and requested the general lend him his belt. He did and York went back in to treat more men.

Meier, John W. (First Award), Technician Fifth Grade, US Army Medical Detachment, 8th Infantry Regiment, 4th Infantry Division

Silver Star

Action: November 30, 1944

> The President of the United States of America, authorized by Act of Congress July 9, 1918, takes pleasure in presenting the Silver Star to Technician Fifth Grade John W. Meier (ASN: 35878008), United States Army, for gallantry in action while serving as a Medical Aidman with the Medical Detachment, 8th Infantry Regiment, 4th Infantry Division, in action in the Hürtgen Forest, Germany, on 30 November 1944. On that date, Technician Fifth Grade Meier accompanied forward infantry elements during a coordinated infantry and tank assault upon powerful Hürtgen Forest fortifications, courageously administering to the wounded during the heat of battle. Hostile rocket fire immobilized and ignited a nearby tank, which was quickly converted into a flaming wreck. Technician Fifth Grade Meier, observing several crew members hastily evacuating the tank, realized that there might be others in the vehicle who were unable to dismount because of injuries. He dashed to the burning vehicle, where he discovered the tank commander, severely burned and wounded. Although heavy enemy fire was still directed at the vehicle, Technician Fifth Grade Meier deftly extricated the wounded man from the tank and placed him in a covered position. Running through direct hostile machine-gun fire delivered from a point only 30 yards away he procured an assistant and a litter, whereupon he ran the gauntlet of enemy fire a second time in reaching the stricken tank commander. Assisted by his companion, he then evacuated the casualty to the forward aid station, where timely medical treatment saved his life. Technician Fifth Grade Meier's exemplary display of courage and proficiency under fire and his complete display of courage and proficiency under fire and his complete subjugation of self-interest in behalf of the wounded are in keeping with the finest traditions of the military service.

Mabry, George L., Jr., Lieutenant Colonel, US Army, 2nd Battalion, 8th Infantry, 4th Infantry Division

Medal of Honor

Place and date: Hürtgen Forest near Schevenhutte, Germany, November 20, 1944

> He was commanding the 2nd Battalion, 8th Infantry, in an attack through the Hürtgen Forest near Schevenhutte, Germany, on 20 November 1944. During the early phases of

the assault, the leading elements of his battalion were halted by a minefield and immobilized by heavy hostile fire. Advancing alone into the mined area, Lieutenant Colonel Mabry established a safe route of passage. He then moved ahead of the foremost scouts, personally leading the attack, until confronted by a booby-trapped double concertina obstacle. With the assistance of the scouts, he disconnected the explosives and cut a path through the wire. Upon moving through the opening, he observed three enemy in foxholes, whom he captured at bayonet point. Driving steadily forward, he paced the assault against three log bunkers, which housed mutually-supported automatic weapons. Racing up a slope ahead of his men, he found the initial bunker deserted, then pushed on to the second where he was suddenly confronted by nine onrushing enemy. Using the butt of his rifle, he felled one adversary and bayoneted a second, before his scouts came to his aid and assisted him in overcoming the others in hand-to-hand combat. Accompanied by the riflemen, he charged the third bunker under point-blank small-arms fire and led the way into the fortification from which he prodded six enemy at bayonet point. Following the consolidation of this area, he led his battalion across 300 yards of fire-swept terrain to seize elevated ground upon which he established a defensive position which menaced the enemy on both flanks, and provided his regiment a firm foothold on the approach to the Cologne Plain. Lieutenant Colonel Mabry's superlative courage, daring, and leadership in an operation of major importance, exemplify the finest characteristics of the military service.

Garcia, Marcario, Staff Sergeant, US Army, Company C, 22nd Infantry, 4th Infantry Division

Medal of Honor

Place and date: Near Grosshau, Germany, November 27, 1944

While an acting squad leader of Company B, 22nd Infantry, on 27 November 1944, near Grosshau, Germany, he single-handedly assaulted two enemy machine-gun emplacements. Attacking prepared positions on a wooded hill, which could be approached only through meager cover, his company was pinned down by intense machine-gun fire and subjected to a concentrated artillery and mortar barrage. Although painfully wounded, he refused to be evacuated and, on his own initiative, crawled forward alone until he reached a position near an enemy emplacement. Hurling grenades, he boldly assaulted the position, destroyed the gun, and with his rifle killed three of the enemy who attempted to escape. When he rejoined his company, a second machine gun opened fire and again the intrepid soldier went forward, utterly disregarding his own safety. He stormed the position and destroyed the gun, killed three more Germans, and captured four prisoners. He fought on with his unit until the objective was taken and only then did he permit himself to be removed for medical care. Staff Sergeant (then Private) Garcia's conspicuous heroism, his inspiring, courageous conduct, and his complete disregard for his personal safety wiped out two enemy emplacements and enabled his company to advance and secure its objective.

It is said by those who were there that when President Truman put the Medal of Honor around Marcario Garcia's neck during a White House ceremony after the war, he said, "I'd rather have earned this Medal than be President of the United States."

4th Infantry Division casualties

November

Killed in Action (KIA)

	Officers	42
	Enlisted Men	390

Missing in Action (MIA, many later listed as KIA)

	Officers	10
	Enlisted Men	245

Seriously Wounded in Action (SWA)

	Officers	20
	Enlisted Men	318

Lightly Wounded in Action (LWA)

	Officers	133
	Enlisted Men	2,895

Total

	Officers	205
	Enlisted Men	3,848

CHAPTER 13

"THE COLD SHOULDER OF THE BULGE"

On December 12, the 8th Infantry reached the Duchy of Luxembourg and while the 12th Infantry maintained its position near the town of Echternach the 22nd Infantry continued active patrolling along its front in the vicinity of Mondorf. Contact with the Germans was described at the time as being "light and infrequent." This was regarded as an innocuous, quiet sector where the Ivy men could rest and replenish their seriously depleted ranks.

Meanwhile General Patton, not known for keeping his opinions to himself, was uneasy about the large gap between the First and Third Armies and had remarked that "The First Army is making a terrible mistake in leaving VIII Corps static, as it is highly probable that the Germans are building up to the east of them." Patton had placed his Third Army in the Alsace region of France. He was sure that the Germans were still capable of mounting a major counterattack and wrongly assumed that it would occur there. He wasn't getting it all his own way at that time. In the 12th Army Group's southern sector, Metz had proved to be a particularly difficult objective and fighting there had continued almost unabated since November 8.

One of the critical problems facing Eisenhower on the eve of the Battle of the Bulge was a severe shortage of infantrymen. General Omar Bradley had reported on December 15, that his army group had a deficit of around 17,000 riflemen because of casualties caused by the previous combat and weather-related conditions. In response to this Eisenhower ordered the reclassification of as many support personnel as possible so that they could be redesignated as infantrymen. Either way there were only four US divisions stretched out along the Ardennes from just below Aachen all the way to Luxembourg because this was regarded as the "quiet sector" by Allied commanders.

At 0530 hours on December 16, 1944 three German armies poured over the western borders along an 87-mile front. The 7th German Army, commanded by Erich Brandenberger, on the southern shoulder of the Bulge had been given the task of surrounding Echternach and then moving on Luxembourg in order to block Patton's advance if he decided to move his Third Army northwards. Brandenberger was a studious and methodical commander who had seen a lot of action on the Eastern Front and although he wasn't particularly well liked among his peers and was often derided for being a typical product of the general staff system, he was nonetheless a competent leader. It wasn't his intention to orchestrate a breakthrough to the west on the southern shoulder of the attack front. Brandenberger had considerably more modest ambitions that entailed preventing counterattacks from General Patton's Third US Army rather than launching a major drive to the west.

The 4th Infantry Division was one of the US divisions in the line. The situation on the morning of December 16 when the Germans attacked was far from favorable. At the time all the infantry battalions in the 4th were considerably under strength. Consequently three battle-weary regimental combat teams were holding a front of approximately 35 miles that extended along the west banks of the Sauer and Moselle rivers in Luxembourg. The recommended front for a whole division at that time was normally 5 miles. Communications between the battalions were strained because of the shortage of radio equipment.

The attached 70th Tank Battalion, which had also suffered terribly in the Hürtgen Forest, was preoccupied with repairing its vehicles. Only 11 of its 54 medium tanks were in working order at that time. In the process they discovered that obtaining parts for the purpose of repair was problematic and consequently many tanks remained static and inoperable for the duration.

North of Luxembourg city, in the town of Wiltz, some 28th Infantry Division GIs had taken a couple of German prisoners along the Luxembourg/German border who reliably informed them that a massive counterattack was being prepared. Unfortunately none of the officers took this information seriously.

In the 12th Infantry sector, at around 0600 hours on the morning of December 16, reports had disclosed that there had been some light enemy patrol activity but nothing to cause major concern. When the attack began the towns of Berdof, Lauterborn, Alttier, Osweiler and Dickweiler became the unwitting targets of powerful artillery barrages with one of the largest concentrations falling on the small picturesque town of Echternach. The barrages lasted several hours and were accurately directed at CPs, severely disrupting all wire communications.

Shortly after 0900 hours, the enemy began to penetrate 4th Infantry Division's forward positions with reconnaissance forces that were later reinforced with substantial infantry formations. Reports covering those first few hours were scant because of the lack of wire communications and the initial failure of radios, particularly those at outposts which had a very limited range over the uneven terrain around Echternach and Berdorf, often referred to as "Little Switzerland," and it was only by late afternoon that a clearer picture of the situation began to develop.

Frank Douglas, Company F, 2nd Battalion, 8th Infantry Regiment

We could see the open plains leading right down to the Rhine Valley open country in front of us after our fight through the Hürtgen Forest. The 83rd Division relieved us, and Captain Reborchek was glad to get us out of there. There were 28 left in our company that day as we got onto trucks to head out to get some rest and be regrouped. I'll never forget our truck ride out of those woods. My word! What memories of all those we left behind.

Once on the trucks (only to haul what was left of Company F) we headed south to Luxembourg and ended up in a 16th-century chateau. We were in reserve. We slept on the floor of the second story of the building. Chapman, Moody, Rene, and others were to get passes to Paris. I loaned Chappie 20 dollars. That night, a rifle sergeant, Peter Ramsey, had an appendicitis attack, so off he went to the hospital. Back at the chateau we were informed that all passes had been canceled. The next morning, Saturday, December 16, we were told there was a big emergency. We wondered what the past few months had been. Of course, we soon found out. The Battle of the Bulge was on.

The next day we moved out and climbed up on a rocky bluff along a ravine. The following day we went further along that ravine, and in an open field we set up the guns. The field was on two levels with about a 5–6 foot ridge down the middle. At the base of this steep ridge, we dug in. We also dug in the guns, a few yards away from our holes. Because the ground was soft we were able to dig down quickly and deeply

The next day we were ordered to attack. Since Company E had 50 men, they led this futile attempt. In short order the plans were changed to "hold at all costs." That's different. The mortars fired hundreds of rounds on the Krauts on the next ridge and down along the road in a ravine near a small river. One lucky shell knocked out a Kraut tank. Engineers put mines on and near the road. Jerry knew where we were, so they sent over 88s via direct express. The shells screamed right over our ridge and landed in the nearby woods. We built up our pillbox-like foxholes and made them deeper. We filled empty shell boxes and tubes with dirt and mud. Then one night, it got very, very cold. Everything and everybody froze solid. The fog lifted, and the air corps now had perfect targets. They really went after the Krauts.

The problem of regimental control and coordination within the 4th Infantry Division was impaired by the wide dispersion of its units along an extended front which created tactical isolation in these areas of dense pine woods interspersed by deep gorges and huge ravines—not entirely unlike the previous location in the Hürtgen. 4th Infantry Division orders had designated the 12th Infantry as division reserve and at the time of the attack they had only five companies in the line.

At around 0930 hours, General Barton had warned his regiments to be on the alert because reports were arriving from the 28th Division area in the north regarding a marked increase in enemy activity. This intelligence was later confirmed by a phone call to Barton from General Middleton. At this juncture General Barton issued the following statement: "There will be no retrograde movement in this sector."

As the Battle of the Bulge got under way the 4th Infantry Division's 12th Infantry were one of the first units to bear the brunt of the German attack. In their sector, a powerful artillery barrage announced the arrival of German troops who crossed the Sauer River in significant numbers. By 1100 hours the 70th Tank Battalion were told to move out and initially some elements were ordered to displace immediately to support the 12th Infantry at their regimental CP, which was located at Junglinster.

By the time this supporting armor had reached forward battalion areas, Company F, 12th Infantry, had been completely surrounded in Berdorf and rescue plans were being formulated that entailed bringing up the 12th Infantry's Company B riding on tanks. The Germans were initially driven out of part of the town but only after a vicious firefight that occurred around the southern perimeter and continued until dark, and despite this contact with Company F had not been effectively restored. When a full-strength German battalion had pounced on Berdorf, the location of the company headquarters, only one rifle squad, two antitank squads and a four-man mortar squad defended the town. These defenders had taken refuge in the town's prestigious Parc Hotel, where they placed a rifle in every other window, and transformed the place into a WWII version of the Alamo.

Wayne Brown, Marshalltown, Company F, 2nd Battalion, 12th Infantry Regiment

I was in a convalescent hospital when the Battle of the Bulge breakthrough came. We were helping the nurses decorate the tent hospital for Christmas, which we assumed would include us. On December 24, a group of doctors came through the tent asking every man that could stand to do so. A doctor looked at my chart, and I told him that I still had stitches, which he quickly removed and said, "Back to active duty."

That afternoon, we were loaded on "forty and eight" railroad cars and sent back to our units in Luxembourg and Belgium. What a way to spend Christmas. I missed most of the battle Company F had at the Parc Hotel in Berdorf but knew a lot of the fellows who were there, such as Master Sergeant Ed Potts from Hudson Falls, New York, and others. From that day on, the weather was horrible. I thought Iowa winters were bad but when someone is trying to kill you, it is worse. I went days without taking off my combat boots, which were wet. No wonder so many men had trench foot. Walking through a foot or two of wet snow with a heavy army overcoat on was very tiring and also made us good targets against the white snow. We didn't receive any white camouflage suits until well into February, after most of the snow was gone. Anyone who lived through the Battle of the Bulge should give thanks every day.

A tremendous example of the fighting spirit and tenacity of the Ivy men was demonstrated on December 16, when Lieutenant McConnell was driving toward Consdorf to relay information about the German offensive and the dismal state of all communications. During his return journey he inadvertently came across some German soldiers who were just a few hundred yards from the Parc Hotel in Berdorf. The lieutenant had a working knowledge of Yiddish, which has a lot of German words, so he knew enough to complain vociferously when the Germans relieved him of his watch and a $5,600 payroll intended for his men. A German sergeant was ordered to accompany Lieutenant McConnell to the Parc Hotel that was at that time home to 31 Ivy men. The Americans were surrounded, seriously outnumbered and outgunned. The lieutenant had been instructed to request that the American commander tell his men to lay down their arms and surrender.

Twelve German soldiers began walking toward the hotel with the lieutenant and stopped in a small meadow in sight of the hotel entrance. A GI stuck his head out of an upper-floor hotel window and shouted to the lieutenant "Are those your prisoners?" "Hell no!" retorted the lieutenant, "I'm their prisoner." Meanwhile as this small interchange was occurring, within the confines of the hotel Lt. John Leake was making a few calculations. He surreptitiously managed to get Lieutenant McConnell's attention and make a few practical suggestions.

The Germans were completely oblivious to this exchange but Lieutenant McConnell knew precisely what he had to do. He shouted up to Lieutenant Leake "Don't shoot!" and then sotto voce he added "Don't miss." Leake told every GI in the hotel to "Pick your targets and go slow, it's just like shooting ducks in a gallery." A wide smile spread across Lieutenant McConnell's face as he looked at the German sergeant stood beside him. Suddenly an enfilade of shots rang out from the hotel, one of the first striking the German sergeant between the eyes causing him to slump lifeless to the floor. All of McConnell's captors fell dead or wounded except one.

Other nearby Germans responded as McConnell used the lone survivor as a human shield as he bundled him into the hotel. Over the next few days the besieged garrison at the Parc Hotel were augmented by an additional 21 GIs from another outpost. Over the next five days they resisted and repelled repeated German attacks. Even when enemy artillery demolished the hotel's roof and part of the third floor, these indomitable Ivy men simply relocated to the ground floor and kept on firing. They would hold this position against a numerically superior German force right up until the moment when they received the order to abandon the hotel. Lieutenant Leake miraculously managed to get every man to the tanks and half-tracks that were stationed in and around Berdorf roughly 800 yards from the hotel. All 54 men survived.

On December 16 simultaneous operations were initiated to relieve other besieged Ivy men at 12th Infantry outposts—Company E was surrounded in Echternach and Company G that was reported isolated in Lauterborn. Company A reached Lauterborn after a light skirmish.

There were only two platoons at Dickweiler and three at Osweiler. As German units infiltrated these locations, the 70th Tank Battalion brought up another batch of GIs from Company K mounted on their vehicles just in time to thwart the German attacks but despite putting up a brave fight, they were seriously outnumbered and surrounded by the close of the day. Because of the frenetic activity in the 12th Infantry's sector throughout the following day all units were placed on full alert and plans were initiated to reinforce the 12th Infantry Regiment.

Conrad "Frenchy" Adams, Company E, 2nd Battalion, 8th Infantry Regiment

Company E was very short of men as the Battle of the Bulge went on. Many men had been killed or wounded. As a machine-gun assistant, I was told to go on a 24-hour stakeout. At that time, the snow was knee deep—and that was a lot of snow for a country boy from Louisiana, who had only seen snow once in his life—and I had to walk three quarters of a mile down a ravine to get to my post. As night fell, I started to expand the foxhole that someone before me hadn't finished. I hit rocks, and the German soldiers started firing 88s at the place where the sound was coming from. I had to stop digging and set up my shelter half. It started to snow harder during the night, and my shelter half fell on me. I couldn't move until the next night because the Germans would have seen me if I had moved.

With the snow on me all night, I became hoarse and could not talk for a month. Although I couldn't talk, I was never taken to the rear for a checkup. As I said, we were short of men, short of new replacements, and that was a hell of a feeling ... but we kept on going. Also, I remember one time the GIs were drinking cognac or schnapps, and I didn't drink. We hadn't taken off our shoes for a couple of months, so I put some of the liquor in my helmet, after removing the liner, took off my shoes and soaked my feet in the helmet, boy did that feel good.

By 16 December the 8th Infantry hadn't made any significant contact with the Germans and remained occupied with patrolling around its position to the north of the 12th Infantry sector but they had already been alerted to expect the enemy at any time. Meanwhile no enemy activity had been reported in the 22nd Infantry's sector but their 2nd Battalion had received orders to be prepared to move to support the 12th Infantry at a moment's notice.

The following day the full weight of the German attacks was being felt all along that painfully thin line and the gravity of the situation began to dawn on the US commanders. On the southern shoulder the 4th Infantry Divisions began committing more troops to the battle. The 12th Infantry had risen early that day to contact all isolated elements and attempt to restore previous outposts. By daybreak the 22nd Infantry's regimental reserve was ordered to go to the 12th Infantry command post at Junglinster where they were joined by two tank platoons but by now the 12th Infantry was now receiving a hard pounding from the whole 212th Volksgrenadier Division, which had spent three years on the Eastern Front. After being withdrawn from the Lithuanian sector in September they had been sent to Poland for urgent refitting and replacements, many of these hailed from Bavaria and a significant number were barely 17 years old.

Despite the ferocity and accuracy of these attacks the 12th managed to repel most of them and hold their ground for the duration. Only fifteen artillery pieces belonging to the 42nd FA Battalion were in range to offer assistance to the 12th Infantry who were curbing this German advance alone between the town of Berdorf and the Schwaise-Ernz River valley, a sizeable ravine that provided a natural chasm between the 4th Division and the 9th Armored Division. Six days before the Germans went on the offensive the 9th Armored Division commanded by General Leonard had been sent to hold a 3-mile sector on the VIII Corps front roughly between the 28th Infantry Division and the 4th Infantry Division boundaries. Most of 9th Armored Division were untried in battle and the majority of the division had been assigned as VIII Corps' reserve to the west of the line.

At around 0930 hours a large concentration of German troops and armor were observed advancing along the base of this ravine. Shortly after they began attacking 9th Armored Division positions. General Barton voiced his concern that if the Germans were able to force their way through that ravine it would seriously compromise the safety of the 4th Division's northwestern flank. Meanwhile, east of the Sauer and Moselle, the Germans maintained a defensive stance against combat teams assembled from the 8th and 22nd Infantry Regiments and it was becoming apparent that despite the horrendous losses incurred during the fighting in the Hürtgen Forest the 4th Division was still a force to be reckoned with.

Jack Capell, HQ, 8th Infantry Regiment

I was a member of the 4th Infantry Division, 8th Infantry Regiment, Headquarters Company from D-Day until the end of the war, including the Battle of the Bulge. I was a combat infantryman. I am arranging these recollections in a series, rather than giving continuous narration, because I think it is a matter of record as to what the 4th Infantry Division did during the Battle of the Bulge, and I see no reason I should go over that or include many numerous details. I will give you some of the memories that I have of that period.

The first recollection begins just prior to the outbreak of the battle. When we arrived in Luxembourg on December 12, 1944 we had been fighting in the Hürtgen Forest and had been severely battered, were battle weary, exhausted, had suffered terrible casualties, and were seriously depleted in manpower and much in need of replacements. We were removed from the Hürtgen Forest and sent to the Luxembourg front in the Ardennes Forest.

The 28th Infantry Division had a similar experience. They also were among those divisions that were spread out alongside of us. We were, at the time, near the town of Senningen, Luxembourg, just to the west of the Moselle River near the Luxembourg/German border. Supposedly, we were facing a rather weak German unit and it was considered to be a quiet front. Some of the veterans of the Hürtgen Forest, especially those who had been in for the full time, were allowed 48 hours at a hospital rest camp in Arlon, Belgium. I was one of the first to be able to go and was to leave on December 15. There were about ten of us loaded on a two-and-a-half ton truck early in the morning to head back to Arlon.

The camp was in a large stone building, and there were cots complete with sheets, blankets and mattresses; hot water showers; and a supply of clean-laundered clothing. Good hot food was served in a mess hall, and it was pure luxury.

We spent December 15 with great pleasure and looked forward to a full night's sleep. We expected to have another enjoyable day on the 16th. However, early in the morning on the 16th we were ordered to get ready to go back. We were shocked and thought there must be a mistake. We loudly proclaimed that we had one more day to stay in Arlon. The officer who gave the order insisted there was no mistake and we were to go back. We protested loudly, and a major then came on the scene and ordered us to get ready to go out and to be ready to leave in a very short while. He said there was a problem at the front, and if we didn't go and follow orders we would be charged with refusing duty, so we reluctantly complied but complained bitterly.

We were loaded onto a two-and-a-half ton truck and headed back. The weather had turned cold that day, and there was a biting wind that blew through the back of the truck. We were not only extremely angry, but miserable from the cold. After a time we stopped to refuel. While waiting, we went inside the fuel dump shack to get warm for a few minutes and heard an English-language broadcast on a radio the men had there. Suddenly, we forgot how cold we were when we heard about a German counterattack and specific mention of the fact that the 4th Infantry Division had been annihilated in the fighting. We were stunned, since we were all from the Headquarters Company of the 8th Infantry Regiment, 4th Infantry Division. We frantically interrogated the driver, who was from division headquarters, and asked him where he was taking us. He said he knew nothing about it except that he was to take us to division headquarters for instructions. From then on, there was no further concern about the cold, but there was great anxiety.

At division headquarters, the driver was instructed to take us to the town of Senningen. Then we left. My foxhole, or shelter trench, had been half a mile forward from Senningen. When we returned, we came right back to the town and found that members of our company were in the cellar of a stone building in the center of Senningen. Immediately upon arriving, we were issued TNT and dynamite caps, or blasting caps, to set off the TNT in order to blast foxholes in frozen ground. We were also issued more grenades that we strapped around our belts and were ordered to check our M-1 rifles. If there were any malfunctions, there were a few replacement rifles for which we could exchange them. Immediately we were marched to a position near Senningen on the front and ordered to hold the position. By this time we had learned about the German counterattack and about how our division had survived. We found there were few, if any, casualties in our company, but those who were around the town of Echternach, Luxembourg, were in serious trouble and probably were all killed or captured. That seemed to be the area where the 4th Infantry Division had suffered the worst losses. Otherwise, except for some minor withdrawals, the line was being held.

Artillery, mortar, and small-arms fire were intense. We had begun hearing heavy artillery fire even before we reached Division Headquarters when we were coming back. The Germans had broken through just to the north of us, but had failed to penetrate very far into the 4th Infantry Division sector and the 4th Infantry Division was now forming the southern border of the new front. Our division had lost Echternach and the area around it, but we fought very hard to keep from yielding any more ground and we apparently *did prevent the Germans from breaking through to Luxembourg City. In just a 24-hour period, we had gone from paradise back into hell again. This concludes my recollection of how I first learned about the Battle of the Bulge.*

My second recollection concerns Christmas Day, 1944.

The weather had cleared somewhat, but it was still very cold with snow having come on or about December 20. I recollect the Christmas Day situation because of its irony. We were promised we would have hot Christmas dinners on Christmas Day even though we were still holding the line at the front. I didn't know how this would be possible. On that day our kitchen truck came up to regimental headquarters about a quarter of a mile back from where I had chiseled a shelter trench out of the snow and ice. One by one we were allowed to go back to the kitchen truck and get our Christmas dinners. I had the mess kit lid (I had discarded the rest of it) and my canteen cup. I walked back through the ice and snow and was given servings of turkey, reconstituted dehydrated potatoes, some cranberry sauce and a cup of coffee. I was ordered to return to my hole and not to stay by the same truck and eat it there. So with my rifle over my shoulder, I precariously made my way back through the snow and ice, trying to keep from spilling my coffee and dinner until I finally arrived at my hole. When I sat down to eat it, I found the cranberry sauce had frozen to the mess kit and everything was ice cold, including the coffee. I chiseled out the cranberry sauce and had my Christmas dinner. It was the most unusual Christmas dinner I had ever had.

Another recollection occurred sometime during that period, but I am not quite sure what date. We had been warned about English-speaking Germans in American uniforms infiltrating our units. A rumor was circulating that our command post had been visited by mysterious strangers who left unidentified. My good friend, Horace Sisk, from Illinois, was the regimental clerk. I knew he could tell me what had happened, if anything. He told me that a jeep driven by one enlisted man and two men wearing uniforms of high-ranking American officers as passengers arrived at regimental headquarters. The party passed the guard without being questioned after stating they were from corps headquarters. While the driver stayed in the jeep, the two officers walked into the regimental headquarters building and immediately asked for Colonel McKee, who was the 8th Infantry Regiment Commander. They were told he was not there but was expected back soon. They expressed anger and said that he had told them he would be there to meet with them, and they demanded to see the next in command. They were quite irate. They were directed to Lieutenant Colonel Strickland, with whom they spoke briefly. They then preceded to lower-ranking officers, particularly a captain who apologized for the fact that McKee was not there. The officers continued to express their anger, and to appease them, he answered their questions about 8th Infantry positions and strategy, as well as detailed information about the deployment of our troops. The officers quickly left.

Colonel Strickland finally became suspicious and went to the captain. The captain said that since the officers had already talked to Strickland, he assumed that Strickland had identified them. Strickland realized they had been duped. The officers were imposters. When Colonel McKee returned to the Regimental Headquarters, he became extremely upset and terrified because he had made no appointment. The imposters must have known that Colonel McKee was not at regimental headquarters. Possibly they had monitored radio transmissions from Division HQ and knew he was there.

The fourth recollection I have took place on December 31. By that time, we had moved to the town of Wecker, Luxembourg. The civilians had been evacuated. The German guns were quieter than usual. It was still cold, but it was a bright day, and I had gone into the lower floor of an evacuated two-story frame house to relax and get a bit warmer. Soon I heard bombs whistling, then suddenly a jarring explosion followed by one after another. I was struck with a terrible shock and deafening noise very close to the house. The air was filled with dust and debris, and I was aware of things falling on me. I quickly exited the house and returned to my foxhole. The bombing continued a while longer. Medics were coming to treat our wounded. I soon learned that one of my very good friends, a man from Pennsylvania by the name of Sepik, had been killed. Some of the men said they had seen the aircraft through some high clouds and they identified them definitely as American heavy bombers—B-17s, as I recollect. We were completely puzzled because we were not on the front at the time. We were back in reserve and wondered why they would bomb so short. We concluded that somehow or another there had been some American heavy bombers captured by Germans, and these were actually being flown by Germans. We could not believe that American pilots could be that far off target. However, it had happened once before. Prior to the St. Lô breakthrough on July 25, it happened when the line marking to the target on the German side drifted over us. We lost many men in that bombing.

On the following day, January 1, 1945, the weather was even brighter. We were still in and around the town of Wecker, and we were astounded to see American P-38 fighter planes swoop down over our area and begin strafing us. This was the second day in a row we were hit by American planes. We immediately laid out cloth panels showing the American insignia. They had to be visible to the aircraft, but the strafing continued. Our regimental history indicates that there were 12 P-38s involved in this raid. After the raid, according to my friend in Regimental HQ, Horace Sisk, a command car came up to visit. It was carrying American officers with no identifying insignia. We learned that they were American air corps officers investigating what had gone wrong. Their identification was kept secret because of concern over what some of our men might have done had they learned who they were. That concludes the fourth memorable recollection.

The fifth recollection is probably the most memorable of all. It took place during the cold, snowy, winter weather during the latter part of December and January. Some of us still had no overcoats, and although we had the new longer and heavier field jackets, they were not sufficient protection against the cold. We had wool gloves and the new combat boots. They had leather tops, which replaced the old leggings, but they were not any more protection against severe cold. We wore rubber overshoes to help insulate, but had a deadly fear that we might rip an overshoe such that snow could work its way in.

Once the snow melted from the body heat, and then one stopped to rest, the foot would quickly freeze. Trench foot was a serious problem. It may have caused more casualties than actual battle wounds during that particular period. We supplemented our clothing by cutting up burlap sacks found in farmhouses. We wrapped those around our heads, necks, and legs. The Germans did the same thing, and some of the prisoners we took were so wrapped up they looked like mummies.

At night many of the men, in groups of two or three, would make a shelter from trunks of trees. I carried a crosscut saw in one of our company vehicles for this purpose. We would huddle together and use body heat to help keep us warm. Sometimes we half-filled a C-Ration can with gasoline and lit it. It would burn slowly, giving off enough heat to help considerably. This, of course, could only be done if the low, steady flame could be obscured somehow by having it in a shelter, or at least in a pup tent with snow heaped around so that the enemy could not see the light.

Sometimes I would be sent on a mission and return after dark. Being unable to take adequate protection against the cold, I would find myself unprotected from the cold for the night. I would sometimes seek a manure pile. There were huge manure piles in front of the peasant houses. They were flattened on top, and by throwing some boards on top of the manure, one could crawl on top and keep warm as the manure fermented. It was so warm that the snow would melt off, and steam rose. There was strong methane gas being given off, and the pungent odor meant that one could survive only a short time without getting away for some fresh air. Then I would have to spend the rest of the night in the cold.

One cold and dark night, I was alone without protection. Searching for a building to get into, I found in the darkness a shed or a barn of some sort with an open door, and I sensed the feeling of warmth. I reached down to find a floor of concrete, which was warmer than would be expected. I felt around on the floor until it felt even warmer. At that spot, I lay down and immediately went to sleep. Shortly afterward, I was awakened by something nudging me in the back. I reached over and felt a furry leg and a hoof. I realized I was sleeping by a cow that was resting on its side. I went back to sleep. When daylight came, I found I had spent the night sleeping between the cow's legs and considered that to be an excellent way to beat the cold.

The worst times in the cold were when we did sentry duty. There was little one could do to protect from the biting wind. More than once, after a seemingly endless session on sentry duty, I returned to my hole for shelter so cold and thoroughly fatigued that I was afraid to fall asleep for fear of freezing. I was often assigned to take the weapons carrier to get back to division headquarters and pick up supplies and ammunition as well as a number of other miscellaneous missions. I often accidentally got into enemy territory. Sergeant Mike Camarote, who was wounded and being returned to the regiment, noticed what I was doing and volunteered to accompany me for some extra protection.

One time when Mike and I were together we were carrying a supply of TNT and dynamite caps for blowing foxholes. The explosives compartment was directly behind the driver's seat in the weapons carrier. As Mike and I were driving back on a narrow icy road, on top of a dike, we encountered a two-and-a-half ton GMC truck approaching from the other direction. It was impossible for both vehicles to come to a stop, and there was not room *for both of us on top of the dike. We collided, and the weapons carrier went into a spin as the heavier GMC truck went on without stopping to see what happened.*

We spun and slid off the edge of the dike, then dropped 8 to 10 feet. The vehicle was lying on the driver's side where the TNT was stored. When we hit, Mike bounced on top of me. I was not injured, and I asked Mike if he was OK. He was just shaken up a little bit. Then I said, "What do you think, Mike? Are we in another world now, or, if by some miracle that TNT and dynamite did not explode when we hit?" Mike gasped. "My God, I had forgotten about that!" Then he laughed and said, "Well, must be the same old world. I'm just as cold as ever."

Another major recollection also has to do with events that occurred during the extremely cold weather. We were on a ridge with a valley going down to a creek bed. An American tank column was attempting to move along the steep slope on the other side of the draw. An infantry column was also moving up about the same time. The lead tank began to attempt to traverse the side of the hill. The commander was standing with his upper body extending out of the hatch. The tank slid sideways and rolled over. The tank commander was crushed. The other tanks following stopped before attempting to traverse the slope. I looked back to see a most entertaining sight. The next tank was traversing the slope with ropes extended out from the front and rear of the tank and at least 50 infantrymen holding on to ropes to keep the tank from sliding sideways.

It was like a tug of war with the tank in the middle. Suddenly, one infantryman lost his footing and slid downhill toppling a dozen or so men. The same thing happened on the other rope, and this happened time and time again—the tank sliding sideways a few feet each time, but still making some progress forward. Eventually, all the tanks went across the slope. That would have been a great scene to capture on film as an example of sheer ingenuity and perseverance. There was an element of comedy as one man would lose his footing and topple a dozen or so, or more like dominoes. All of them would scramble to regain their feet and get going once more. Again, the foot soldier proved his worth.

General Barton ordered all divisional rest camps from sites as far north as Arlon to be moved so that they were in proximity to the regimental CPs. He then instructed his commanders to maintain only small forces along the line that ran parallel to the river outposts on the Sauer and Moselle while keeping the main body of these regiments in nearby villages. Just before midnight on December 16, General Barton had received a welcome call from the 10th Armored Division that was stationed at the Third Army area in Thionville around 75 miles south. He was informed that "Combat Command A" would head out to join the 4th at daybreak the following day. While their sister unit CCB headed for Bastogne, CCA of the 10th Armored covered those 75 miles and got up to Echternach in one single day. The Ivy men wouldn't have to fight it out alone anymore.

General Barton wasn't aware of the logistic problems that General Brandenberger's 7th Army were experiencing as they attempted to advance into this densely forested country. Despite the difficulties experienced attempting to move heavy artillery pieces Brandenberger managed to put a serious dent in the 12th Infantry's line and threaten the northern flank. The fighting that occurred on December 17 in the 4th Division sector was mainly in the 12th Infantry garrisoned areas around their left flank at Berdorf, Consdorf, and Mullerthal, then in the center along the Echternach–Lauterborn–Scheidgen road, and on the right in the Osweiler–Dickweiler sector. The Germans forced inroads at all these places but these penetrations were mild stabs, not deep cuts and on most occasions they were driven back.

By December 18, General Barton felt confident enough to launch a counterattack. On hearing the news some 4th Infantry Division soldiers were so enthusiastic at the prospect that as soon as units from CCA arrived in the 12th infantry area they immediately went up to the line. The plan was that supporting armor from CCA would advance in three task forces. The first one, Task Force Chamberlain (Lt. Col. Thomas C. Chamberlain), would advance to the Schwarz Erntz gorge, then in the center Task Force Standish (Lt. Col. Miles L. Standish), was dispatched to assist the 2nd Battalion, 12th Infantry clear the enemy from Berdorf, so they headed out up the Consdorf–Berdorf road. Then Task Force Riley (Lt. Col. J. R. Riley) would go through Scheidgen to reach Echternach.

An estimated company of enemy moving on Dickweiler from Girst posed the only serious threat to this region but this attack was successfully repulsed and the Germans were compelled to resort to harassing the defenders with long-range artillery. Then the 12th Infantry's 3rd Battalion organized a successful supply mission to Echternach that tipped the balance in favor of the defenders even further.

In Echternach, the central part of 12th Infantry's sector, Company E were holding out while Companies A and G were still dug in near Lauterborn.

At 0800 hours, Task Force Riley began to offer assistance to the Ivy men by initiating an attack. First they moved towards Michelshof and then when they reached Scheidgen they encountered some concerted German resistance but managed to deal with the situation. To prevent being held there up they left a token force in place and continued on to Echternach where they established a line approximately 300 yards southwest of the town, which allowed them to bring up supplies to the men in Echternach. When they arrived they discovered that morale in Company E was unexpectedly good. Task Force Riley offered to evacuate them from the town but the company captain Paul H. Dupuis declined on the basis of his previous order from General Barton concerning retrograde movements.

At the same time Task Force Standish advanced through Consdorf to support infantry and tanks that had been assembled in Colbet, a mile and a half south of Müllerthal the previous day. This collection of infantry and tanks was designated as Task Force Luckett. It comprised the 803rd Tank Destroyer Battalion and the 2nd Battalion, 8th Infantry. Task Force Luckett consolidated its defense and maintained its positions on the high ground to the south of Mullerthal against a sizeable German force. Around mid-afternoon the task force attacked simultaneously with Task Force Chamberlain and reached Mullerthal. They stopped in front of the steep ravine there on the premise that it could prove to be a veritable tank trap.

Meanwhile elements of the 2nd Battalion 8th Infantry and the 4th Engineer Combat Battalion had reached their objectives on the high ground overlooking Mullerthal, which provided them with a panoramic view of the whole area.

The following day, under a veil of dense mist, all units in the 4th Infantry Division sector resumed the attack. Task Force Luckett launched a coordinated attack with Task Force Chamberlain at 1000 hours. The 8th Infantry's Company E was confronted with the heaviest resistance. Then the CO of Task Force Luckett received orders that his mission was solely intended to prevent the Germans from using the road network near Mullerthal. After a sustained and damaging German artillery barrage

Company E was pulled back from the line and Task Force Chamberlain was ordered to withdraw to Consdorf.

Berdorf became a scene of intense activity as a team from Task Force Standish and a platoon of armored engineers were tasked with mopping up German infantry holed up in houses on the north side of the village. It was precarious and laborious work that involved a lot of house-to-house, hand-to-hand fighting. The modus operandi was that first a 10lb pole charge would be exploded against a wall or house. This would be the signal for a tank to advance and discharge shells into the gap. When this had occurred the infantry would get stuck in and deliver the coup de grace to stunned Germans with small arms and hand grenades.

In the Berdorf–Echternach area Task Forces Standish and Riley continued their counterattacks but it was becoming increasingly clear to all units in the line that although fighting had been intense along the left flank, the Germans were losing momentum. Pockets of German resistance were encountered all along the rest of line but most of these were effectively neutralized by the close of the day. Luxembourg city had been spared but at that time US commanders had no idea that this wasn't the objective of the attacking Germans, who had only planned to advance as far as Mersch, 8 miles north of the city.

December 20 saw further intense combat in the 4th Infantry Division sector as the 4th Infantry Division and the 10th Armored began to disengage their advance elements and regroup along a stronger main line of resistance where they could reinforce defensive positions. Although the 4th Infantry Division were regarded as being part of the First Army, owing to the proximity of Patton's Third Army they were transferred to his command on December 20.

The most vulnerable section of the 4th Infantry Division line was in the east opposite the 212th Volksgrenadier Division, which made an attempt to reach its original objective and occupy good defensive terrain in the Consdorf–Scheidgen–Michelshof area. During the afternoon of December 21 the Germans headed out along the main Echternach–Luxembourg road while a simultaneous German attack was launched with the purpose of taking Osweiler. Two companies of the 22nd

Infantry's 2nd Battalion effectively halted this enemy advance. In the late afternoon, the 2nd Battalion of the 22nd Infantry, supported by two tanks of the 70th Tank Battalion, attacked west of Osweiler toward the high ground against an enemy force estimated to be about 400 strong. Contact was made after an advance of between roughly 500 –700 yards, and the Germans were dislodged from their positions but as nighttime descended neither side were able to advance so the engagement was halted because a stalemate had been reached.

A fierce fight developed on the left flank of the 12th Infantry sector when two German companies attempted to take Consdorf. A classic ambush ensued as American tanks and infantry stayed low and held their fire until the Germans had left the cover of the woods and were fully deployed on the exposed incline in front of the town. Then the order was given to open fire. Suddenly a terrible fusillade from the US positions poured into the area. Around 60 Germans fell down dead or wounded and the rest began to retreat back to the woods.

George Knapp, Chaplain, HQ, 12th Infantry Regiment

On Christmas of '44, in a small town close to the river separating Luxembourg and Germany, I conducted a candlelight service in a barn alongside the road leading to the front line. Candelabra and candles came from a bombed-out church in town. Men of all faiths attended. We only had a trio to sing as the other member of an intended quartet had been captured with others from Company K. Men from another outfit were going on the road past the barn, on the way to relieve our men up in the foxholes at the front. I was glad for my men, but sorry for the replacements getting into those front-line foxholes on Christmas Eve. The next morning, my Christmas Day Services were conducted in a two-lane bowling alley in another town a bit farther away from the front. Other services were held that Christmas Day of 1944.

When we eventually left Luxembourg, the officer in charge of a chateau in Luxembourg City said to me, "Chaplain, everything is cleaned up, but here is a set of golf clubs. Can you take them?" He knew that I had a jeep and a trailer, so I did. I still have that set of golf clubs.

The stand made by the 4th Infantry Division during those first days of the Battle of the Bulge proved invaluable in preventing the 7th German Army from advancing to the west. Temperatures frequently dipped below -20c and many 4th Infantry Division men succumbed to frostbite and hypothermia. Nevertheless General Barton had said, "The best way to handle these Heinies is to fight 'em." The American counterattack was initiated on December 22. Each side jockeyed for position but it was becoming increasingly apparent to all that the German effort to charge through Luxembourg was beginning to dissipate. When the skies cleared above the province on December 24, XIX Tactical Air Command made good use of perfect flying weather and set to work unopposed. The 405th Fighter Group flew eight missions during the day, dropping fragmentation and napalm bombs at strategic points along the Sauer River, then strafing and bombing German positions east of there. When the Battle of the Bulge ended depended on largely where your unit was at a given time. The fighting in Luxembourg went on through January and well into February but now the Third Reich was visibly beginning to crumble both internally and externally. The definitive end was in sight.

General Barton had been a tenacious, inspirational commander of the 4th Infantry Division but after two and a half years and nine successful operations, he was transferred on December 27. For his magnificent efforts he was awarded the Silver Star and a Distinguished Service Medal. His replacement was Brig. Gen. Harold W. Blakeley, an experienced artillery commander who ultimately would lead them to victory in the Battle of the Bulge.

Later on Lt. Gen. George S. Patton, Jr., wrote to Maj. Gen. Raymond O. Barton, then division commander:

No American division in France has excelled the magnificent record of the 4th Inf. Div., which has been almost continuously in action since it fought its way ashore on the 6th day of last June; but in my opinion your most recent fight, when such a depleted and tired division you halted the left shoulder of the German thrust into the American lines and saved the City of Luxembourg, is your most outstanding accomplishment.

CHAPTER 14

SEEING IT THROUGH!

The first two weeks of January 1945 saw all three regiments of the 4th Infantry Division in Luxembourg continuing to defend along the west banks of the Sauer and Moselle Rivers while maintaining one battalion in reserve. Long before daybreak at 0300 hours, January 18, the 8th Infantry prepared to endure winter's most inclement weather conditions when they crossed the seasonally swollen Sauer River. Battered by a tempestuous north wind that whipped up freezing blizzard conditions the men ploughed ahead regardless. Trucks and trailers slid and skidded along precipitous ice-covered roads while the 4th Engineers struggled and cursed as they assembled a bridge over the Sauer. To the north of this position the 12th Infantry attacked Fuhren and occupied high ground near the town of Vianden. By January 21, the Division had captured and secured all its objectives. On January 27 the Ivy men became part of General Troy Middleton's VIII Corps.

A rotation plan had been introduced and implemented earlier in the month to insure that the outposts were manned while carrying on an extensive training program within all units not actively engaged. As the days passed defensive was transposed into offensive along with the momentum to move east. During the last two weeks of January, the 4th Infantry Division moved along the Luxembourg border and crossed into the German-speaking part of Belgium. The 22nd Infantry were placed in reserve while the other two continued to harass and pursue the Germans back to their domestic frontier. By the beginning of February the Ivy men were retracing their steps, getting back on German soil and taking the fight to the enemy. They found themselves hitting the Siegfried Line again in the area where two regiments of the 106th Infantry Division had been routed at the start of the Battle of the Bulge. The Ivy Division resumed the attack and continued the pursuit through the Siegfried Line, following almost the same route that it had traversed in September 1944. The Ivy men had earned some furlough and from the beginning of February every third day throughout the month, a total of 16 officers and 55 enlisted men were given permission to go to Paris on 72-hour passes. Major General Troy Middleton, VIII Corps commander, presented the DSC to Colonel C. T. Lanham, commanding officer of 22nd Infantry. Lanham had served the 22nd Infantry and the 4th Infantry Division with tremendous leadership skills that endeared him to his men and gained him the respect of many superior officers.

The Germans continued to provide sporadic and occasionally concerted resistance to these encroachments into their territory but it was becoming obvious to all but the blind that this was becoming a losing battle for the Third Reich.

On February 9, the 8th Infantry orchestrated another river crossing at the Prüm River and two days later, after a heavy fight, the 22nd took the adjacent city of Prüm. At this time the 4th Infantry were facing the German 5th Parachute Division augmented by elements of the 34th Volksgrenadier Division who were disposed along the high ground to the east of the Prüm River. According to 4th Infantry Division reports the enemy offered stiff resistance and defended with heavy small arms, automatic weapons, rocket artillery, and mortar fire. The enemy was well dug in and covering all approaches with an unusually large number of machine guns, and minefields. Tanks were also operating in the area. It was noted that German morale was marginally better than the Wehrmacht average had been over the past few weeks.

By mid-February the 12th Infantry and elements of the 22nd Infantry found themselves once again in proximity to the German city of Prüm. The enemy continued to vigorously defend their positions and sent out occasional patrols to determine the strength and direction of the advance. Meanwhile as the remainder of VIII Corps continued assaulting the Siegfried Line the 4th Infantry Division continued to organize and defend within its sector. Forward elements received intermittent artillery fire throughout the period.

Marvin A. Simpson, Company D, 4th Medical Battalion

In March 1945, stationed near Prüm, Germany, I was given a three-day pass back to Paris. This happened the day after I had won $300 in an all-night poker game. Wow, was I ever excited and happy. I boarded a train with other comrades and arrived in Paris. Suddenly, I was in a different world. I took in all the sights, peed in an outdoor latrine on the sidewalks of Paris, rode in a two-seat taxi pulled by a bicycle and took in the shows and nightclubs. I had come a long way from the farm in Iowa to the streets of Paris. It was a tremendous 72-hour pass.

At the beginning of March, VII Corps was pushing eastward through a hard-won gap in the Siegfried Line to the Kyll River a tributary of the Moselle. In the center of this drive the 4th Infantry Division, supported by the 11th Armored, led the corps as they pushed on to cross the Kyll River in the vicinity of Gerolstein. Both divisions encountered some staunch resistance as the Ivy men gathered its forces to secure a bridgehead for the armor. The 22nd Infantry relieved forward elements of the 11th Armored Division in the half-mile-deep bridgehead across the Kyll River, and sent patrols into Hillesheim.

Throughout the rest of the Division sector, the Germans continued their delaying actions while withdrawing most of their troops and equipment across to the east bank of the Kyll River. Then a task force under Brigadier General Rodwell made a dramatic 24-hour dash that covered more than 20 miles eastward and in the process captured the towns of Adenau and Reifferscheid. During the night and early morning hours of March 9, the town of Honerath, Adenau, Rodder and Reiffersheid were cleared of enemy opposition and little resistance was reported. The following day the 4th Infantry Division began assembling in preparation for departure from the Third Army sector to the VIII Corps area to the south in the vicinity of Luneville, France. Since the liberation of Paris the 4th had been in combat for almost 1999 days. During the entire operation to drive east, over 1,500 POWs were taken while 4th Infantry Division losses were two killed in action and four wounded.

It was a proud day when the 4th Infantry turned over Adenau over to Maj. Gen. Troy Middleton, VII Corps commander, who had been an officer in the old 4th Division that had occupied the town 27 years earlier after World War I. At the end of March the 4th Infantry Division were in the vicinity of Neustadt, Germany, conducting the maintenance and cleaning of vehicles and equipment. Then orders were received for the entire division to cross the mighty Rhine River. A heavy-duty pontoon bridge had been assembled at the town of Worms and within a few hours all the units were across and well on their way to the new division sector in the vicinity of Heppenheim.

Clive Clapsattle, 22nd Infantry Regiment

I joined the 4th on April 6, 1945, or about then. I know the last town we were in was Kircheim, and that is where this story begins. When we left Kircheim the platoon took over the hill. We "did in" two Germans, and as we continued on I told my BAR man to be my backup as there were more Germans close to the road where HQ was going to be. I went around a tree and ran into a German. He swung his rifle, so I had to shoot him. That is when I was shot in the neck (a half-inch from my artery) and part of my left ear. My BAR man was not around—gone—and boy, did I swear.

I fixed myself up with sulfa and tried to decide what to do. The platoon had already gone over the hill, and I could not connect with them, as there was a German behind me somewhere. Well, I loaded up and started firing to about where I thought he was. He finally said, "Camerade!" and surrendered. I took him prisoner. Going down the road into town, I picked up five more Germans. I had to take them about a half mile and tried not to pass out, which I did about 100 feet from a forward aid station. Medics fixed me up, and I wanted to go back and have a talk with my BAR man, if not shoot him.

They sent me to a MASH unit where they operated on me and then sent me to a hospital in France. I came back to the unit in Ausbach. I signed in with Staff Sergeant Ivan Johnson and then started looking for my BAR man. I found him and was mad, but I passed it over.

Before this, I was connected with SHAEF and in charge of perimeters when Ike, Churchill, Marshall, and others were meeting in little towns outside London. I was in intelligence and security. I was hooked up with G2 and had the job of seeking out Germans dressed as GIs. I followed all outfits, including the 4th Infantry Division, to Paris where I set up a HQ. I worked with both the 3rd and 7th Armies all along the German border.

Marvin A. Simpson, Company D, 4th Medical Battalion

On VE Day our camp was near Starnburg, Germany. What a day to remember. We thought the war was over. A month later, however, we were on our way across the Atlantic for a 30-day leave before going to the Pacific for the invasion of Japan. After arriving back in the States and traveling by train to Cedar Rapids, Iowa, I waited a long time for my wife to appear. It was there I realized I was getting a "Dear John" letter in a very subtle way. I was right—the marriage that began at the beginning of the war for me was over at the end. VJ Day came during my furlough, and I was discharged soon after with the rank of Staff Sergeant.

I went to Chicago and lived with my wartime buddy, Jim Saxton. I married the sweetest, most wonderful girl, Mary Fellmer. During our 52 years of marriage, I have experienced many breathtaking moments. Our first son, James, was born in 1949, then our second son, John, in 1953. My wife and I attended the 50th Anniversary of D-Day, lived with a French family in Normandy who called us "liberators," walked through the rows of white crosses at the Normandy American Cemetery, and, with tears in our eyes, we prayed.

After a short rest, the 4th moved across the Rhine 29 March at Worms, attacked and secured Wurzburg and by 3 April had established a bridge-head across the Main at Ochsenfurt. Speeding southeast across Bavaria, the Division had reached Miesbach on the Isar, 2 May 1945, when it was relieved and placed on occupation duty.

The 4th Infantry Division advanced northeast in the direction of Wurzburg with the 8th and 22nd Infantry Regiments abreast and the 12th Infantry in division reserve. Resistance was encountered through-out but it was now more likely to be characterized by scattered rifle shots and an occasional hand grenade thrown by soldiers in civilian clothes or by civilians venting their anger against the occupying Allied forces. Some mention was made of enemy jet-propelled aircraft at this time but the psychological effect of these aircraft was considerably more substantial than any material damage they inflicted.

As with many Allied units pushing deep into the Reich, the 4th were witnessing the last dying gasps of a nation on the brink of total annihilation. There were still occasional skirmishes and during the night of April 3/4, the 8th Infantry was the focus of an organized raid on the regimental command post area. The raiding force was estimated to have numbered around 25 enemy soldiers armed with bazookas and incendiary grenades. Apart from causing temporary havoc at the CP they succeeded in destroying approximately a dozen vehicles and killing a GI.

As the month of April unfurled the Nazi Reich began to reveal some of its most terrifying and heart-rending secrets. During the march into southern Germany in late April, the 4th inadvertently discovered the site of a Dachau sub-camp near Haunstetten that had been built to service a Messerschmitt aircraft plant. Haunstetten was one of the biggest sub-camps in Nazi Germany. It was only one of many concentration and POW camps that were being liberated by the Allies. When the war ended on May 8, 1945, the 4th Infantry Division had the distinction of having participated in every single Allied campaign in the ETO from the Normandy beaches to Germany. On July 11, 1945, they sailed back over the Atlantic and returned to New York harbor. From there they went to Camp Butner, North Carolina to prepare for the invasion of Japan. Then at 0815 hours on the morning of August 6, 1945, an atomic bomb exploded over Hiroshima. In 1992 the US Army's Center of Military History and the United States Holocaust Memorial Museum officially recognized the 4th Infantry Division as a "liberating unit." The Ivy men had done their duty.

Command and Staff, 4th Infantry Division World War II

Commanding General

January 28, 1944	Major General Raymond O. Barton
September 18, 1944	Brigadier General Harold W. Blakeley
September 21, 1944	Major General Harold R. Bull
September 30, 1944	Brigadier General James A. Van Fleet
October 5, 1944	Major General Raymond O. Barton
December 27, 1944	Brigadier General Harold W. Blakeley
March 18, 1945	Major General Harold W. Blakeley

Assistant Division Commander

January 28, 1944	Brigadier General Henry A. Barber
July 9, 1944	Colonel George A. Taylor
August 1, 1944	Brigadier General George A. Taylor
September 19, 1944	Brigadier General James A. Van Fleet (Acting)
October 10, 1944	Colonel James S. Rodwell
December 7, 1944	Brigadier General James S. Rodwell

Artillery Commander

January 28, 1944	Brigadier General Harold W. Blakeley
December 28, 1944	Colonel Richard T. Guthrie
July 2, 1944	Major Guy O. Deyoung, Jr.
October 20, 1944	Lieutenant Colonel Guy O. Deyoung, Jr.

Assistant Chief of Staff G-5

April 10, 1944	Major Philip A. Hart, Jr.
May 31, 1944	Lieutenant Colonel Dee W. Stone

Commanding Officer, 8th Infantry

January 28, 1944	Colonel James A. Van Fleet
July 2, 1944	Colonel James S. Rodwell
September 22, 1944	Colonel Richard G. McKee

Commanding Officer, 12th Infantry

January 28, 1944	Colonel Russell P. Reeder, Jr.
June 11, 1944	Colonel James S. Luckett
November 21, 1944	Colonel Robert H. Chance

Commanding Officer, 22nd Infantry

January 28, 1944	Colonel Hervey A. Tribolet
June 26, 1944	Colonel Robert T. Foster
July 19, 1944	Colonel Charles T. Lanham
March 3, 1945	Lieutenant Colonel John F. Ruggles
April 22, 1945	Colonel John F. Ruggles

DATE	CORPS	ARMY	ARMY GROUP	
	Assigned	Attached	Assigned	Attached
January 10, 1944		First	ETOUSA	
January 14, 1944	V	First		
February 2, 1944	VII	First		
July 16, 1944	VIII	First		
July 19, 1944	VII	First		
August 1, 1944	VII	First	12th	
August 22, 1944	V	First	12th	
November 8, 1944	VII	First	12th	
December 7, 1944	VIII	First	12th	
December 20, 1944	III	Third	12th	
December 21, 1944	XII	Third	12th	

January 27, 1945	VIII	Third	12th	
March 10, 1945	–	Seventh	12th	6th
March 20, 1945	VI	Seventh	–	6th
March 25, 1945	XXI	Seventh	–	6th
April 8, 1945	–	Seventh	–	6th
May 2, 1945	–	Third	12th	
May 6, 1945	III	Third	12th	

COMPOSITION

8th Infantry
12th Infantry
22nd Infantry
4th Reconnaissance Troop (Mechanized)
4th Engineer Combat Battalion
4th Medical Battalion
4th Division Artillery
29th Field Artillery Battalion (105mm Howitzer)
42nd Field Artillery Battalion (105mm Howitzer)
44th Field Artillery Battalion (105mm Howitzer)
20th Field Artillery Battalion (155mm Howitzer)

Special Troops

704th Ordnance Light Maintenance Company
4th Quartermaster Company
4th Signal Company
Military Police Platoon
Headquarters Company Band

PART 3

THE VIETNAM WAR

CHAPTER 15

MAKING END TERM OF SERVICE

This volume would not have been possible without the gracious and generous assistance of Bob Babcock so it's only fitting that his account of his experiences in the Vietnam War should open this section.

Bob Babcock, Bravo Company, 1st Battalion, 22nd Infantry Regiment, 4th Infantry Division

The most memorable year of my life was the one I spent serving with 4ID in Vietnam as a rifle platoon leader and executive officer with Bravo Company, 1st Battalion, 22nd Infantry Regiment. As part of the lead 2nd Brigade of 4ID who departed Fort Lewis, WA, on the troopship USNS Nelson Walker, on 21 July 1966, we landed in Qui Nhon on 6 August 1966. It was exactly 22 years and two months after the 4ID had landed on Utah Beach on D-Day in WWII to start that well-known fight across Europe.

We who landed on that hot day and flew to Pleiku in the central highlands to help establish what would become known as Camp Enari were the vanguard of a stream of Ivy Division Soldiers who would come and go from Vietnam over the next four and a half years. The 4ID's colors returned to Fort Carson, CO in early December 1970, ending the Vietnam chapter of our history. Over 2,500 Ivy Division Soldiers made the ultimate sacrifice in Vietnam, thousands were wounded, and seventeen earned the Medal of Honor. All of us came home with memories and friends that will last us a lifetime. A typical tour of duty was one year, a year unlike any that most of us had experienced before or since.

My memories come from leading my first combat patrol just days after arriving in country; six weeks patrolling along the coast south of Tuy Hoa, protecting the rice harvest; then almost two months on a never-ending search and destroy mission as part of Operation

Paul Revere IV *in the dense jungle where the Ho Chi Minh trail came into Vietnam from Cambodia.*

Christmas 1966 saw us returning to base camp for a brief rest and refit. In early January 1967, the same 4ID units returned to the same area of operations along the Cambodian border for another six months of slugging it out with the enemy. In the summer of 1967, we original "boat people" returned home, ending our tour of duty. Many of us left the Army and returned to civilian life. We were replaced by fresh soldiers, mostly individual replacements, to continue the fight. Names like Suoi Tre, Nine Days in May, Dak To, Tet '68, Kontum, Ben Het, Chu Moor Mountain, and other obscure places known only to those who fought there became part of 4ID history.

In 1985, before a long-delayed welcome home parade for Vietnam vets in Chicago, Gen. William Westmoreland, our overall US commander in Vietnam, came to a group of us 4ID vets assembled for the parade and told us, "You 4ID guys never got the credit you deserved in Vietnam. You had the largest AO (area of operations), extremely rugged terrain, a relentless enemy coming down the Ho Chi Minh Trail, and were far enough away from Saigon that the press corps seldom ventured out to report on your accomplishments." That, ten years after the fall of Saigon in 1975, was the first time anyone had ever acknowledged our accomplishments. It felt good. I'm proud to call myself a 4ID and Vietnam vet.

I remain, Steadfast and Loyal.

> Bob Babcock
> President/Historian
> National 4th Infantry Division Association
> B/1-22 Infantry 1966–1967 Vietnam

Never has a war been so contentious and raised more questions than answers than the Vietnam War. It won't be possible to do it full justice here, but a soldier is a soldier and a veteran is a veteran wherever they fought, and the ones who fought the Vietnam War deserve our respect and admiration for the service they did. There were other wars before this one that affected more people, had a greater impact on the world, and entailed more devastation, but no war can invoke images and sounds in people's minds like the Vietnam War. The mere mention of the name conjures up images of Huey Bell helicopters flying to the musical accompaniment of Wagner's *Valkyrie*, palm trees, hills and jungles. It marked and defined a whole generation. Its theme tunes were the recognizable anthems such as Eric Burden's rasping vocal hammering

We got to get out of this place to Jimi Hendrix rendering *All along the Watchtower*, this war had a sound, a million voices, to the uninformed it was rock and roll meets napalm and to those who survived it Vietnam left an enduring legacy. The protagonists were the "baby boomers" whose fathers fought World War II for a better world. They were raised on a tangible diet of fervent patriotism, anti-communism, Audie Murphy, John Wayne and a veritable host of indomitable heroes to emulate and admire.

This was their war. The one they didn't want, despite the longhaired protests, the civil disorder and all the other tumult it provoked. Some things had changed but some things hadn't. When a young guy from Hicksville was confronted with the hateful reality of what "real war" entailed he looked to his friends sharing the same foxhole, he looked to his NCOs and decided that good, bad or indifferent, this was "his" war and somehow, someway he was going to get back to the "world."

The 1960s were a time of great social and cultural upheaval. Young Americans had witnessed the assassination of a president, the rise of the black civil rights movement, hippies and their psychedelic lifestyles, and music from the British "invasion." It was a time of unprecedented change. African American college students staged sit-ins, freedom rides, and protest marches to challenge segregation in the South. Their efforts led the federal government to pass the Civil Rights Act of 1964, prohibiting discrimination in public facilities and employment, and the 24th Amendment and the Voting Rights Act of 1965, guaranteeing voting rights.

Youth culture was empowered and further enhanced by the superfluous availability of marijuana, LSD and free love. In retrospect hippies could have meant hypocrites because they didn't share much love with returning Vietnam veterans. During WWII an infantryman could expect to have spent at least 10 days in combat in the course of one year but there were notable exceptions among the 4th Infantry Division. In Vietnam that could have been up to 240 days in combat in one year. These were the men and women who really needed love and peace, but they weren't going to get much of either in Nam!

Bud Roach, 1st Battalion, 22nd Infantry Regiment, 4th Infantry Division

No one had told us what to expect when we landed. I was thinking we would be shot at getting off the plane. Cam Ranh Bay was very hot but it was on the beach of the South China Sea. The sand was pure white and the water was clear blue, however, we did not have time or the will to enjoy it. The days there were busy doing paperwork and getting outfitted for our assignment. I do remember late in the evening looking inland and seeing what I thought were thunder clouds. At least that what it would be if I was in Texas. It turned out that I showed my flatlander background. The "thunder clouds" were mountains where the coastal plain rises.

I was assigned to the Fourth Division at Camp Enari near Pleiku in the central highlands. I did not know anything about the reputation of any of the units and I did not know the strategic location of the Fourth Division's area of operations but I soon found out.

The central highlands are just what it implies—mountains. And not just mountains but mountains covered with triple canopy jungle. I was assigned to C Company, 1st Battalion, 22nd Infantry Brigade (C/1/22). The day I reported to C Company in the field it was raining. I should say that Vietnam has two seasons—wet and dry. During wet season it rains and rains and rains. The first morning I was with C Company we packed and changed locations. My initiation was marching under full pack in the rain up and down steep hillsides. I was in great physical condition but I was struggling. I would have been soaked with sweat if I hadn't been drenched by the rain. After a few days this became routine.

One reminder of Vietnam was the red dirt. During monsoon season it was a sloppy mess. The red mud was everywhere and there was no way to get it off. In the dry season the red dirt made clouds of dust that got into everything. If a helicopter landed the dust from the prop wash was blinding. We were assigned convoy security a couple of times. When we got to the end of the trip everyone was covered from head to toe. When we were on firebase security we would wash but no sooner had we cleaned up than the wind would blow the dust right back on. There was no relief.

Charlie Company stayed in the boonies about three weeks out of every month. We ate C rations that were dated for WWII. We didn't bathe for weeks at a time and kept the same clothes on round the clock for days. If we camped near a stream we would bathe but that wasn't very often.

We were in jungle much of the time that was so dense that objects just a few feet away were impossible to see. The enemy could be very close without detection. There were trails laced throughout the area that led from village to village. However, the trails were dangerous because of the threat of ambushes. This was the war from early September until early October.

I did not see many unusual animals but the jungle had many. I saw huge scorpions four inches or more in length. Snakes were huge and small. There were cobras, pythons, and the dreaded Bamboo Viper. The Bamboo Viper was a small snake but his venom would kill a man quickly. It was called the two-step viper. Rumors of tigers were common. There are several stories of tigers killing soldiers. Much of the area we patrolled is now a protected area for tigers. I still have scars around the top of where my boots were from leeches. In the swampy damp areas leeches were common. They would be attached before you knew they were a problem. There were several ways to get a leech off from spraying them with mosquito repellant to holding a lit cigarette close to them until they released. Monkeys were very common. Some of the guys at the firebase had monkeys as pets. Birds of all shapes and sizes were always around. The jungles were usually noisy with birds chirping and monkeys chattering. If we went into an area that was very quiet it set off an alarm to those experienced in the jungle.

The Vietnam War was blamed for inciting ghetto rioting, and a militant antiwar movement that contributed to a political backlash, which would have consequences for the Republican Party for many years to come. It was a war incited by politicians as most wars are, but most of these politicians successfully avoided the draft. They were draft dodgers in extremis who left the fighting to those mainly hailing from less privileged backgrounds—that's also been the case as long as there have been wars to fight. Nevertheless the Vietnam War was a war with a difference. It's where the Cold War communist paranoia of the previous decade became white hot and bothered. It spawned a new dialogue and new vocabulary that replaced previous "War" terminology. US soldiers in Vietnam wrote history with words as well as weapons and the incumbents further alienated the outside world by inventing their own terms and phrases. Who caused it and who was behind it didn't make the slightest bit of difference to the grunt humping the boonies or the FNG (Fucking New Guy) who had to learn it fast or risk going "Dien cai dao" and not making ETS (End Term of Service) in one piece. The enduring legacy is that much of the language used in the war has since worked its way into contemporary use and in the process generated even greater respect for those who were there.

Veterans returning from the Vietnam War were seldom if ever lauded with ticker tape parades or brass bands. More often than not, and due to no fault of their own they were jeered at, derided and denigrated by the errant youth of a nation living comfortable lives in a democracy that so many had fought and died for. It was the first real media war that was filmed, recorded and scrutinized by journalists and displayed on TV screens throughout the world and peculiarly enough news coverage was not subjected to government censorship. For those of a certain age it was "our war." The veterans were in some cases ostracized by an ungrateful nation; they had done their duty and sacrificed their young years to serve a country that initially didn't want to know.

By the end of the 1970s and into the 1980s there was renewed interest in the war through a plethora of highly successful movies such as *Apocalypse Now*, *The Deer Hunter*, *Full Metal Jacket*, *Platoon* and *Hamburger Hill*, which appeared to be the catharsis needed to remind America and the world that these courageous men and women had earned and deserved their admiration. The Director of *Platoon*, Oliver Stone, served in the 22nd Infantry Regiment in Vietnam, when they were part of the 25th Infantry Division (the 2nd and 3rd Battalions switched from 4th ID to 25th ID on August 1, 1967 while 1st Battalion remained with 4th ID in Vietnam for the duration). Hollywood may have reconciled the situation to some extent but it didn't provide the cure to the many thousands that were maimed or suffering from post traumatic stress disorder (PTSD). Many Vietnam veterans continue to carry internal and external scars to this day. Their war never ended as wars rarely do.

Vietnam was the longest war in American history. Technically the United States did not lose the war in Vietnam because they were never officially "at war" with Vietnam; the US forces were supposedly only in situ as advisors without Congressional approval to fight.

It was a war that had no precedent, where victories weren't measured by territorial gain but by body count. By May 1966 there were 280,000 troops in Vietnam, and by January 1967 that had risen to 389,000 of whom one third were volunteers. US troop strength peaked in 1969 with a staggering 543,482 US military personnel in the country.

The people of Vietnam, Laos and Cambodia suffered greatly after US forces pulled out when they came under Communist rule after the war, which had resulted in nearly 60,000 American deaths and an estimated 2 million Vietnamese deaths. Nevertheless there were those who regarded it as a necessary war and a noble cause, intended to protect the South Vietnamese from the spread of communism and a totalitarian government. The reasons for fighting it were least important considerations for those who got sent to "Nam." They had other more pressing considerations such as taking on the NVA and the Vietcong on their own turf. The VC name is reputed to have first been used by the South Vietnamese President Ngo Dinh Diem to demean the rebels, he was quoted using this reference in various Saigon newspapers in 1955. Việt Nam Cộng-sản" means "Vietnamese Communists and this was abbreviated to just Việt Cộng or VC.

The overwhelming majority of the Viet Cong were recruited in South Vietnam, but they were supplied and trained by regular North Vietnamese Army soldiers who often infiltrated into South Vietnam.

The North Vietnamese Army (NVA) and Vietcong combined were tough adversaries who fought a determined guerilla war of attrition in often deplorable conditions. These soldiers were capable of living off the land and fighting from the confines of their "Cu Chi" tunnel networks that covered tens of thousands of miles including an extensive network running underneath the Cu Chi district northwest of Saigon. Soldiers used these claustrophobic underground routes to house troops, transport supplies and assemble terrifying booby traps. They were elusive, highly dedicated, and cunning.

In January 1966 the 4th Infantry Division was called on again. The US Naval Ship *General Nelson M. Walker* was one of three ships that took the US Army's 4th Infantry Division to Vietnam in 1966. Shortly after, the 4th Engineer Battalion set up its base of operations in Vietnam's central highlands near the town of Pleiku. The 1st Brigade arrived in October and moved into a new camp south of Pleiku. The 2nd Brigade established its headquarters near the coast at Tuy Hoa in September 1966. The Division's 3rd Brigade was dispatched further south outside of Saigon and was assigned to the 25th Infantry Division. For much of November 1967, the 4th Infantry Division was engaged in numerous clashes along the Ho Chi Minh Trail in the area near the village of Dak To, a strategically important location. The 4th destroyed the operational capabilities of two whole NVA regiments and counteracted a planned major NVA offensive.

Charlie Shyab, 3rd Platoon, Company C, 1/22 Battalion, 4th Infantry Division

I was inducted as a conscientious objector into the US Army on June 7, 1967 and sent to Ft. Sam Houston, Texas for training as a Combat Medic in a 20-week program. After leave I was sent to Ft. Lewis, Washington for a jet flight to Cam Ranh Bay, Viet Nam.

I recall a Chinook flight to Pleiku where I would report to the Fourth Infantry at Camp Enari for a unit assignment. As a replacement you were placed on a duce ½ with 15/20 soldiers to be taken to different infantry companies. I was assigned to 3rd Platoon Company C of the 1/22 Battalion, 4th Infantry Division. This random selection reminds one of how your military destiny is shaped by a chance assignment. I was sure I would be in an evac hospital with 3 hots and a cot, not humping the boonies living out of a backpack! A few days after sharing a Thanksgiving meal in camp, I took a chopper to our highlands jungle camp. The first day I experienced combat and a night hike to another location with the company. All I owned was what I had on my back, a 60/70 lb rucksack, containing my shelter half, poncho, 4 days' C-rations, medical supplies, and personal items.

From November '67 to April '68, I lost 40 lb and received numerous tick bites and skin fungus infections. When we would move to a firebase each platoon would take turns patrolling on search and destroy missions. We were combat assaulted to different location for a week at a time during Dec/Jan.

The Chinese New Year, called "TET," was celebrated Feb 1st. The NVA/VC were hoping to use the sound of the celebrations as cover for their attacks on the cities aiming to cause a general uprising! We were airlifted by chopper to provide airport security in the city of Kontum.

Over the course of a week we helped Co D. clear out the NVA imbedded in the Special Forces compound north of the city. I was called forward to give aid to a wounded soldier pinned down in the building complex; as I moved forward an NVA soldier rose out of the rocketed building and started to draw down to aim at me. The men who were near me were able to shoot before he could fully aim on me. They did not have to do that but I pray that I was valuable enough for them to protect me. I had replaced another medic who refused to move forward during a November firefight even when the men drew down on him he would not get off the ground. I knew what to do; whenever and wherever I was need I was to respond. The men always checked where the medic was before going on patrol. All the medics were respectfully called "DOC."

On Feb 5 our company was directed to patrol the firing range east of Kontum. The sights and sounds of a large enemy unit were all around. While 2 platoons broke for lunch a squad provided security at 150 yards away. We heard an explosion and one squad member came running back to say that they had been hit by a rocket and had taken casualties. We ran back to the shell crater where the injured buddy was. Others moved up to form a perimeter for protection as we could hear the AK-47s all around us. Some of the men thought I was at 12 on the perimeter and moved up to cover me and ran into a machine-gun nest that was keeping us pinned down. They found me at 9 and a machine-gun team came to the crater to help. One of the ammo carriers was next to me and received a fatal head injury. I will someday ask the Lord in heaven why I was not hit by that shot. We were in the firefight till about 4 p.m. when a tank took out the machine gun. We lost 8 men in this ambush.

Much more went on that we don't have time for or that I do not recall. We were on patrol during Feb, March and April, doing search and destroy missions till we were sent to Chu Moor Mt. 6 miles from the Cambodian border near Kontum where an NVA regiment was dug in. We attacked the Mt. on the 26, 27 and 28th, each time taking casualties. On the evening of the 27th we received orders to attack the hill on the 28th no matter how many men were left! When we heard that we figured it was all over for us and that we would lose our lives. As senior medic I knew I had to be with my men.

On the morning of the 28th I found a place to read my New Testament and prayed to the Lord that I knew I could do nothing to save myself and that if he saw fit to save me I would serve him by being a teacher according to His will! When the command came for us to leave our bunkers to attack the hill a jet was dropping a 500 lb bomb on the Mt. The NVA used the sound to cover the mortar noise as we were moving up. About 20 ft. away I saw a flash and felt my right hand go numb just like you do when you bump your elbow. I thought I had just lost my hand but I looked down and it was still there; I knew I was hit so I returned to the bunker and told the 1st Sergeant I was hit. He lifted my right collar and his eyes got big as he confirmed the injury. I was also hit in the other arm and both legs but I did not know that. The med-evac chopper came in with 3 gunships to cover us and suppress any NVA fire. Of the 120 men in the company, 30 were KIA and 15 were choppered out; the 70 injured were treated by their fellow soldiers or medics.

My friend Richard Cassano escorted me to the LZ to help load the wounded; he never made it back to his foxhole!

Another great medic, Bud Roach, came in to replace me when I left. Come to find out that there were no other medics on the ground and that I was the last one to leave till he arrived to evacuate the rest of the men.

When the chopper landed at the aid station the corpsmen did not move because we were such a sight; me with no helmet just boonie hat, sunglasses, a 5-day beard and a messy uniform. The sargt. ordered them to get the wounded off because they were hesitant to be in such a mess. Inside the station they thought I was a hippy and moved me to a corner to protest the war!

After I recuperated 4/6 weeks in Japan I was assigned to Dewitt Army Hospital at Ft. Belvoir, VA to assist in the emergency room from June '68 to April '69. After my discharge I finished my Education Degree at CAU and started a 38-year educational career in 1970 as I had promised the Lord.

The beautiful young girl I was dating wrote to me mostly every day and she would send me care packages twice a week to tell me I was not forgotten. I want to thank JO, my family, friends and the VA for being there all these many years and what they have done to show their appreciation for my service.

When you go to the Viet Nam Wall, please go to panel 52 E and see the names of the 30-plus fellow soldiers from Company C who gave their best on Chu Moor Mt. on April 28 of 1968. Since 2003, those that remain have met each June to continue the legacy left by those fallen heroes.

Greater Love hath no man than to give his life for his fellow men!
Will you join me in continuing to cherish their honorable sacrifice?

Department of the Army
Office of the Adjutant General Washington D.C. 10 December 1969

The 4th Infantry Division changed command on 30 November 1968. At that time there was a lull in the fighting because the enemy was withdrawing into sanctuaries in or near Cambodia and Laos. Taking advantage of the lull in enemy activity during November and December, the 4th Infantry Division concentrated its efforts on destroying the Viet Cong infrastructure and disrupting Viet Cong base areas. The primary purpose of this campaign against the Viet Cong was to assist the Government of Vietnam in securing and pacifying its territory, with peace talks imminent, accelerated pacification became the chief goal of the Government of Vietnam and all Free World Military Assistance Forces in order to enhance the South Vietnamese Government's bargaining position. A second objective of the campaign against the Viet Cong was to hamper future operations of the regular North Vietnamese forces, which depend on local Viet Cong to guide their operations in unfamiliar territory and to stockpile foodstuffs and munitions.

To produce an environment in which the government of Vietnam's pacification activities could flourish, maneuver battalions of the 4th Infantry Division, situated from Dak To to Ban Me Thuot, conducted five types of operations: reconnaissance in force into base areas, screening operations, interdiction of routes of communication, cordon and search of selected populated areas, and civic action. Reconnaissance in force operations detected and destroyed enemy base camps, eliminated caches, and whenever possible, detected and destroyed enemy units. These operations inhibited movement of large enemy units, and consequently reduced the enemy's influence upon the civilian populace. Screening operations were conducted extensively in the western portion of the Division area of operations along the Cambodian border. The screening force, composed of the armored cavalry squadron and long- and short-range patrols, was deployed across enemy infiltration routes to the east. This permitted early warning of enemy forces moving into the area of operations while freeing the Division's other maneuver elements to pursue other operations. The screening forces would engage and delay the enemy forces to permit the commitment of other combat elements to destroy the enemy. Screening missions are essential to the economy of force role of the Division.

Interdiction was the mission of short-range patrols and long-range patrols. Composed of four men, these patrols remained in position from 48 to 72 hours, reporting enemy activity *and adjusting indirect fire upon the enemy both day and night, without disclosing their own positions. Saturating the avenue of approach to villages with ambushes and short-range patrols, the battalions of the 4th Infantry Division restricted the enemy's movement and reduced his ability to make contact with the Viet Cong infrastructure to acquire food and labor from the civilian population. Free from the Viet Cong's influence, the people were able to respond to the government's pacification programs.*

Cordon and Search operations were designed to detect and eliminate the Viet Cong infrastructure. For these operations to be effective, close liaison with District and Province Intelligence and Operations Control Centers was necessary. The Static Census Grievance (SCG) representative was one of the key personnel in the DIOCC. He maintained a hamlet book which contained such information as census of families and hamlets, maps and diagrams of villages and category cataloging of all of the residents in his area. When this information was combined with the photographs of suspected VCI and detainees, many times positive identification could be made. Cordon and Search operations provided additional information, which the battalions shared with the Vietnamese agencies. Repeated cordons and search of the same village proved fruitful, even though the initial catch might have been only one or two members of the VCI. Detainees would frequently identify other VCI through the screening of photographs of suspects, enemy dead, and villagers. MEDCAP's (Medical civic action program) were the heart of the battalions' efforts to demonstrate the benefits of cooperation with the Government of Vietnam. While in the villages, the battalions took note of the relative impact of various civic action projects and gathered intelligence. After repeated visits to the villages, the US personnel, along with interpreters and National Police, were able to detect strangers among the regular inhabitants. Many of these strangers were detained for interrogation. The central function of the MEDCAP was to provide the people with needed medical personnel to recognize and treat the afflictions common among the Montagnard (The indigenous Montagnards were recruited into service by the American Special Forces in Vietnam's mountain highlands, where they defended villages against the Viet Cong and served as rapid response forces).

Medical personnel assigned to battalion civic action teams also trained Montagnard personnel to recognize and treat these common afflictions so that they might help themselves in the absence of US MEDCAPs. The battalions found that repeated face-to-face contact generated interest in MEDCAP, gave us a better insight into problem areas and cultivated an attitude among the people that permitted the Volunteer Informant Program to flourish. As the Montengnards gained confidence in the US forces, the US forces gained confidence in their own efforts.

During the Vietnam War, although roughly two-thirds of the American soldiers volunteered to serve their country, the rest were selected for military service through the draft system. When the war started the names of all young, eligible American men were gathered by the Selective Service. When someone's name was chosen he was obliged to report to his local draft board, the manner by which the selection would occur was by design subject to notorious abuse and often used as a way to settle family or community disputes.

This is why most of those drafted during the Vietnam War hailed from poor working-class areas that provided fodder for the blue-collar industries. The demographic of American forces that served in Vietnam was roughly 25% poor, 55% working-class and 20% middle-class men; very few were drafted from Ivy League stock. There was always a way out if one was well connected. While career politicians such as Bill Clinton and Dick Cheney were accused of having avoided the draft thanks to their connections, others hightailed it to Canada and were labeled with the derogatory term "Draft dodgers." By the end of the 1960s it was becoming all too apparent that the selection system for the draft was corrupt and unworkable. Something had to be done. They system needed to be overhauled to pacify the public's outrage.

The initial spark for US involvement in Vietnam came with the Gulf of Tonkin Incident. As the 1960s got under way the United States was closely monitoring developments in Southeast Asia. McCarthyism and the paranoia that it had induced were still resonating and for all intents and purposes, according to some sections of the media, communism appeared to be destined to envelop and consume the whole region. The "Bay of Pigs" debacle had highlighted the dangers that communism posed to world peace and rekindled seething contempt for this totalitarian ideology. On August 2, 1964, three North Vietnamese torpedo boats engaged the USS *Maddox* in the Gulf of Tonkin. A couple of days later, there was another apparent incident involving the *Maddox* and another destroyer, the *Turner Joy*. President Johnson referred to these alleged assaults as "open aggression on the high seas," and retaliated by launching air strikes against the North Vietnamese naval bases harboring the enemy vessels.

Declassified documents revealed in 2005 that the second reported attack was pure invention, pure fabrication. It never happened. It didn't matter back then because this was the necessary excuse the US Congress would use to pass the "Tonkin Gulf Resolution," which gave carte blanche to President Lyndon B. Johnson to intervene in the face of blatant "communist aggression" and escalate US involvement in Vietnam. The joint resolution "to promote the maintenance of international peace and security in southeast Asia" was passed on August 7, 1964 and became the subject of great political controversy over the course of the undeclared war that ensued.

During the 1950s the 4th Infantry Division had been on duty in Germany and was largely inert during the Korean War but in 1958 they returned to the United States and were sent to Fort Lewis to become part of the Strategic Army Corps, which provided basic training to thousands of young draftees.

On September 25, 1966, the 4th Infantry Division was called on to begin a combat assignment against the North Vietnamese Army that would last until December 7, 1970. In the summer of 1966 the 4th Engineer Battalion established its base of operations near Pleiku, a town in Vietnam's central highlands. The 1st Brigade arrived in October and moved into a new camp south of Pleiku. The 2nd Brigade established its headquarters near the coast at Tuy Hoa in September 1966.

The Division's 3rd Brigade was sent further south outside of Saigon and was assigned to the control of the 25th Infantry Division. With the 25th ID's 3rd Brigade already operating out of the Pleiku area, the decision was made to reflag both organizations in August 1967. In August 1966, led by the 2nd Brigade, the Ivy Division headquarters closed into the central highlands of Vietnam. The Ivy men were at war yet again.

Bill French, 1/22nd Infantry Regiment, 4th Infantry Division

I will forever be grateful for a telephone call I received from Ray Warner in the spring of 2010 encouraging me to attend the Charlie Company reunion in Branson Missouri. Ray's call was the first conversation with a 1/22nd soldier since I left Vietnam in June 1968. Had he not called me I would not have come to the reunion. Attendance at the reunion, and the one to follow provided the opportunity to be in the presence of the best of America's citizen soldiers. Being somewhat of a "base camp commando," I considered it an honor just to be in the same room with these true American heroes and to listen to them connect the dots of experiences long past. The people that attend the reunion are the true "boots on the ground" soldiers and I treasure every moment of the reunions. Meeting family members and friends of these soldiers is a valued blessing.

So how did a kid from Iowa end up in Vietnam? My destiny was to graduate from college and return to Fairfield Iowa to teach math. Well, obviously that never happened. When I enrolled in college the military was the furthest thing from my mind. I never really knew anyone who had been in the military other than an aunt who was a nurse in WWII and an uncle who was in the infantry. They did not say much about it. In college, the first two years of ROTC were mandatory. I found the classes interesting and the military instructors to be fascinating. I had not known people who had been the places they had been and done the things they had done. One of the ROTC instructors' name is on THE WALL. By my junior year, Southeast Asia was in the news and it was obvious that some type of military service was in my future, so I elected to sign up for the last two years of ROTC to receive an officer commission upon graduation. To the surprise of some of my professors I actually graduated on time and was commissioned in the Medical Service Corps in June 1966. At that time I signed up for the last two years of ROTC the prediction was that to serve in Vietnam you would have to be at least a captain and be in a combat arm. Well that obviously did not happen quite that way as I spent my first anniversary of graduation from college in Vietnam with the 1/22 Infantry as a Second Lieutenant Medical Platoon Leader.

I arrived in Vietnam the first week of June 1967 on a commercial charter aircraft. Except for the fact that everyone was in a military uniform, the plane could have been headed to any foreign destination for pleasure or business. The stewardesses (they were called that then) were dressed in their customary uniforms and the pilots kept us informed of the flight information. Similarities to a pleasure flight ended there. When the plane landed in Vietnam it looked like the wing tip was practically touching the barbed wire running along the runway. When the door of the plane opened the anticipated blast of hot humid air I had heard so much was anything but that. It was surprisingly cool! Waiting on the runway was the muddiest group of GIs I had even seen, emitting the unforgettable ammonia smell of days-old human sweat. As soon as we were off the plane they clamored on and the plane immediately took off. The look on the stewardess's faces was something to behold. Obviously there had been a change in plans.

Things seemed a little strange. I was on orders to go to one of the Surgical or Evacuation hospitals and was supposed to land in Saigon. I had received a letter on Medical Command Letterhead informing me that I was to bring stateside fatigues and civilian clothes as I would not be issued the combat jungle uniform. The letter also informed me that the hospitals had recreational facilities, to include tennis courts. So, based on this information, I showed up with a set of matched luggage, and of course, a tennis racket. For some reason the plane was diverted from Saigon to Pleiku with a resulting change of orders from the 44th Medical Brigade to the 4th Infantry Division. I sometimes still hear "Hey Lieutenant, what are you going to do with that tennis racket??" ringing in my ears. Still have the tennis racket and have yet not learned how to play tennis.

All junior officers were put through an orientation course upon arrival to the 4th Infantry Division. This covered in about three days what you should have learned in basic about small arms if you were paying attention. One of the training stations was throwing hand grenades. I had just finished this station and had moved on to the next training station which was a lecture on the importance of safety. During the middle of the safety lecture an NCO came running to our group yelling that there were injured soldiers in the grenade pit. Evidently a grenade was dropped in the pit. The NCO in charge, who was due to DEROS (Date Eligible for Return from Overseas) in a couple days, tried to pick it up and throw it when it exploded, killing him instantly. All six of the other soldiers in the pit were severely injured and probably died. There were no medical supplies available and no radio to call for a dust off chopper. Helmets were passed and filled with combat dressings and belts for tourniquets. THERE WAS NO MORPHINE. Some of us still had white T-Shirts and used them to spell out "HELP" on the ground to attract the attention of choppers flying overhead. After an eternity a chopper finally arrived and I was introduced to the sound of the Huey while loading muddy, blood-soaked soldiers onto a chopper. I was angered about things that happened in Vietnam and this was definitely one of them. The training set up was totally wrong, with 5–6 people throwing grenades from a single pit. I had been in country less than a week and already saw people die! In war people get hurt, but there is no excuse for sloppy training and not being prepared to provide immediate care, whatever the source of injury. I vowed that I would do everything in my power to not let something like this happen on my watch in Vietnam.

Being a Medical Service Corps officer in an infantry battalion is a unique experience in that you are the only person in the battalion with that specialty. One of the greatest challenges was convincing the combat arms officers what you were actually supposed to be doing. On more than one occasion it was suggested that I be the Recon Platoon Leader! Even a greater challenge was educating them that it was really not a good idea to put the medic, who was supposed to be supporting an entire platoon, in a two-man listening post. The medical platoon was a part of the Battalion Headquarters Company. As the medical platoon leader it was my responsibility to assist the Battalion Surgeon (doctor) in attaching medics to the platoons and company headquarters; obtaining supplies for the medics; operating aid stations in the fire bases, brigade trains areas and the base camp. Fortunately I had received additional training as a Battalion Surgeon's Assistant right after officer basic. It provided additional training in combat first aid, diagnosing of diseases unique to Vietnam and decision making in when and how to call for a Dust Off chopper. It also provided additional training in medical logistics, but I will talk more about this later. As it turns out I actually got to use this training, which would not have been of much use in a hospital. At full strength there were about 40 medics in the medical platoon spread out with five companies and the numerous aid stations. Although I did not meet all of the medics face to face, I certainly heard if they were doing a good job and 99% of the time the information back from all of the battalion companies was that "Doc was the best."

So let's talk about medical logistics in Vietnam. The first thing I learned was to not believe all of what was taught in the Medical Field Service School at Fort Sam Houston.

The second thing I learned was that there were a lot of medical supplies in Vietnam; they were just not necessarily in the right place. It was a matter of finding out where they were and what you had to trade for what you could not get through the Division Medical Supply Office. Although these people tried to supply what you needed, they frequently responded with a "Due Out" notice. Fortunately some of the best, shall we say, "creative scroungers" were the medics in the base camp aid station. If they could not get it from the Division Medical Supply people they went on their own to other aid stations in base camp or the medical battalion units to get what was needed. I learned early not to ask a lot of questions. I did some pretty good trading myself.

Getting medical supplies was not necessarily the end of the challenge. Getting it to the medics was not always easy. White adhesive tape was a particularly hard item to get enough of. It was needed to reinforce combat dressings and for a variety of bandage applications. On one occasion 25 rolls were obtained and sent to the fire base to go out to the platoon medics. Unfortunately they were appropriated by a Battalion Headquarters officer to outline the Regulars motto on the LZ before I could send them out to the medics. Did I mention earlier that there were some angering moments!

Yet another challenge was getting the equipment the medics actually needed. The Army has a document called a TO&E (Table of Organization and Equipment). This document lists the equipment that a particular unit is authorized. If it is not on the list, you don't get it. One of the items sorely needed in the Aid Stations was an "Ambu-Bag." This is a device to help a person breathe. It consists of a mask, which goes over the nose and mouth and a bag, which is squeezed to force air into the lungs. These were not on our TO&E so we did not have any. It took some creative procurement by trading things we did have, but I probably should not specifically identify, to get a couple. Another item we sorely needed was a small refrigerator to preserve immunizations. The stateside refrigerator that came over with the Battalion had received one too many mortar fragments and no longer worked. Although we were not authorized a refrigerator, by now the property book officer realized that we no longer accepted that answer, so he agreed to order one. He only wanted to know how many cubic feet it should be. He ordered exactly the size I said. Well, when it showed up in the Brigade Trains area it was in the back of a duce and a half, and took about a squad to unload. It was really heavy and had walls about a foot thick. It was a laboratory refrigerator designed to freeze tissue samples so they could be thinly sliced for viewing under a microscope. It froze a test sample six pack solid in a matter of minutes. It went back on the truck it came on. Next time I was in base camp I bought a small refrigerator at the PX.

As I mentioned earlier, compared to the men of Charlie Company, I was a "base camp commando." I probably spent less than half my time in a firebase, with the rest divided among the Brigade Trains and the Base Camp. I actually preferred the firebase with the battery of artillery; the crew-served weapons of the weapons platoon and fully trained infantry providing security. The most helpless I felt was in base camp. When there was incoming all you could do was dive into a poorly constructed bunker and wait until it was over. I remember my last night in Vietnam. I had turned in all my equipment. All I had *was the uniform I was to wear home. That night base camp was attacked. I headed for the bunker with just my boots on. I was darned if I was going to get my going home uniform dirty.*

I also had the experience of often not being where the action was. On more than one occasion the fire base got hit between the time I left and I arrived at whereever I was going. For some reason people wanted me to stay where I was! Yes, I got shot at, but it was nothing like the men of the 1/22nd infantry companies experienced.

So what do I remember most from Vietnam?

The brave, courageous people in Vietnam. People who did amazing things under tough circumstances. Many of them were drafted into the military; others were there because it was their profession.

I remember Bill Zimmerman returning to his platoon. This was the greatest example of personal leadership I witnessed in 28 years in the military.

I remember medics volunteering to go back out to platoons when the medic was wounded or killed. They had been there before and knew what was going to happen. Bud Roach was one of them. He volunteering to go back to Charlie Company during the battle of Chu Moor after Charlie Shyab was evacuated. He had already done his time in the field. He was the man for the job and he took on the responsibility.

I remember the medical platoon receiving a care package from the family of one of the medics who was KIA. It meant a lot to us. It was around Christmas.

I remember that many of the medics were conscientious objectors and did not carry weapons. They honored their beliefs while serving their country. They are good people and every bit a soldier as those that did carry a weapon.

I remember men coming into the firebase after weeks in the field, their uniforms in shreds, their bodies covered with jungle rot. I know it must have hurt when we scraped and washed off the jungle rot, but they did not show it. And here we were ready to stick needles in their arms! I would not have blamed them if they punched me out.

I remember being told that I was a father for the first time by one of the medics who heard it on the company radio. I think it was Charlie Shyab who told me. I never did hear from the Red Cross. My son was born February 18, 1968. It was during TET. I remember the endless casualties coming through the aid station, particularly during the TET offensive, and the heroic efforts made to save them. Some did not make it. I can still hear the sound the zipper on a body bag makes.

Being at the Firebase, I spent a lot of time in the Battalion Tactical Operations Center (TOC). I remember being in the (TOC) when plans were made to move unit symbols on the map from one hill top to another, knowing what it was going to cost the men ordered to do it. There was a lot of turnover on the Battalion Command Staff so senior officers could get field time on their records. I sometimes wonder if they all understood what it took by the men that were represented by those unit symbols to move those symbols around that map.

My next assignment after Vietnam was to Fitzsimons Army Center in Aurora, Colorado. There were over 1,200 beds in the hospital, most of them filled by Vietnam injured and sick. Here I daily witnessed the struggle and determination of hundreds of wounded soldiers to recover. I remember the soldier who lost most of the function of his arms explaining to his buddies during lunch how he was able to tie a necktie. He would close one end of it in the dresser draw and step back to tighten the knot. I remember a lieutenant who was in my squad in basic training and was in Vietnam the same time as I who lost both legs and an arm in Vietnam. He came to our friend's wedding in dress uniform and was able to walk into the chapel, seat himself, get up from his seat and walk out of the chapel without assistance. It took a while, but he did it, and no one was impatient waiting on him to do it.

I remember the medical staff, many of whom had volunteered or had been drafted out of their medical practices, who dedicated their skills to the wounded and sick soldiers. I remember the occupational therapist who taught multiple amputees to ride horses and snow ski to regain a sense of accomplishment and purpose.

I remember after returning from Vietnam being a "Survivor Assistance Officer." This duty entailed personally notifying parents of two Vietnam casualties, presenting the folded flag to the parents during the military funeral and helping them through the maze of "benefits" of being a surviving NOK. One of the soldiers was KIA; the other was simply in the area of a "fragging" incident. It was the third child the parents had lost and he was the oldest. I do not know how you could have been a Survivor Assistance Officer if you had not been to Vietnam. The families were desperate for some meaning in their sons' deaths. The one comforting thing I could tell them was that they were with people that cared about them when they died, that they did not die alone.

I spent a total of 28 years in the military and now receive a retirement check every month. I am one of the lucky ones. I truly appreciate the opportunity to have experienced the people I met over the years. There is not a day goes by I don't think of the soldiers of the 1/22nd Infantry Battalion. They taught me the true meaning of courage.

The 1/22nd Infantry Regiment served in Vietnam from August 1966 through until January 1972. The regiment saw action in the precarious dense jungles of the central highlands as an integral part of the 4th Infantry Division and in the hotly contested areas west of Saigon as part of the 25th Infantry Division. The 2nd and 3rd Battalions earned the Presidential Unit Citation for their actions at the battle of Soui Tre.

It didn't take long for US troops in Vietnam to discover that their opponents were skillful operators and not to be underestimated. They would employ every devious tactic possible to undermine and frustrate US attempts to defeat them. They were referred to as "Charlie," VC, or Gooks and despite protestations to the contrary they regarded Vietnam as their country. The 4th Infantry Division had a tough job on its hands as they attempted to adapt and implement new strategies to deal with this new enemy. As always, adversity brought out the best in the Ivy men and they rose to the challenge. As the months passed they would become as wily and adept as their enemy. They would go into inhospitable terrain, try to avoid "punji-sticks" and Two Step snakes and take the fight to the NVA and VC.

Frustrated by their failure to effectively match the US troops in combat, sometime in 1966 the NVA began using new tactics. One of these became known as the "Hill Trap" maneuver that attempted to cunningly manipulate existing strategies used by US forces by luring them into mountainous terrain for one purpose. To prepare a veritable killing ground that had no recourse. South Vietnam's four corps areas were meticulously prepared as forced laborers dug veritable fortresses complete with bunkers, tunnels and trench systems. These areas were situated mainly in I Corps territory in and around the strategic A Shau–Da Krong War Zone, west of Hue, and in the strategic Tri-Border–Chu Pong War Zones, west of Dak To, in the region where II Corps operated.

To ensure that these preparations were not impeded, NVA troops occupied the A Shau Valley in early 1966 and established strong anti-recon screens to the west. The same procedure was followed between the Tri-Border Zone and Dak To. The 4th Infantry Division began scouting these places in early 1967. They had already experienced combat with the NVA further south along the Cambodian border, near the Ia Drang River. Further skirmishes ensued when the NVA launched rocket attacks against Pleiku in June 1967.

By August 1967, ARVN (The Army of the Republic of Viet Nam) became embroiled in a running battle with the 2nd Battalion, 174th NVA Infantry Regiment, near Dak To. It was becoming apparent that the NVA were establishing a chain of hill fortifications concentrated on and around Hill 1416. Ten miles to the south of Dak To, the 32nd NVA Infantry Regiment executed similar deployments, occupying another series of fortified mountain redoubts. Further redoubts were set up along the 32nd's intended line of retreat in the direction of the Cambodian border. General Peers, commander of the US 4th Infantry Division observed that the NVA had set up a well-prepared battlefield, complete with intricate bunker and trench complexes. The general was also well aware that the enemy had moved ample supplies and ammunition in preparation for an extended stay.

The NVA's 1st Infantry Division had assigned a formidable collection of units in these hill fortresses, totaling around 7,000 combatants, or the equivalent of seven USMC battalions. They were however quite sparsely dispersed over roughly 900 square miles of jungle terrain and their fortified mountain redoubts were too far apart to provide mutual logistic support and assistance. Most of these locations were in densely foliated arboreal areas with steep slopes covered with mixed bamboo and scrub brush. This was the type of terrain that the 4th Infantry Division were expected to fight in. They had been in the trenches in WWI, stormed the beaches and fought in the dense forests of the Hürtgen in WWII and now they had to contend with more inclement terrain and an entirely different enemy. Charlie Company was involved in at least four battles that involved these "hill trap" maneuvers during 1967–1968: November 17, 1967 in Ban Blech; February 5, 1968 in Kontum; April 22–30, 1968 at Chu Moor Mountain; and June 28, 1968 in VC Valley.

Homer R. Steedly Jr., 1/8th Infantry, 4th Infantry Division

2 Nov. 1968

After the incident with the giant Anaconda yesterday I noticed that when we moved out this morning the point man moved forward much more slowly than the day before. We found no evidence of any casualties from the road runner artillery firing last night, except a single Ho Chi Minh sandal left hastily on the trail. We are moving to a hilltop about 3 klicks away to set up a base to run squad-sized ambush patrols out of for a few days. The fact that this ridge line has such a clear trail on top means that it is being used regularly. The patrols are told to set up alongside the trail, put out claymores, prefire some artillery targets and wait for someone to come along. When the enemy is in the kill zone, they are to blow the claymores, fire a mad minute, and pull back to our perimeter as the artillery is fired behind them in a blocking maneuver. No one is spotted the first night, but we do see some flashlights on the opposite ridgeline and call in some 105mm artillery fire on them. The next day the CO wants us to send someone over to see if we got anyone. I tell him that it almost killed us getting up the ridge the first time. To go down, then up the other, search it, come back down only to have to climb back up this ridgeline again is simply not an option. If they made contact while on the opposite ridge, I could not get to them in time to help. He tries real hard to get me to do it, but I refuse. He then orders me to break up into three night ambushes instead of the one. I send out two reinforced squads, one in each direction along the ridge and keep the third with me in the perimeter we have set up. That night we heard movement about halfway down the ridge towards the valley. They had obviously spotted us and were going around our position by traveling in the valley. I made the mistake of telling the CO what I thought and of course he wanted us to set up an ambush in the valley. Now that was real dumb, so I made another suggestion. Why not sneak off and move to the other ridgeline where we had sighted the lights and set up a platoon-sized ambush on that trail. He liked the sound of that, so we packed up and began the move. I had one squad stay behind and make enough noise to keep the enemy thinking we were still all there. I also fired some blocking artillery targets along the ridge to discourage anyone from moving up on the stay behind element. We split up their packs and took most of their gear with us, so they could make good time when I called them to move out and catch up with us. By 11:00 a.m. we were in the valley filling our canteens in the stream. It was not as hot as it had been the last time we climbed a ridge, but it was still over 90 degrees. About noon, just after we started climbing the ridge, it started raining. The cool rain really felt good and soon cooled things down quite a bit. The ground was so hot that there was steam everywhere. It became so humid that the sweat just poured off us, irritating our eyes. While we appreciated the respite from the heat, the rain also made the red clay very slippery. About an hour up the ridge, someone slipped down the hill nearly 50 feet, stopping when he was impaled on a stump of bamboo cut by the point man while clearing a path.

He was in total agony. I came back to his position and was shocked by what I saw. He had about a foot of bamboo jammed right up his butt. Doc had given him some morphine to calm him down and ease the pain. Everyone was stumped about what to do next. Doc said that if we lifted him off the bamboo, he would probably bleed to death before we could get him to an LZ. I sent the first squad up to the top to find an LZ, then called Battalion and told them the situation. We decided that we had to cut the bamboo off and leave it in place, then carry him up the hill to the LZ for Medevac. The only thing we had to cut the bamboo with was the serrated back of a K-bar knife. Four of us held the guy while they cut at the bamboo. It was nearly two inches in diameter and every saw with the K-bar was agony for the poor guy even with the morphine.

Finally we got him free. We made a litter from his poncho and two bamboo poles, then tied him into it. Them we just took a rope and tied it to the litter and had five or six men up front pull, while several of us on either side lifted the litter. Each heave would get him about 3 feet up the ridge, then the rope guys would hold him until we moved up alongside again and we would then hold the litter in place until the rope guys were in position to pull again. I still do not know where we found the strength to keep that up long enough to reach the top. At first the adrenalin helped, but that soon wore off and it was sheer willpower. When we got him to the top, the first squad took over and moved him to the LZ, which was only a 50-meter section of elephant grass about 50 meters down the ridge line. The chopper had to hover with only one skid on the ground as we loaded him into the cargo bay. That, of course, ruined all chances of any surprise ambush on the ridge line, so we were sent to a hill top about 4 klicks south to set up a company-sized perimeter in preparation for the rest of the company to join up with us the following day.

Another pressing problem confronting the US forces in Vietnam was the capacity of the NVA and VC to resupply their operational units. The Ho Chi Minh trail was an intricate system of mountain and jungle trails that connected North Vietnam to its allies in the South Vietnam, Cambodia, and Laos. It was the main artery for deploying troops, vehicles, and supplies and comprised more than 12,000 miles of roads and paths through some of the world's most inhospitable terrain. With the largest assigned area of operations of any division in Vietnam, the Ivy division was charged with screening the border of South Vietnam as the first line of defense against infiltration down the Ho Chi Minh trail through Laos and Cambodia, with a purpose of attempting to preempt any offensive on the more populated lowlands. US ground troops were not allowed to venture into Laos and Cambodia but no such restriction applied to the US air forces. During the Vietnam War around 2.4 million bombs were dropped on the Ho Chi Minh trail—almost twice the amount US air forces dropped on Germany during WWII. It didn't succeed in stopping the resupply chain. There were even discussions at the Pentagon about the possibility of employing nuclear weapons to deal with the problems caused by the Ho Chi Minh trail.

Public opposition to the war in the United States was increasing and in an attempt to pacify this General Bruce Palmer, Jr., one of Westmoreland's commanders made the audacious claim that "the Viet Cong has been defeated" and that "He can't get food and he can't recruit." Westmoreland was even more emphatic in his assertions when he publicly reported that, as of the end of 1967, the communists were "unable to mount a major offensive." In a further attempt to sway the public Westmoreland claimed that the NVA & VC were "losing the war."

All US forces were placed on maximum alert when shortly after midnight on January 30, 1968, all five provincial capitals were attacked. This was the beginning of what became known as the "Tet Offensive." Tet was the name used by the Vietnamese for the lunar New Year and was regarded as a major holiday in their calendar. One of these provincial capitals was located in Kontum, the capital of Kontum Province a key Central Highlands province capital. As NVA and VC troops swept into the area it was the South Vietnamese Army who faced them first and prevented the enemy from taking complete control of the city. This area was within the region in which the 4th Infantry Division were operating and it was they who were tasked with clearing the enemy out of the city and pursuing him into the countryside. Ground command of the operation was directed under the auspices of Lt. Col. William P. Junk, commander of 1st Battalion, 22nd Infantry, who was in charge of all 4th Infantry Division forces in the area. For the duration of the operation the elements at his disposal were organized into Task Force 1-22. The vicious fighting that ensued lasted 14 bloody days and became known as the battle of Kontum. The Ivy men turned potential defeat into victory and for its efforts the 1st Battalion, 22nd Infantry was awarded the "Valorous Unit Citation" for actions in the defense of the provincial capital of Kontum, during the Tet Offensive of 1968.

Bud Roach, 1st Battalion, 22nd Infantry Regiment, 4th Infantry Division

From the middle of November '67 until the end of January '68 it was unusually quiet. Charlie Company was on firebase security during the Christmas ceasefire. Christmas '67 was a memorable time. I was homesick and lonely … everybody was. We laughed about Santa Claus finding us and made jokes but it was a low time. We played football with a rolled-up sand bag for a football. It was the dust bowl. We shared the goodies sent from home. We went back in the boonies in January '68. The entire battalion was moved to base camp for a stand down late in the month. A stand down is a time to pull a unit off line for some reason, usually for equipment. There was no such need this time. In retrospect it is obvious why there was little enemy activity and why we were pulled back to base camp. On February 1 the NVA started the 1968 Tet offensive. It was a major attack on every important city. Kontum City is the provincial capital of Kontum Province and it came under heavy attack. All of the units of the 1/22 infantry were committed to the battle to retake Kontum City.

C Company arrived by helicopter into the airfield at Kontum. We were to secure the landing strip. Sounds of war were all around us. Air strikes by jets were constant as were attacks by helicopter gunships. The NVA had infiltrated the city and it was our job to push them out. On the first morning D Company was in heavy contact and C Company was called to reinforce them. When we joined D Company the two units were able to retake a group of buildings that were the Provincial Government headquarters. This was heavy fighting and many NVA were killed, wounded, or captured. The second day we began going from house to house clearing everyone out of the city. At the end of the second day we camped on the edge of an open field behind a dirt levee near the government buildings. After dark we were under strict orders not to use any kind of light. We passed hand grenades to the people on the perimeter. The instructions were to not fire a shot because the muzzle flash would show our location. The grenades were to be used until the NVA came over the levee. These were very unusual orders but by knowing the orders we all knew what a dire situation we were in.

Puff the Magic Dragon was slang for an airplane equipped with guns that could fire 100 rounds per second. It was an awesome and devastating weapon. Puff the Magic Dragon flew a figure eight pattern over us all night firing all around us. The next morning we went out into the open field. As a medic I was instructed to find any wounded enemy and patch them up for interrogation. The field was full of dead NVA. You could literally walk across the field on bodies. I did not find one alive. Puff the Magic Dragon kept our unit from being overrun and wiped out.

In two or three days the city was cleared and secure. Kontum was a beautiful oriental city with white stucco buildings and blue-green tile roofs. When we left the town was in shambles. The terrain around the city was rolling hills covered with a thick growth of scrubby trees. After the city was cleared our mission became the pursuit of the retreating NVA. On February 5 the unit I was with was patrolling a short distance outside the city. We had just stopped to take a break around noon and I had laid down using my medic bag for a pillow when all hell broke loose. A squad that had been sent out to secure the area around where we stopped was ambushed. I grabbed my bag and ran through the scrub trees to get to the wounded. I slid in on my stomach next to a wounded soldier. Fellow medic Charlie Shyab and I tended to him. He was very seriously wounded. He had lost an arm at the elbow and a leg was hanging on by a small strip of skin at the thigh. As I lay beside him the ambush continued. A machine gun kept opening up and bullets were hitting everywhere. The bullets were hitting so close that dirt was hitting my face. It was very hot that afternoon and no breeze at all could reach the small clearing. There was a haze in the air from guns being fired and the explosion of grenades.

A lieutenant was killed that day who had arrived in the field the day before. He lasted one day—his only firefight. His inexperience probably was the reason the group walked into the ambush. A close friend was killed also. He was the person who taught me the inside information about survival when I first arrived in the boonies. He was from Pennsylvania and a great high school athlete.

There is a myth that bullets make a noise when they go by. My experience was that there was no noise at all. When a bullet hits a person it makes a dull thud sound. In movies a person who is hit by a shot flies through the air. I did not experience this. When a person is wounded they just drop in their tracks. The person next to you could be shot while you are talking to him and you wouldn't know until you looked.

I had to plan how to get the wounded soldier out. I figured that at some point I would throw him over my shoulder and run, if so, I planned to amputate his leg. We were there for about four hours until a tank came and rescued us. I did not have to make a decision about severing the leg. He died in the helicopter before he reached the field hospital. I cried that night because I lost him. After keeping him alive for hours I lost him. I also shed tears because at that point I didn't see any way I would survive doing what I had to do. We lost eight men that day. I knew them all very well. After a few more days of intense fighting things were quiet for a while. Forty years later I still try to save that soldier in my dreams.

As a new decade dawned American military presence began to wind down, even veterans began protesting against US involvement and media interest in the Vietnam War began to wane. By 1975 it had spluttered to an ignominious end with the fall of Saigon. Tom Brokaw called those who served in World War II the "greatest generation" but he overlooked the undisputable fact that the two and a half million United States citizens who served in Vietnam were by far the greatest of their generation. Their average age was 22 years old and they displayed just as much courage, just as much fortitude and heroism as any generation had before or since. They were all heroes.

There have been other books written about the heroic deeds of the Ivy men during the Vietnam War and 11 additional battle streamers would be added to the 4th Infantry Division colors as they fought in places that would become synonymous with that war.

The Ia Drang Valley, Plei Trap Valley, Fire Base Gold, Dak To, the Oasis, Kontum, Pleiku, Ben Het, An Khe, and Cambodia. They held the largest assigned area of operations of any division in Vietnam and the 4th Infantry Division earned more Medals of Honor during the Vietnam War than in all the other wars combined. They went above and beyond the call of duty on numerous occasions. They remained "steadfast and loyal" as they had done in other wars. Their gallantry and valor will not be forgotten.

Bellrichard, Leslie Allen (posthumously)
The Medal of Honor
Vietnam Veterans Memorial Panel 20E Line 54
Rank and organization: Private First Class, US Army, Company C, 1st Battalion, 8th Infantry, 4th Infantry Division.
Place and date: Kontum Province, Republic of Vietnam, May 20, 1967
Entered service at: Oakland, California
Born: December 4, 1941, Janesville, Wisconsin

For conspicuous gallantry and intrepidity in action at the risk of his life above and beyond the call of duty. Acting as a fire team leader with Company C, during combat operations PFC Bellrichard was with 4 fellow soldiers in a foxhole on their unit's perimeter when the position came under a massive enemy attack. Following a 30-minute mortar barrage, the enemy launched a strong ground assault. PFC Bellrichard rose in face of a group of charging enemy soldiers and threw hand grenades into their midst, eliminating several of the foe and forcing the remainder to withdraw. Failing in their initial attack, the enemy repeated the mortar and rocket bombardment of the friendly perimeter, then once again charged against the defenders in a concerted effort to overrun the position. PFC Bellrichard resumed throwing hand grenades at the onrushing attackers. As he was about to hurl a grenade, a mortar round exploded just in front of his position, knocking him into the foxhole and causing him to lose his grip on the already armed grenade. Recovering instantly, PFC Bellrichard recognized the threat to the lives of his 4 comrades and threw himself upon the grenade, shielding his companions from the blast that followed. Although severely wounded, PFC Bellrichard struggled into an upright position in the foxhole and fired his rifle at the enemy until he succumbed to his wounds. His selfless heroism contributed greatly to the successful defense of the position, and he was directly responsible for saving the lives of several of his comrades. His acts are in keeping with the highest traditions of the military service and reflect great credit upon himself and the US Army.

Bennett, Thomas W. (posthumously)
The Medal of Honor
Vietnam Veterans Memorial Panel 32W Line 10
Rank and organization: Corporal, US Army, 2nd Platoon, Company B, 1st Battalion, 14th Infantry, 4th Infantry Division.
The only conscientious objector to receive the Medal of Honor in Vietnam
Place and date: Chu Pa region, Republic of Vietnam, February 9–11, 1969
Entered service at: Fairmont, West Virginia
Born: April 7, 1947, Morgantown, West Virginia

For conspicuous gallantry and intrepidity in action at the risk of his life above and beyond the call of duty. Cpl. Bennett distinguished himself while serving as a platoon medical aid man with the 2d Platoon, Company B, during a reconnaissance-in-force mission. On 9 February the platoon was moving to assist the 1st Platoon of Company D which had run into a North Vietnamese ambush when it became heavily engaged by the intense small arms, automatic weapons, mortar and rocket fire from a well fortified and numerically superior enemy unit. In the initial barrage of fire, 3 of the point members of the platoon fell wounded. Cpl. Bennett, with complete disregard for his safety, ran through the heavy fire to his fallen comrades, administered life-saving first aid under fire and then made repeated trips carrying the wounded men to positions of relative safety from which they would be medically evacuated from the battle position. Cpl. Bennett repeatedly braved the intense enemy fire moving across open areas to give aid and comfort to his wounded comrades. He valiantly exposed himself to the heavy fire in order to retrieve the bodies of several fallen personnel. Throughout the night and following day, Cpl. Bennett moved from position to position treating and comforting the several personnel who had suffered shrapnel and gunshot wounds. On 11 February, Company B again moved in an assault on the well fortified enemy positions and became heavily engaged with the numerically superior enemy force. Five members of the company fell wounded in the initial assault. Cpl. Bennett ran to their aid without regard to the heavy fire. He treated 1 wounded comrade and began running toward another seriously wounded man. Although the wounded man was located forward of the company position covered by heavy enemy grazing fire and Cpl. Bennett was warned that it was impossible to reach the position, he leaped forward with complete disregard for his safety to save his comrade's life. In attempting to save his fellow soldier, he was mortally wounded. Cpl. Bennett's undaunted concern for his comrades at the cost of his life above and beyond the call of duty are in keeping with the highest traditions of the military service and reflect great credit upon himself, his unit, and the US Army.

Evans, Donald W. Jr (posthumously)
The Medal of Honor
Vietnam Veterans Memorial Panel 14E Line 85
Rank and organization: Specialist Fourth Class, US Army, Company A, 2nd Battalion,12th Infantry, 4th Infantry Division.
Place and date: Tri Tam, Republic of Vietnam, January 27, 1967
Entered service at: Covina, California
Born: July 23, 1943, Covina, California

For conspicuous gallantry and intrepidity in action at the risk of his life above and beyond the call of duty. He left his position of relative safety with his platoon which had not yet been committed to the battle to answer the calls for medical aid from the wounded men of another platoon which was heavily engaged with the enemy force. Dashing across 100 meters of open area through a withering hail of enemy fire and exploding grenades, he administered lifesaving treatment to 1 individual and continued to expose himself to the deadly enemy fire as he moved to treat each of the other wounded men and to offer them encouragement. Realizing that the wounds of 1 man required immediate attention,

Sp4c. Evans dragged the injured soldier back across the dangerous fire-swept area, to a secure position from which he could be further evacuated. Miraculously escaping the enemy fusillade, Sp4c. Evans returned to the forward location. As he continued the treatment of the wounded, he was struck by fragments from an enemy grenade. Despite his serious and painful injury he succeeded in evacuating another wounded comrade, rejoined his platoon as it was committed to battle and was soon treating other wounded soldiers. As he evacuated another wounded man across the fire covered field, he was severely wounded. Continuing to refuse medical attention and ignoring advice to remain behind, he managed with his waning strength to move yet another wounded comrade across the dangerous open area to safety. Disregarding his painful wounds and seriously weakened from profuse bleeding, he continued his lifesaving medical aid and was killed while treating another wounded comrade. Sp4c. Evan's extraordinary valor, dedication and indomitable spirit saved the lives of several of his fellow soldiers, served as an inspiration to the men of his company, were instrumental in the success of their mission, and reflect great credit upon himself and the Armed Forces of his country.

Grandstaff, Bruce Alan (posthumously)
The Medal of Honor
Vietnam Veterans Memorial Panel 20E Line 28
Rank and organization: Platoon Sergeant, US Army, Company B, 1st Battalion, 8thInfantry, 4th Infantry Division.
Place and date: Pleiku Province, Republic of Vietnam, May 18, 1967.
Entered service at: Spokane, Washington
Born: June 2, 1934, Spokane, Washington

For conspicuous gallantry and intrepidity in action at the risk of his life above and beyond the call of duty. P/Sgt. Grandstaff distinguished himself while leading the Weapons Platoon, Company B, on a reconnaissance mission near the Cambodian border. His platoon was advancing through intermittent enemy contact when it was struck by heavy small arms and automatic weapons fire from 3 sides. As he established a defensive perimeter, P/Sgt. Grandstaff noted that several of his men had been struck down. He raced 30 meters through the intense fire to aid them but could only save 1. Denied freedom to maneuver his unit by the intensity of the enemy onslaught, he adjusted artillery to within 45 meters of his position. When helicopter gunships arrived, he crawled outside the defensive position to mark the location with smoke grenades. Realizing his first marker was probably ineffective, he crawled to another location and threw his last smoke grenade but the smoke did not penetrate the jungle foliage. Seriously wounded in the leg during this effort he returned to his radio and, refusing medical aid, adjusted the artillery even closer as the enemy advanced on his position. Recognizing the need for additional firepower, he again braved the enemy fusillade, crawled to the edge of his position and fired several magazines of tracer ammunition through the jungle canopy. He succeeded in designating the location to the gunships but this action again drew the enemy fire and he was wounded in the other leg. Now enduring intense pain and bleeding profusely, he crawled to within 10 meters of an enemy machine gun which had caused many casualties among his men. He destroyed the position with hand grenades but received additional wounds. Rallying his remaining men to withstand the enemy assaults, he realized his position was being overrun and asked for artillery directly on his location. He fought until mortally wounded by an enemy rocket. Although every man in the platoon was a casualty, survivors attest to the indomitable spirit and exceptional courage of this outstanding combat leader who inspired his men to fight courageously against overwhelming odds and cost the enemy heavy casualties. P/Sgt. Grandstaff's selfless gallantry, above and beyond the call of duty, are in the highest traditions of the US Army and reflect great credit upon himself and the Armed Forces of his country.

Johnson, Dwight H.
The Medal of Honor
Rank and organization: Specialist Fifth Class, US Army, Company B, 1st Battalion, 69th Armor, 4th Infantry Division.
Place and date: Near Dak To, Kontum Province, Republic of Vietnam, January 15, 1968
Entered service at: Detroit, Michigan
Born: May 7, 1947, Detroit, Michigan

For conspicuous gallantry and intrepidity at the risk of his life above and beyond the call of duty. Sp5c. Johnson, a tank driver with Company B, was a member of a reaction force moving to aid other elements of his platoon, which was in heavy contact with a battalion-size North Vietnamese force. Sp5c. Johnson's tank, upon reaching the point of contact, threw a track and became immobilized. Realizing that he could do no more as a driver, he climbed out of the vehicle, armed only with a .45 caliber pistol. Despite intense hostile fire, Sp5c. Johnson killed several enemy soldiers before he had expended his ammunition. Returning to his tank through a heavy volume of antitank rocket, small arms and automatic weapons fire, he obtained a sub-machine gun with which to continue his fight against the advancing enemy. Armed with this weapon, Sp5c. Johnson again braved deadly enemy fire to return to the center of the ambush site where he courageously eliminated more of the determined foe. Engaged in extremely close combat when the last of his ammunition was expended, he killed an enemy soldier with the stock end of his submachine gun. Now weaponless, Sp5c. Johnson ignored the enemy fire around him, climbed into his platoon sergeant's tank, extricated a wounded crewmember and carried him to an armored personnel carrier. He then returned to the same tank and assisted in firing the main gun until it jammed. In a magnificent display of courage, Sp5c. Johnson exited the tank and again armed only with a .45 caliber pistol, engaged several North Vietnamese troops in close proximity to the vehicle. Fighting his way through devastating fire and remounting his own immobilized tank, he remained fully exposed to the enemy as he bravely and skillfully engaged them with the tank's externally-mounted .50 caliber machine gun; where he remained until the situation was brought under control. Sp5c. Johnson's profound concern for his fellow soldiers, at the risk of his life above and beyond the call of duty are in keeping with the highest traditions of the military service and reflect great credit upon himself and the US Army.

McDonald, Phill G. (posthumously)
The Medal of Honor
Vietnam Veterans Memorial Panel 59W Line 26
Rank and organization: Private First Class, US Army, Company A, 1st Battalion, 14th Infantry, 4th Infantry Division.
Place and date: Near Kontum City, Republic of Vietnam, June 7, 1968.
Entered service at: Beckley, West Virginia
Born: September 13, 1941, Avondale, West Virginia

For conspicuous gallantry and intrepidity in action at the risk of his life above and beyond the call of duty. PFC McDonald distinguished himself while serving as a team leader with the 1st platoon of Company A. While on a combat mission his platoon came under heavy barrage of automatic weapons fire from a well-concealed company-size enemy force. Volunteering to escort 2 wounded comrades to an evacuation point, PFC McDonald crawled through intense fire to destroy with a grenade an enemy automatic weapon threatening the safety of the evacuation. Returning to his platoon, he again volunteered to provide covering fire for the maneuver of the platoon from its exposed position. Realizing the threat he posed, enemy gunners concentrated their fire on PFC McDonald's position, seriously wounding him. Despite his painful wounds, PFC McDonald recovered the weapon of a wounded machine gunner to provide accurate covering fire for the gunner's evacuation. When other soldiers were pinned down by a heavy volume of fire from a hostile machine gun to his front, Pfc. McDonald crawled toward the enemy position to destroy it with grenades. He was mortally wounded in this intrepid action. PFC McDonald's gallantry at the risk of his life which resulted in the saving of the lives of his comrades, is in keeping with the highest traditions of the military service and reflects great credit upon himself, his unit, and the US Army.

McKibben, Ray (posthumously)
The Medal of Honor
Vietnam Veterans Memorial Panel 37W Line 52
Rank and organization: Sergeant, US Army, Troop B, 7th Squadron (Airmobile), 17th Cavalry.
Place and date: Near Song Mao, Republic of Vietnam, December 8, 1968.
Entered service at: Atlanta, Georgia
Born: October 27, 1947, Felton, Georgia

For conspicuous gallantry and intrepidity in action at the risk of his life above and beyond the call of duty, Sgt. McKibben distinguished himself in action while serving as team leader of the point element of a reconnaissance patrol of Troop B, operating in enemy territory. Sgt. McKibben was leading his point element in a movement to contact along a well-traveled trail when the lead element came under heavy automatic weapons fire from a fortified bunker position, forcing the patrol to take cover. Sgt. McKibben, appraising the situation and without regard for his own safety, charged through bamboo and heavy brush to the fortified position, killed the enemy gunner, secured the weapon and directed his patrol element forward. As the patrol moved out, Sgt. McKibben observed enemy movement to the flank of the patrol. Fire support from helicopter gunships was requested and the area was effectively neutralized. The patrol again continued its mission and as the lead element rounded the bend of a river it came under heavy automatic weapons fire from camouflaged bunkers. As Sgt. McKibben was deploying his men to covered positions, he observed one of his men fall wounded. Although bullets were hitting all around the wounded man, Sgt. McKibben, with complete disregard for his safety, sprang to his comrade's side and under heavy enemy fire pulled him to safety behind the cover of a rock emplacement where he administered hasty first aid. Sgt. McKibben, seeing that his comrades were pinned down and were unable to deliver effective fire against the enemy bunkers, again undertook a single-handed assault of the enemy defenses. He charged through the brush and hail of automatic weapons fire closing on the first bunker, killing the enemy with accurate rifle fire and securing the enemy's weapon. He continued his assault against the next bunker, firing his rifle as he charged. As he approached the second bunker his rifle ran out of ammunition; however, he used the captured enemy weapon until it too was empty, at that time he silenced the bunker with well-placed hand grenades. He reloaded his weapon and covered the advance of his men as they moved forward. Observing the fire of another bunker impeding the patrol's advance, Sgt. McKibben again single-handedly assaulted the new position. As he neared the bunker he was mortally wounded but was able to fire a final burst from his weapon killing the enemy and enabling the patrol to continue the assault. Sgt. McKibben's indomitable courage, extraordinary heroism, profound concern for the welfare of his fellow soldiers and disregard for his personal safety saved the lives of his comrades and enabled the patrol to accomplish its mission. Sgt. McKibben's gallantry in action at the cost of his life above and beyond the call of duty are in the highest traditions of the military service and reflect great credit upon himself, his unit, and the US Army.

McNerney, David H.

The Medal of Honor

Rank and organization: First Sergeant, US Army, Company A., 1st Battalion, 8thInfantry, 4th Infantry Division.

Place and date: Polei Doc, Republic of Vietnam, March 22, 1967

Entered service at: Fort Bliss, Texas

Born: June 2, 1931, Lowell, Massachusetts

1st Sgt. McNerney distinguished himself when his unit was attacked by a North Vietnamese battalion near Polei Doc. Running through the hail of enemy fire to the area of heaviest contact, he was assisting in the development of a defensive perimeter when he encountered several enemy at close range. He killed the enemy but was painfully injured when blown from his feet by a grenade. In spite of this injury, he assaulted and destroyed an enemy machinegun position that had pinned down 5 of his comrades beyond the defensive line. Upon learning his commander and artillery forward observer had been killed, he assumed command of the company. He adjusted artillery fire to within 20 meters of the position in a daring measure to repulse enemy assaults. When the smoke grenades used to mark the position were gone, he moved into a nearby clearing to designate the location to friendly aircraft. In spite of enemy fire he remained exposed until he was certain the position was spotted and then climbed into a tree and tied the identification panel to its highest branches. Then he moved among his men readjusting their position, encouraging the defenders and checking the wounded. As the hostile assaults slackened, he began clearing a helicopter landing site to evacuate the wounded. When explosives were needed to remove large trees, he crawled outside the relative safety of his perimeter to collect demolition material from abandoned rucksacks. Moving through a fusillade of fire he returned with the explosives that were vital to the clearing of the landing zone. Disregarding the pain of his injury and refusing medical evacuation 1st Sgt. McNerney remained with his unit until the next day when the new commander arrived. First Sgt. McNerney's outstanding heroism and leadership were inspirational to his comrades. His actions were in keeping with the highest traditions of the US Army and reflect great credit upon himself and the Armed Forces of his country.

Molnar, Frankie Zoly (posthumously)
The Medal of Honor
Vietnam Veterans Memorial Panel 20E Line 64
Rank and organization: Staff Sergeant, US Army, Company B, 1st Battalion, 8th Infantry, 4th Infantry Division.
Place and date: Kontum Province, Republic of Vietnam, May 20, 1967
Entered service at: Fresno, California
Born: February 14, 1943, Logan, West Virginia

For conspicuous gallantry and intrepidity in action at the risk of his life above and beyond the call of duty. S/Sgt. Molnar distinguished himself while serving as a squad leader with Company B, during combat operations. Shortly after the battalion's defensive perimeter was established, it was hit by intense mortar fire as the prelude to a massive enemy night attack. S/Sgt. Molnar immediately left his sheltered location to insure the readiness of his squad to meet the attack. As he crawled through the position, he discovered a group of enemy soldiers closing in on his squad area. His accurate rifle fire killed 5 of the enemy and forced the remainder to flee. When the mortar fire stopped, the enemy attacked in a human wave supported by grenades, rockets, automatic weapons, and small-arms fire. After assisting to repel the first enemy assault, S/Sgt. Molnar found that his squad's ammunition and grenade supply was nearly expended. Again leaving the relative safety of his position, he crawled through intense enemy fire to secure additional ammunition and distribute it to his squad. He rejoined his men to beat back the renewed enemy onslaught, and he moved about his area providing medical aid and assisting in the evacuation of the wounded. With the help of several men, he was preparing to move a severely wounded soldier when an enemy hand grenade was thrown into the group. The first to see the grenade, S/Sgt. Molnar threw himself on it and absorbed the deadly blast to save his comrades. His demonstrated selflessness and inspirational leadership on the battlefield were a major factor in the successful defense of the American position and are in keeping with the finest traditions of the US Army. S/Sgt. Molnar's actions reflect great credit upon himself, his unit, and the US Army.

Roark, Anund C. (posthumously)
The Medal of Honor
Vietnam Veterans Memorial Panel 61E Line 18
Rank and organization: Sergeant, US Army, Company C, 1st Battalion, 12th Infantry, 4th Infantry Division
Place and date: Kontum Province, Republic of Vietnam, May 16, 1968
Entered service at: Los Angles, California
Born: February 17, 1948, Vallejo, California

For conspicuous gallantry and intrepidity in action at the risk of his life above and beyond the call of duty. Sgt. Roark distinguished himself by extraordinary gallantry while serving with Company C. Sgt. Roark was the point squad leader of a small force which had the mission of rescuing 11 men in a hilltop observation post under heavy attack by a company-size force, approximately 1,000 meters from the battalion perimeter. As lead elements of the relief force reached the besieged observation post, intense automatic weapons fire from enemy-occupied bunkers halted their movement. Without hesitation, Sgt. Roark maneuvered his squad, repeatedly exposing himself to withering enemy fire to hurl grenades and direct the fire of his squad to gain fire superiority and cover the withdrawal of the outpost and evacuation of its casualties. Frustrated in their effort to overrun the position, the enemy swept the hilltop with small arms and volleys of grenades. Seeing a grenade land in the midst of his men, Sgt. Roark, with complete disregard for his safety, hurled himself upon the grenade, absorbing its blast with his body. Sgt. Roark's magnificent leadership and dauntless courage saved the lives of many of his comrades and were the inspiration for the successful relief of the outpost. His actions which culminated in the supreme sacrifice of his life were in keeping with the highest traditions of the military service, and reflect great credit on himself and the US Army.

Smith, Elmelindo R. (posthumously)
The Medal of Honor
Vietnam Veterans Memorial Panel 15E Line 51
Rank and organization: Platoon Sergeant (then S/Sgt.) US Army, 1st Platoon, Company C, 2nd Battalion, 8th Infantry, 4th Infantry Division
Place and date: Republic of Vietnam, February 16, 1967
Entered service at: Honolulu, Hawaii
Born: July 27, 1935, Honolulu, Hawaii

For conspicuous gallantry and intrepidity at the risk of his life above and beyond the call of duty. During a reconnaissance patrol, his platoon was suddenly engaged by intense machine-gun fire hemming in the platoon on 3 sides. A defensive perimeter was hastily established, but the enemy added mortar and rocket fire to the deadly fusillade and assaulted the position from several directions. With complete disregard for his safety, P/Sgt. Smith moved through the deadly fire along the defensive line, positioning soldiers, distributing ammunition and encouraging his men to repeal the enemy attack. Struck to the ground by enemy fire which caused a severe shoulder wound, he regained his feet, killed the enemy soldier and continued to move about the perimeter. He was again wounded in the shoulder and stomach but continued moving on his knees to assist in the defense. Noting the enemy massing at a weakened point on the perimeter, he crawled into the open and poured deadly fire into the enemy ranks. As he crawled on, he was struck by a rocket. Moments later, he regained consciousness, and drawing on his fast-dwindling strength, continued to crawl from man to man. When he could move no farther, he chose to remain in the open where he could alert the perimeter to the approaching enemy. P/Sgt. Smith perished, never relenting in his determined effort against the enemy. The valorous acts and heroic leadership of this outstanding soldier inspired those remaining members of his platoon to beat back the enemy assaults. P/Sgt. Smith's gallant actions were in keeping with the highest traditions of the US Army and they reflect great credit upon him and the Armed Forces of his country.

Willett, Louis E. (posthumously)
The Medal of Honor
Vietnam Veterans Memorial Panel 15E Line 37
Rank and organization: Private First Class, US Army, Company C, 1st Battalion, 12th Infantry, 4th Infantry Division
Place and date: Kontum Province, Republic of Vietnam, February 15, 1967
Entered service at: Brooklyn, New York
Born: June 19, 1945, Brooklyn, New York

For conspicuous gallantry and intrepidity at the risk of his life above and beyond the call of duty. Pfc. Willett distinguished himself while serving as a rifleman in Company C, during combat operations. His squad was conducting a security sweep when it made contact with a large enemy force. The squad was immediately engaged with a heavy volume of automatic weapons fire and pinned to the ground. Despite the deadly fusillade, Pfc. Willett rose to his feet firing rapid bursts from his weapon and moved to a position from which he placed highly effective fire on the enemy. His action allowed the remainder of his squad to begin to withdraw from the superior enemy force toward the company perimeter. Pfc. Willett covered the squad's withdrawal, but his position drew heavy enemy machine-gun fire, and he received multiple wounds enabling the enemy again to pin down the remainder of the squad. Pfc. Willett struggled to an upright position, and, disregarding his painful wounds, he again engaged the enemy with his rifle to allow his squad to continue its movement and to evacuate several of his comrades who were by now wounded. Moving from position to position, he engaged the enemy at close range until he was mortally wounded. By his unselfish acts of bravery, Pfc. Willett insured the withdrawal of his comrades to the company position, saving their lives at the cost of his life. Pfc. Willett's valorous actions were in keeping with the highest traditions of the US Army and reflect great credit upon himself and the Armed Forces of his country.

4th Infantry Division Vietnam War

Location of 4th Infantry Division Headquarters in Vietnam
Pleiku, September 1966–February 1968
Dak To, March 1968–April 1968
Pleiku, April 1968–February 1970
An Khe/Pleiku, March 1970–April 1970
An Khe, April 1970–December 1970

4th Infantry Division Commanders in Vietnam

Brigadier General David O. Byars, August 1966
Major General Arthur S. Collins, Jr., September 1966
Major General William R. Peers, January 1967
Major General Charles P. Stone, January 1968
Major General Donn R. Pepke, November 1968
Major General Glenn D. Walker, November 1969
Major General William A. Burke, July 1970
Brigadier General Maurice K. Kendal (acting), December 1970

1st Brigade, 4th Infantry Division Commanders

Colonel Joseph E. Fix III, April 24–October 23, 1968
Colonel Hale H. Knight, October 24, 1968–January 31, 1969

1st Battalion, 8th Infantry Division Commanders

Lieutenant Colonel William W. Tombaugh, March 2–September 1, 1968
Lieutenant Colonel William D. Old, September 2, 1968–January 19, 1969
Lieutenant Colonel William E. Haas, July 1–December 16, 1969
Lieutenant Colonel Allen M. Buckner, January 20–January 31, 1969

February–March 1969, 1/8th Infantry Commanders

Bn XO, Major Donald W. Androsky

Bn S-3, Major John M. Trebbe

Bn S-2, Lieutenant Terry W. Ward

Bn S-3 Air, Captain Garnett L. Jarrett

Company A, Captain David Hockett. Captain Gerald R. Gold (unconfirmed)

Company B, Captain James Deroos

Company C, Captain Stephen J. DeHart. Captain Herbert F. Gagne

Company D, Captain Ted N. Yamashita

Company E, Lieutenant James R. Ghent

1st Battalion, 8th Infantry

2nd Battalion, 8th Infantry (Mechanized)

3rd Battalion, 8th Infantry

1st Battalion, 12th Infantry

2nd Battalion, 12th Infantry (to 25th ID, August 1967–December 1970)

3rd Battalion, 12th Infantry

1st Battalion, 14th Infantry (from 25th ID, August 1967–December 1970)

1st Battalion, 22nd Infantry (Separate, November 1970–January 1972)

2nd Battalion, 22nd Infantry (to 25th ID, August 1967–December 1970)

3rd Battalion, 22nd Infantry (to 25th ID, August 1967–December 1970)

1st Battalion, 35th Infantry (from 25th ID, August 1967–April 1970)

2nd Battalion, 35th Infantry (from 25th ID, August 1967–December 1970)

2nd Battalion, 34th Armor (to 25th ID, August 1967–December 1970)

1st Battalion, 69th Armor (from 25th ID, August 1967–April 1970)

2nd Battalion, 9th Artillery (105 mm) (from 25th ID, August 1967–April 1970)

5th Battalion, 16th Artillery (155 mm)

6th Battalion, 29th Artillery (105 mm)

4th Battalion, 42d Artillery (105 mm)

2d Battalion, 77th Artillery (105 mm) (to 25th ID, August 1967–December 1970)

1st Squadron, 10th Cavalry (Armored) Division Reconnaissance
4th Aviation Battalion
4th Engineer Battalion
4th Medical Battalion
124th Signal Battalion
704th Maintenance Battalion
43rd Chemical Detachment
4th Military Intelligence Company
Dedicated reconnaissance elements
Company E, 20th Infantry (Long Range Patrol)
Company E, 58th Infantry (Long Range Patrol)
Company K (Ranger), 75th Infantry (Airborne)
4th Administration Company
4th Military Police Company
374th Army Security Agency Company
Division Support Command and Band

Decorations of 4th Infantry Division in Vietnam

Presidential Unit Citation (Army) for Pleiku Province (1st Brigade only)
Presidential Unit Citation (Army) for Dak To District (1st Brigade only)
Republic of Vietnam Cross of Gallantry with Palm 1966–1969
Republic of Vietnam Cross of Gallantry with Palm 1969–1970
Republic of Vietnam Civil Action Honor Medal, First Class 1966–1969

Vietnam casualties

2,531 killed in action
15,229 wounded in action

PART 4

GLOBAL WAR ON TERROR

CHAPTER 16

IRAQ: WE GOT SADDAM!

After the Vietnam War the 4th Infantry Division resumed training and became involved in various "Cold War" missions. They were in residence at Fort Carson, Colorado from 1970 until 1995. During this period, the Division experienced a major overhaul and was ironically converted to a mechanized organization as it had been in 1940 before reverting back to an infantry division. Meanwhile they frequently sent units to Europe to continue their Cold War mission of standing against the potential Communist threat. It was during their time in Fort Carson that the Division assumed the nickname, "Ironhorse."

In December 1995, HHQ and several brigades were relocated to Fort Hood, Texas where as part of the downsizing of the US Army the illustrious "Hell on Wheels" 2nd Armored Division was deactivated. Combining five armor battalions of the 2nd Armored Division with four mechanized infantry battalions of the 4th Infantry Division, the Ivy Division again became the experimental division of the Army, as it had been in the early 1940s. Until completing the mission in October 2001, the Ivy men and women led the United States Army into the 21st century under the banner of Force XXI. The 1st BDE (a.k.a. the "Digital Brigade") developed and tested state-of-the-art digital communications equipment, night fighting gear, advanced weaponry, organization, and doctrine to prepare the United States Army for wars in the new century, in addition to being ready to deploy to any hot spot in the world.

After the devastating terrorist attacks of September 11, 2001, The United States military geared up for action in Afghanistan, and other potential locations with the purpose of taking the fight to terrorist breeding grounds. While the 4th ID didn't see any action there when troops were initially deployed, within a year they were preparing to deploy to Iraq for the subsequent phase of the Global War on Terror (GWOT). The new century would be defined by a glut of these acronyms. War would become more precise, more technical and the military would employ every available piece of technology to streamline the procedures and focus on accuracy.

Nevertheless it would still need "boots on the ground" to do the job properly. For the foot soldier it would still entail patrolling, face-to-face contact with potential and actual enemy insurgents and all the risk factors that entails but the latter would now be quantifiable and subject to analysis like never before. The objectives and targets would be meticulously compiled and subjected to military planning on a staggering scale but, as with all conflicts, there would still be casualties. Although the survival rates increased dramatically in contrast to other wars and conflicts of the previous century, there would still be the wounded and the maimed, there would still be those who died and there would still be broken hearts to carry the overwhelming burden of irreplaceable loss of a loved one. Technology has improved some elements of warfare dramatically, but this mutual quasi-symbiotic alignment of machines and people couldn't remove or nullify the emotional toll that war incurs. Some things never change.

For the purposes of this section, the emphasis will be on events that occurred in 2003–2004, which remains to this day one of the most significant deployments the 4th has been assigned in modern times. During that year, the Division settled Tikrit and the Sunni Triangle (using tactics very different than those used in other areas of the country), handled the initial onset of terrorist insurgency, and captured Saddam Hussein. The rest of this section will focus on a few instances of sustainment operations in both Iraq and Afghanistan. Because of the fragmented nature of the Brigade Combat Team concept, it is very difficult to take a close look at every single

4th deployment from 2004–present without producing a separate volume in its own right but that's been the case with every individual section.

When the orders came through for the Ivy men to ship out and join the fight they executed the most rapid deployment of heavy armored forces in history. Lt. Gen. Campbell was part of the team that helped pave the way to catching Saddam Hussein.

Lt. Gen. Donald M. Campbell (then Colonel), 1st Brigade, 4th Infantry Division

Following the invasion our HQ was set up in Tikrit, which was an especially dangerous location due to a high population of regime loyalists and Republican Guard there.

I was at Fort Hood (Texas—Killeen/Waco area) when we got wind something was gonna happen with regard to Iraq in Summer 2002. I was taking part in an exercise at Fort Carson, Colorado when I was called back a day early to meet with Major General Odierno (4th ID CG) about a potential deployment. When I arrived, the Chief of Staff of the Army (Gen Shinseki) was there as part of the discussion, so I knew it was big. Nobody was sure what was gonna happen, but planning cells at 4th ID HQ and the brigades (1st, 2nd, and 3rd) began looking at Iraq-based scenarios (starting Fall 2002) and they were planning down to battalion level. In very late 2002 or early 2003, 4ID were notified of the deployment.

It would include all three brigades (one of which was at Ft. Carson), artillery, division support command, 4th Bde Aviation (Apaches, UH-60, and a division Cav squadron of tanks and Bradleys) along with an attached unit of Engineers (555—Triple-nickel), a platoon of RQ-7 Shadows under 1st Brigade

There really was no plan to invade through Turkey, and it was all part of an elaborate deception to fool the Iraqis. It fooled most people in the Army too. We sat at Fort Hood waiting for word to move out, while ships full of equipment floated aimlessly in the eastern Mediterranean and Red Sea waiting for instructions on where to berth and off-load. I recall that General Odierno was pretty frustrated that we weren't in the fight yet. We watched the invasion on CNN from Fort Hood.

In March, 4th ID was notified to move out, and within a week, we were in Kuwait— Camp Pennsylvania, to be exact (which was closed in 2004). It was the location of the first fragging incident since the Vietnam War, when Sgt Hasan Akbar (from the 101st) threw four grenades into a tent, then fired at his fellow soldiers in the ensuing chaos. Two men were killed and fourteen were wounded. Akbar was sentenced to death, which was appealed in 2015, and reaffirmed. I arrived just after the incident and remembered seeing yellow crime scene tape around the tent where the fragging occurred.

I arrived in Kuwait about 1 April. Odierno wanted 1st, 2nd, and 3rd Bde ready to move north within three weeks. That was later cut in half, then became less than 1 week! Then Odierno said "You're moving out Saturday!" That was the night of 5 April.

1st Bde was selected by Odierno to be the lead brigade. 1st Brigade was the Army's first "digital" brigade, we had all the cool bells and whistles, including "Blue Force Tracker" and FBCB2 (communication platforms designed for commanders to track forces on the battlefield).

Odierno was always impressed with 1st Bde, not just because of our certified status as the first digital brigade, but because we were always on our game. The Division transportation officer was a busy guy, it took the lead elements of the 1st Brigade 44 hours to convoy north and halt at the southern edge of Baghdad. This was due to break spots for refueling that could sometimes last a couple of hours.

Few people had issues with sleep because most soldiers and commanders were "wired!" Adrenaline was high. I remember the MKT (mobile field kitchen) broke down, was left behind, and within 24–48 hours, the Iraqis had stripped it bare.

Coming up through southern Iraq, the 4th ID was generally welcomed by Iraqis. Some people were cheering, others giving a thumbs-up, saying "thank you," etc, but by the time we got to Karbala (south of Baghdad), people were not welcoming us anymore, and we were getting angry glares. I gave the order to lock and load when we got near Baghdad.

South of Baghdad, 4th ID met up with elements of 3rd ID. The next night, we set off for Taji, which was projected to be a logistics hub because of its sizeable runway (Taji was a chemical weapons site and Republican Guard center of gravity during the Saddam era; it is in the Sunni Triangle). This required moving through Baghdad at night, which took 2–3 hours. It was pretty spooky, the power was largely still out because of the "shock and awe" air campaign, so the entire place was dark and looked like a ghost town.

Taji put up some resistance and there was a good fight there. It was our first real gunfight. Samarra was next. The 4th ID left Balad/Taji and elements of the 3rd ID (from Baghdad) backfilled them once the fight ended. The intention was to link up with Marines in Samarra. Fighting in Samarra for another large airfield produced the first Purple Heart in the 4th ID when a soldier was hit with shrapnel. Once Samarra was secured, the 1st Brigade moved for Tikrit. Once established at Tikrit, the big missions became reestablishing governance, restoring utilities and finding bad guys.

I recall that we had to remove all the images of Saddam we could find such as statues, posters, framed portraits, etc. They were everywhere especially in Tikrit—his home town and base of support. At one point, a battalion commander was with his troops on a Saddam-image-removal mission, and noticed a fence that had a poster of his likeness. Convinced he'd seen it removed earlier, he thought about it and realized someone had put it back up. He approached carefully and upon inspection, found a booby trap explosive. It was disabled, but this was a big intelligence indicator that we were starting to face insurgency-like resistance, and was an indicator of what the future might hold.

1st Brigade was the first to get Iraqi freedom fighters. It was one company of about 75–100 men, mostly a part of the Iraqi diaspora from outside the country who came home to fight and get rid of Saddam. "Al," who was an expat from Canada, led them. I remember asking him if he would come back to Iraq with his family to stay after it was stable, his answer was "Hell no." He would go back to Canada. Freedom fighters were integrated with 1st Bde and some were pretty rough with prisoners, which caused some minor headaches for 1st Bde leadership. We had to tell "Al" that his guys needed to be real careful because it could create problems for us. The Freedom fighters participated in raids with the 1st Brigade, rooting out bad guys in the "Card Deck" and other Ba'ath Party sympathizers. They ended up getting one individual in Ad Dawar, in the forties on the Iraqi card deck. This was a big deal because in most cases these HVTs (High Value Targets) were captured by Special Forces not regular Army troops.

Elements of the 1st Bde surrounded Ad Dawar upon an intelligence tip-off and rounded up all military-age men. A man looking like Al-Douri was captured, but we weren't sure it was him. The 1st Brigade S3 (Maj. Mike Sullivan) and his Iraqi counterparts struggled with identification, but 4th ID HQ ultimately confirmed Al-Douri's identity. It was an exciting moment for 1st Brigade and the Iraqi freedom fighters, they were thrilled!

In coordination with the initiatives designed to tackle the Global War on Terror the 4th Infantry Division received orders to deploy in late 2002 under the command of Major General Ray Odierno. Elements intended for this deployment consisted of units primarily based at Fort Hood, Texas, and Fort Carson, Colorado.

During the preparatory stages, the 4th were ordered to enter Iraq from the north through Turkey, but in anticipation of the volatile Turkish government denying US troops this route, cargo ships had been positioned in the Mediterranean Sea. Meanwhile troops were waiting for word on where they'd stage in southeast Turkey prior to entering the combat zone. By the time the Turks had denied access to the northern route, the 3rd ID had already "crossed the berm" from Kuwait into Iraq, and they were beginning to engage in combat. Soon after, the 4th's cargo ships were diverted and traveled through the Red Sea to Kuwait, followed simultaneously by the personnel elements.

Within a week, the 4th crossed into Iraq, ultimately traveling through Baghdad, seeing brief action at Taji and Balad. They eventually settled in Saddam Hussein's hometown of Tikrit, to the north of Baghdad.

Cody Hoefer deployed to Iraq with the 4th ID during the initial push into Iraq, as well as a subsequent deployment in later years. He appeared on the cover of *Time* Magazine in 2003.

Cody Hoefer, 1/22nd Infantry Regiment, 4th Infantry Division

At 17 I began my Army time assigned to the 163rd, a National Guard unit in Montana. In mid-2000 I became an infantryman (11M mechanized infantry—Bradley vehicles) my MO was merged with 11B (light infantry), and everyone became "infantry." After 9/11, I decided to go on to active duty and was sent to Bosnia in 2002. I requested assignment at Fort Hood, because I knew they were about to get deployed to Iraq. I was assigned to 1/22 Infantry.

A week and a half after arriving at Fort Hood, I was in Kuwait (May 2003 time frame) where I took some training, and headed north to join the rest of the 4th ID. I recall seeing body bags being dropped off by C-130s, which left quite an impression on me. The 4th was already near Tikrit when I got on site; HQ was already set up there. I was a combat replacement for people who had gotten hurt or were being added to existing forces to beef up the strength of our unit. Many showed up to Kuwait without weapons and about 50% went without them for the entire 2-hour drive to Tikrit. They still had gun trucks on their convoys but it was nerve wracking. When we got to Tikrit, we were finally issued weapons. On arrival at battalion the sergeant major split the group up and assigned people to different companies (A, B, C, HQ) respectively. The Sergeant Major needed a new driver but I told him in no uncertain terms "I don't wanna be no damn driver!" I'd always been an infantryman throughout my whole service. When we saw drivers we used to say "Oh, look at that asshole! I don't wanna be THAT guy." Anyway I ended up being Steve Russell's driver for my whole deployment. During Operation Iraqi Freedom, Steve Russell, currently a Congressman, commanded the 1st Battalion, 22nd Infantry.

I spent about two weeks learning about communications equipment he wasn't familiar with such as FBCB2 computer systems battle tracking, staff orientation, how to perform command and control and send messages to Lieutenant Colonel Steve Russell's driver if he wasn't in the vehicle. It was more than just talking on a radio and driving.

Over the next few weeks there was a shift in the community. Instead of people waving and smiling and being nice, it went to a more ominous tone. We began asking "Are they tired of us already?" Then we got into a firefight. Russell was doing a visit to a checkpoint around curfew time when a massive explosion resonated while we were heading south, distinctly RPG. The next step was to go cut them off. I saw an ambulance and knew that some of them were being used to escort insurgents into hot zones.

Russell told me to turn left by the ambulance—all in blackout (no lights). We saw a Toyota Love pickup come around a corner opposite us also in blackout. We could make out the silhouette of a guy in the back with an AK-47. We knew what was going to go down.

We knew there were no Iraqi police officers rolling around like that. Russell said, "STOP THEM!" There was some confusion over what that meant. We decided to ram the truck as it headed directly toward them. I was launched forward (nobody was wearing seatbelts) and hit my head on the windshield, which caused some minor bleeding. I looked at Russell to make sure he was OK, but he wasn't in his seat. Sergeant Major Martinez told me, "If the colonel's dead, you better be dead beside him."

Lt Brian Luke (riding in the back seat) was launched into the front end of the vehicle where the radios are located. I heard Russell's initial gunshots. I pulled myself up as the vehicle began receiving return fire and I saw several tracers began flying past. I brought my M-16A4 rifle over the top of the windshield and began to fire with one hand to provide suppressing fire. A street fight ensued and I saw muzzle flashes from Russell's rifle on the passenger side of the vehicle hitting the right flank of the enemy truck. Then I dismounted and set up next to the driver's side, careful to give Lt Luke enough room to get out and set up to begin firing. I went through 3 magazines on single-shot mode (M-16 has two modes—single-shot, and 3-shot burst). I hit the passenger of the vehicle. Another guy went down beside him, and that individual used the body of his buddy as a shield. I thought he's not a sandbag, so bullets will go through him. On my right peripheral, I saw Russell get up and start walking around to get at the back of the enemy vehicle so I followed with similar movement to the left. Another truck came up behind me that was part of our original convoy and driven by my buddy Garcia. Garcia jumped out and began moving up with me, Russell and Luke. Then things got very quiet. My legs felt like they were full of concrete, it took a conscious effort to make them work. I didn't know who was dead or who was alive, so I popped off a round into the engine block of the enemy truck to see if anyone moved in response. Nobody moved, but we discovered a guy hiding around the back corner.

All were dead except for one enemy who had between 30–50 rounds in him and was remarkably enough still alive! We were obliged to render aid to the injured man who was laying in gasoline. Garcia said we needed to get him away from the leaking gas, he was very heavy, but we managed to lift him on to the sidewalk. His arm was so destroyed, only attached by some sinews that it began to separate from his body. Then a US medic came up and said, "I can't do anything for him." Russell said, "Try and make it easy on him, do the best you can." The individual ended up dying about 20 minutes after we got him on the sidewalk. Quick reaction force Charlie Company arrived and secured the area to allow for easier intel gathering.

My group was among the first to encounter IEDs. Several of my buddies and people I knew in other units had gotten gravely injured. We would often use our convoys as IED "bait" to draw out the insurgents because our Humvees were a lot faster than many of the other vehicles. Many times we'd draw fire, but other times not, the running joke became "Always take a right turn, never take a left turn,"—every time we took a left turn, something bad happened.

On one occasion we took a right turn and drove right past an IED. It was down in a storm drain. After the second vehicle behind ours passed the IED location, it went off, the third truck had not reached the site yet because it was lagging behind a bit. My first reaction was "Oh, SHIT!" because up to this point we'd only heard rumors about IEDs in Baghdad and mines being used on buses. We couldn't see the third truck from our position, so we got out and began looking for it and the trigger man. It quickly became clear the third truck was OK, and the IED hadn't hit anything because of the placement in the storm drain, the blast went straight up and did no damage but it made us pucker a little. We couldn't find the triggerman, but knew he must have been listening, so we began yelling at him in Arabic: "You dumbass! Figure out what you're doing before you bring your game back!"

During another IED incident, our Charlie Company Commander was hit. We'd gone back out afterwards to do some sensitive site exploitation, find out what they were using and how they were being made. To this day, Steve Russell thinks that particular bomb was made for our vehicle. There were two IEDs, one hit the C Co Commander, but the other didn't go off. The bomb was hidden behind the concrete curb, and it was a good one. We'd parked our trucks right next to it and didn't even know. Russell was doing a press interview and said, "You're usually looking for wires sticking out, ball bearings, anything out of the ordinary, etc." Then the reporter looked down and said, "You mean kind of like the one we're standing next to?" The reporter had found the second bomb. We soon evacuated the area. Because we were so short on Explosive Ordinance Disposal teams, we ended up detonating it ourselves with our own small-arms fire, a single M-16 round accompanied by a tracer would usually take out an IED. On this occasion it blew the crap out of the storefronts. I was peppered with debris on the other side of the road where I was performing security detail.

Over time the IED thing became so repetitive and annoying. One gets sick of it. You look at dead animals, trash, rocks, etc. You become deadened and complacent to the threat. By the time of the end of the deployment, guys would stop to investigate a potential threat, kick the suspicious item and say, "it's clear, let's go." Complacency is bad. We worked with local trash pickup people to get them to pick up all the debris along the road so our soldiers wouldn't have to. I deployed to Iraq for a second time in 2004 after being promoted to sergeant.

Following the initial deployment and invasion of Iraq, the US Army made significant changes to precisely how they deployed. A new concept known as the Brigade Combat Team (BCT) concept was introduced, which was intended to structure small "pieces" of larger divisions into fully autonomous units, like a division in miniature (typically led by a colonel). This led to the "piecemealing" of large divisions (such as the 4th) and assigning brigade-sized units to a command element that might be similarly "piecemealed" from another large division (such as the 101st). This concept effectively did away with the deployment of large divisions, as was done during the initial 2003 invasion of Iraq, and led to conglomerations of combat power from different divisions under a single commanders.

When the BCT concept was implemented, small units of the 4th ID deployed to Iraq and Afghanistan. This meant that at any given time, some element of the 4th was deployed.'

During sustainment operations in Iraq and Afghanistan, this is how the Army deployed, this was radically different to how they did things during the initial invasion, when the entire 4th deployed.

One of their missions would lead to the capture of notorious Iraqi dictator Saddam Hussein. Following the collapse of Hussein's regime, the 4th Infantry Division occupied the area in and around Hussein's family home of Tikrit, also deployed throughout the area in the summer of 2003. Several tactical HUMINT (Human Intelligence) teams consisting of US Army interrogators, counterintelligence agents, and interpreters, interacted with local Iraqi citizens on a daily basis, generating a vast amount of information about Hussein's previously undisclosed family network. Although many high-ranking Iraqi officials and Hussein family members had been caught, the US forces were still no closer to catching Hussein himself because his political power base was fractured and dispersed when the Iraqi regime tumbled. Army Intelligence personnel realized that capturing political leaders was not the best way of discovering the whereabouts of Saddam Hussein.

Instead, analysts needed to focus on Hussein's personal connections. Intelligence analysts with the 4th Infantry Division's 1st Brigade Combat Team developed a process of elimination that became known as the "Three Tier Strategy" which was based around five families who had personally known Hussein since his youth.

Army Intelligence personnel with the 1st BCT and Special Operations Task Force 121 created "Link Analysis Diagrams" that depicted Hussein's network. They began with personal relationships between his closest confidantes and family members. As individuals were captured or detained, interrogations revealed further connections, all of which were plotted on the diagrams. Raids of suspects' homes netted additional evidence of unexpected connections in the network. On the basis of all the fresh information collected by painstaking research from various sources, Army intelligence personnel soon homed in on the Al-Muslit brothers, members of Hussein's inner circle of bodyguards.

According to Master Sergeant James Ferguson, former Intelligence Analyst with the 4th Infantry Division, "The Muslit family was the key as far as they provided all the inner circle of bodyguards. We did a raid on Omar Al-Muslit, who was the patriarch of the family on his farm and that provided us with a ton of pictures of who these people were. So we actually now had something to look for."

On October 11, the youngest Al-Muslit brother was apprehended and transferred to the 4th Infantry Division. During interrogation, he revealed that Basim Latif, the driver and close friend of Ibrahim Al-Muslit, was one of the few people Hussein trusted, and could therefore be a possible key to finding his location. Basim, previously interviewed and released, was returned for further questioning. During the interrogation, he finally revealed Ibrahim Al-Muslit's current location and confirmed that he reported directly to Saddam Hussein. This was the proverbial spark intel needed.

Events began to gather momentum after the Basim interrogation. Early in the morning on December 13, 2003, Task Force 121 raided one of the locations provided by Basim and captured Ibrahim Al-Muslit. "We knew we were close," Ferguson said. "One of the task forces had captured Ibrahim Al-Muslit, and that's the one everybody was tracking as being the key." During interrogation, Ibrahim finally revealed that Hussein was hiding at a farm in Ad Dawr, south of Tikrit. Later that evening as part of Operation *Red Dawn*, the 1st Brigade Combat Team and Task Force 121 targeted two farmhouses near the Tigris River. The initial search failed to locate Hussein, but two cooperating HUMINT sources eventually revealed his actual hiding spot.

On the evening of December 3, the 1st BCT (Brigade Combat Team) command group set out at 1800 hours en route to the attack position in a walled corn granary, about 4 miles from the "Iron horse" FOB (Forward Operating Base). A platoon from the BRT (Brigade Reconnaissance Troop) secured the attack position prior to their arrival. Shortly after the arrival of the command group, the second Brigade Reconnaissance Troop platoon arrived. At approximately 1845 hours, the assault teams and HQ elements from SOF arrived at the assault position.

The assault team leaders conducted final coordination with the BRT platoon leaders. Final checks and last-minute inspections were complete. At approximately 1945 hours there was a power cut in Ad Dawr. The city was reduced to almost total darkness, which was to the task force's advantage because it helped to conceal their movements as they entered the city. There was no civilian traffic along Highway 24. The force entered the objective area at 1955 hours. G Troop established the inner cordon while 4-42 Field Artillery established checkpoints both north and south along Highway 24, in order to prevent all traffic from entering or leaving the city.

Upon the establishment of the inner cordon, SOF (Special Operations Forces) began to search and exploit both objectives. The combined BCT and SOF command post was positioned in the south with observation of the soldiers on both objectives but at that time there was nothing significant to report. The lead SOF assault team accompanied by Cpt. Bailey with 1st Platoon, G Troop moved directly to the palm groves to search for a reported underground hiding place. Source 1 led the assault team to a mud hut. One of the occupants at the location attempted to flee, but was immediately detained. Another occupant vehemently denied knowing anything about Saddam Hussein and attempted to lead the assault team away from the objective. Before he could do so, Source 1 identified and pointed out the location of a potential hiding position near the edge of the orchard. The assault team cleared the entrance to the hole of dirt, debris, and mats, and removed the Styrofoam insert. Converging on the newly revealed location, Task Force 121 discovered the concealed hole in which the former dictator was hiding.

The person inside the hole put his hands in the air and responded to the question, "Who are you?" with "I am Saddam Hussein, the President of Iraq, and I am willing to negotiate." With that, a soldier from the assault team responded with, "President Bush sends his regards," and Saddam Hussein was pulled from the hole. After a search of the area, a helicopter landed and evacuated Saddam Hussein. By 2015 hours, initial reports of a "Jackpot" were sent to Raider 6. At 2026 hours "Jackpot" was confirmed. Col. Hickey (3rd Battalion Commander) and the SOF (Special Operations Forces) commander were less than 200 meters away from Saddam's location when the word, "Jackpot" came to them. The leaders shared a smile, and a quick hug acknowledging the historic event, and then their total focus was on preparing for the rapid evacuation of High Value Target No. 1 (HVT #1) and the expected enemy response, which never came. Col. Hickey was able to quietly inform Command Sergeant Major Wilson of the capture. Raider 7 responded with his signature smile. In the meantime, A/1-10 CAV had successfully moved into the area north of Ad Dawr, significantly increasing the security of the assault elements. With that, the 1BCT command group moved up to the objective area. After congratulating the soldiers, Raider 6 and his command team secured $750,000 discovered on the objective. The SOF detained the remaining two occupants of the mud hut. The operation demonstrated the BCT's ability to act swiftly on intelligence and to plan, coordinate, and execute on a moment's notice. The capture made headline news around the world, and it was all made possible thanks to the indomitable Ivy men.

Captain Dez Bailey, 4th ID G5, 1st Brigade Golf Troop

We were on the objective with the call signs "Wolverine 1" and "Wolverine 2." The place Saddam was thought to be hiding was a dangerous location. High ground on three sides and a river on the other, we were in a bowl. With the platoon leaders we secured all the high ground. The concern was that there were sympathizers in the area who might figure out something was happening or happened already. This might provoke retaliation attacks. We had the element of surprise. It was also a large effort with numerous teams around several houses, with two units of air cover, backup in reserve with an outer cordon set up, robustly outside the small area we figured Saddam was in. It went like this. At 1300 we received notification that a capture op was going to happen so between that time and 1600 we began refitting and rearming. We were not happy because it was my unit's day off because we'd just been out in the western desert for 30 days. Some of my guys said "Man, here it is my day off and I'm doing this damn raid."

I was in Beiji and got a phone call from 1st Brigade Commander Lt. Gen. (then Colonel) Don Campbell that said "get down here, we're doing a raid tonight that's of utmost importance. He brought everyone back down to Tikrit.

At around 1600 we drove close to the objective and linked up with the SOF (Special Operations Force) and then the planning efforts commenced, followed by back-briefs on the plan to our superiors. At 2000 we drove to site and arrived at the objective. While SOF was going after Saddam, my guys provided a secure cordon.

I saw the pretty much the entire thing. I remember thinking "Well, I think we got him." I actually witnessed Saddam's removal from the hole but it was from a short distance away. We found Saddam in a hole, snatched him out, and brought him away—it was fairly anti-climactic. I had envisioned a big gun battle similar to when Qusay and Uday Hussein were killed by the 101st. Saddam was out in 30 minutes.

If they'd waited 2–3 days to put together some kind of elaborate plan, it would never have happened correctly, we may not have gotten Saddam at all. After Saddam was captured, one soldier said "Does this mean we need to go home?" Press knew of capture about 24 hours later. After the capture there was RADIO SILENCE on the way back to Brigade compound and no one was allowed to get on internet, etc.

US President George Bush warmly congratulated the combined efforts that led to the capture and detainment of Saddam. He said "Yesterday, December the 13th, at around 8:30 p.m. Baghdad time, United States military forces captured Saddam Hussein alive. He was found near a farmhouse outside the city of Tikrit in a swift raid conducted without casualties. And now the former dictator of Iraq will face the justice he denied to millions."

Saddam may have been apprehended but the trouble was far from over. On Easter Sunday, March 23, 2008, tension rose again in Baghdad. Up until that juncture attack rates, which had been reduced by 63% between September 2007 and February 2008 began increasing during the closing days of March. Sadr City was recognized as the primary source of this dramatic increase in mortar and rocket attacks. IED, small arms, and indirect fire attacks were launched against the Multi National Defense Bagdad and Iraqi Security Forces bases. The attacks also targeted convoys, and patrols at with a frequency and intensity which had not been experienced since early in 2007. Through April into mid-May, MND-B forces built a dividing wall that effectively separated the southern portion of Sadr City from the volatile northern section and systematically set about eradicating the insurgents. The result was a new level of calm for the entire city of Baghdad and by early summer, the uprising of the Jaysh al-Mahdi militia was stopped.

The emphasis now turned to the eventual handover of the security in Iraq to indigenous Iraqi Security Forces. That was accomplished on schedule with the ISF taking lead as the New Year came in. On January 31, 2009, successful provincial elections were conducted, without a significant enemy attack on election day. A few weeks later, the 4ID once again returned to Fort Hood, ending their third deployment to Iraq since 2003.

KIA figures for the three deployments to Iraq:

2003–2004 4ID/Task Force Ironhorse soldiers	84
2005–2006 4ID/Multi-National Division—Baghdad soldiers	235
2007–2009 4ID/Multi-National Division—Baghdad soldiers	13

CHAPTER 17

AFGHANISTAN

After initial deployments to Iraq in 2003, the 4th ID (along with other large US Army units) was deployed in smaller units under the "Brigade Combat Team" system. Small units were detached from the 4th and deployed to augment other units in theater under a non-4th ID commander (this is known as one unit being "chopped" to another). While the construct was effective in terms of combat power, large divisions have not regularly deployed as one unit as they did in previous conflicts and the initial stages of the Iraq War.

On June 18, 2004, soon after their return to the US from Iraq, Major General James D. Thurman assumed command of the 4th Infantry Division. The Division was again subject to massive reorganization, forming combined arms battalions consisting of infantry, armor, and engineer companies, with support units also assigned in each unit. The Division now had the possibility to field a 4th Brigade Combat Team, which brought the total strength of the Division to just over 20,000 personnel. In July 2009, Major General David Perkins took command to become the 56th commanding general of the 4th Infantry Division. With this change of command, even more significant events happened as the 4th Infantry Division ended its residence at Fort Hood, and returned to Fort Carson, where it had served from late 1970 through late 1995. Immediately, the Division's brigades started preparing for their next return to combat.

In 2004, the 1st Brigade, 4th Infantry Division was reorganized and redesignated as the 1st Brigade Combat Team, 4th Infantry Division.

The 4th Forward Support Battalion was reorganized and redesignated as the 4th Brigade Support Battalion and, along with the 4th Battalion, 42nd Field Artillery, was reassigned to the 1st Brigade Combat Team, 4th Infantry Division. Engineer, military intelligence, military police, and signal elements were incorporated into a new brigade special troops battalion.

January 2006, the 1st Brigade Combat Team (Raider), 4th Infantry Division was operating in Camp Taji, an Army base approximately 10 miles northwest of Baghdad, fulfilling their second rotation in support of Operation *Iraqi Freedom*. Then in May 2009, soldiers of the 4th BCT deployed in support of Operation *Enduring Freedom* and became the first Ivy soldiers to enter the war in Afghanistan. They deployed in July 2010 and operated in two regional commands in the south and west of Afghanistan. Combined Task Force Raider fought and trained side by side with the Afghan National Security Forces (ANSF) and International Security Assistance Forces (ISAF) partners from Herat and Farah to Kandahar and Arghandab. The 4th Infantry Division was faced yet again with another conflict, new rules and new terrain but even though technological advances had made some things considerably easier, the experience of the soldier-in-the-field didn't differ all that much from other wars and conflicts. It was still kill or be killed. It was still the fight to suppress rising panic and trepidation that has been fought by every soldier preparing to go into battle. In that respect 1st Lieutenant (later Captain) Antonio Salinas would concur that he was no different than any other soldier who had gone before him.

It was within this framework that Antonio Salinas deployed to Afghanistan in 2010. Salinas became an infantry officer because he wanted to know what it was like to go to combat. During school, Salinas discovered that he was being assigned to the 4th Infantry Division and that his unit would be going to Afghanistan soon after he reported to 4th Brigade Combat Team (BCT), 2/12th Infantry, 2nd Battalion, 12th Infantry Regiment. Some veterans were assigned with him, and Salinas would be the grateful recipient of a lot of useful information thanks to them.

In August 2008 he reported to Ft Carson but they didn't have a platoon for him yet, so he went to Battalion S-3 plans for a couple of months to learn how to set up rifle ranges, and prepare for combat training. In October 2008 he finally got his platoon—Delta Company (a heavy weapons platoon), which consisted of 20 men, occasionally augmented with extra personnel when necessary. They were deployed to Kunar Province in Afghanistan in May 2009.

Before his deployment Salinas confronted some concerns as most soldiers have done in the past. He would have felt the same trepidation that his companions would have felt when they were told that insurgent and Taliban forces had attacked and swarmed into American company-sized outposts in the past. Nevertheless Salinas was confident that on the basis of his intense preparation and training he and his team would be up to the job. Apart from the inevitable weapons training the Army taught him an additional skill, how to deal with people. He met Afghan interpreters who told him not to trust anyone.

Captain Antonio Salinas Platoon Leader in 2/12th Infantry, 4th ID

I left a little earlier than the rest of my battalion as part of an "advance team" and was deployed as "temporary company Executive Officer to help get everything set up. Once I arrived "in-country" I took over as platoon leader. In May I'd left Fort Carson, Colorado, stopped off in Maine, Germany, and ultimately Manas Air Base, Kyrgyzstan. Manas is regarded as the gateway where one can see the Hindu Kush to the south and just over those hills is Afghanistan.

Then I spent a couple days at Bagram Air Base, north of Kabul before going on to Jalalabad, which was in closer proximity to the front. The size and magnitude of Bagram was extremely impressive.

It was at this point that I hopped a Chinook to depart Jalalabad and go to Forward Operating Base (FOB) Blessing where Battalion HQ was. It was a nighttime movement. Blessing was a "blackout FOB" because mountains surrounded it. I couldn't see the terrain when I was there, this was very disorienting. I awoke the next morning in stuffy barracks, and stepped outside to see stunning mountains. It was very rugged terrain. I immediately understood why the Russians couldn't take this place. It's as dangerous as it is beautiful and I knew that we were in for one hell of a fight.

The Combat Outpost (COP) Michigan where company HQ was located was 10km down the road. Just south of COP Michigan was the Korengal Valley. COP Able Main was just to the east of Michigan. My COP was COP Honaker Miracle, named after a couple fallen men from the 173rd. FOB Asadabad was a few miles away at the confluence of the Pech River and Kunar River. Even though these places were all only a couple miles away from each other, they felt like they were in different states. I stayed at FOB Blessing for a day just absorbing and making notes in my journal, talking to soldiers about their combat experience when suddenly I heard a huge "BOOM" and got up to sprint to my quarters to put on my body armor, but after looking around, I realized nobody was reacting. I realized that's what "outgoing" sounded like.

After that I went to COP Michigan and the following day got right into routine tasks, like weapons accountability with my platoon. The second morning I was there we got shot at. It was a whole different world. We responded to incoming fire with machine guns and 120mm heavy mortars. I heard the whip-snap of a round overhead—some of the dirt fell on my helmet and everything appeared to slow down. This is called auditory exclusion. It hit me then that despite all the training and studying to prepare for this moment, I realized, you cannot replicate fear or the human instinct of self-preservation.

I spent another week at COP Michigan and ended up being in contact with the enemy between 6 and 11 times. After some administrative items and discussions with my company commander I was convoyed to Honaker Miracle. When I arrived, only one of my squad leaders and a few solders were there (in addition to the unit they were replacing, who was preparing to leave) most of my platoon wouldn't get there for another week. My first day on Honaker Miracle, we took mortar fire. Gunfire is one thing—I thought maybe I could live through it if I got tagged—but when mortars land 100m from you with a sickening "Whump" it's something different. The best way to describe being shot at in general in the face of battle is like being in a car going 80mph and you have to slam on your brakes, coming just inches from an accident, it's a climax of fear and invigoration. That sense of "almost-dying" is replicated several times per week, for a year. Being an officer while you're under fire is particularly difficult because you end up asking yourself questions such as can we stay here? Are we outgunned? How much ammo do we have? Is there air support available? If someone does get shot, where is the hot-landing zone (HLZ) gonna be? You get used to the stress, the officer is the eye of the storm, you have to be, you're in charge. The officer can't scream and panic, he has to be cool.

Our mission was to train Afghan National Police (who we were partnered with) on how to patrol, keep order, etc, separate the bad guys from the good guys, mounted movement, fire missions, interaction with the locals, presence, develop the capability of the local National Afghan Security forces. My personal goals were to bring everyone home alive, kill as many bad guys as possible and help as many good people as possible.

My COP Honaker Miracle had two US platoons and one company of Afghan National Army. Our first big engagement occurred in June. The mission was to take an 8-vehicle convoy 2km north then walk to a village called Qatar Kala. We started to get incoming rounds when we were dismounting near Qatar Kala. I could hear the snap-crack of rounds coming in overhead. We made it to the village and remained in enemy contact. I thought,

"Wow, they have all kinds of weapons and firepower." It was a difficult fight and felt I had underestimated my enemy. Being in command is like sipping wine, you get a little bit of a buzz but you can't forget the risks to your men, your supply, etc. unlike a rifleman, which is more like a shot of Jack Daniels, you can embrace the violence. When we arrived back at COP Honaker Miracle about 1800, one of my guys asked me what I thought about the experience, and I replied that it was fucking amazing.

Intel reported that a combat logistics patrol was coming in bringing fuel, water, ammo supply trucks, contracted haulers and a force had to convoy out to do a cover mission to make sure there was no ambush between COP Honaker Miracle and Asadabad. We set up and didn't see anything over several hours. During the drive back to Honaker Miracle, suddenly the ground just exploded. I saw an incoming tracer and thought, why is that tracer going so slow? It was an incoming RPG round and it impacted right next to my vehicle. Sounded like the gates of hell were opening. I shouted "Push through!" We were about 3km from Honaker Miracle. Later on, after we had swapped vehicles we went back out. I could see friendlies on the high ground (appeared to be an Afghan National Police force)— we could see a whole squad. It turned out they were not friendlies, they were actually Taliban. These were supposed to be good guys, the gunners said "What do we do?" I replied "Fuckin take 'em." We fired 50 cal, M240, and 120mm mortars from the COP, plus Air Force assets dropped 100-lb bombs. The battle damage assessment the next day assessed our contact as successful. There was blood and gear, but the bodies had been dragged off.

Afghanistan taught me humility as a westerner, winning hearts and minds and wanting to make a difference is tough because the reality is that the Taliban owns the ground. We only owned what our direct weapons could touch. My analogy for Iraq and Afghanistan is that it's like a cactus—prickly, hard, and ugly. Can you grow grass in the desert? Yes, with lots of water and topsoil but the second the outside resources are removed, the grass dies and the cactuses come back.

Staff Sgt. Clinton Romesha, B Troop, 3-61 Cavalry, 4th Brigade Combat Team, 4th Infantry Division
Medal of Honor

The Soldier earned the medal for actions Oct. 3, 2009, at Combat Outpost Keating in Afghanistan. On that morning, Combat Outpost, or COP, Keating, manned by only 53 Soldiers and situated at the bottom of a steep valley, came under attack by as many as 400 Taliban fighters. During the fight, the perimeter of COP Keating was breached by the enemy. Romesha, who was injured in the battle, led the fight to protect the bodies of fallen Soldiers, provide cover to those Soldiers seeking medical assistance, and reclaim the American outpost that would later be deemed "tactically indefensible."

Staff Sergeant Ty Michael Carter, Bravo Troop, 3rd Squadron, 61st Cavalry Regiment, 4th Brigade Combat Team
Medal of Honor

In May of 2009, Carter deployed for 12 months to Nuristan Province, Afghanistan. In October 2010, Carter was stationed at Fort Lewis, Wash., and joined Alpha Troop, 8th Squadron, 1st Cavalry Regiment, 2nd Stryker Brigade Combat Team, 2nd Infantry Division. In May 2012, he deployed to Kandahar City, Afghanistan.

While on his first deployment in Afghanistan, Carter was stationed at Combat Outpost (COP) Keating in Kamdesh District, Nuristan Province. On October 3, 2009, the outpost came under heavy attack and Carter, then a specialist, distinguished himself in what came to be known as the Battle of Kamdesh.

According to the detailed Official Narrative from the U.S. Army, more than 300 enemy fighters attacked COP Keating from surrounding high ground before 6 a.m. Under intense fire, Carter carried ammunition 100 meters across open ground from near his barracks to a Humvee at the south Battle Position, soon returning across the same distance to retrieve machine gun oil and more ammunition, and traverse that distance a third time to thus resupply the Battle Position. Though wounded within the first half-hour of battle, Carter provided accurate fire under intense pressure to drive back enemy that had infiltrated the camp perimeter. He then crawled under continuing fire to another vehicle, and retrieved needed weapons and ammunition to bring back to the Battle Position. Carter crossed 30 meters of open space to provide life-extending first aid to a wounded soldier, exposed to enemy fire, then carrying him back across the 30 meters to the Humvee. As the battle progressed, Carter ran toward the tactical operations center (TOC) to coordinate reconnaissance and to obtain medical care for the wounded soldier, but, encountering the body of a fallen sergeant, found and retrieved a radio and returned to the Humvee. Carter found a litter, and with a comrade carried the wounded soldier 100 meters across the original distance to an aid station; it was then about noon. The battle extended through nightfall when reinforcements could safely land by helicopter, by which time almost two-thirds of the 53 Coalition soldiers had been killed or wounded.

President Barack Obama awarded Carter with the Medal of Honor in a White House ceremony on August 26, 2013. The following day, Carter was inducted into the Pentagon Hall of Heroes

In addition to the Medal of Honor, Carter's military awards include the Purple Heart, the Meritorious Service Medal, the Army commendation Medal (with 4 oak leaf clusters), the Army Achievement Medal (with 2 oak leaf clusters), the Army Good Conduct Medal, the Navy/Marine Corps Good Conduct Medal, the National Defense Service Medal, the Afghanistan Campaign Medal (with two campaign stars), the Global War on Terrorism Service Medal, the Noncommissioned Officer Professional Development Ribbon (with numeral 2 device), the Army Service Ribbon, the Overseas Service Ribbon, the NATO Medal, the Combat Action Badge, the Expert Infantryman Badge, and the Air Assault Badge. He is also authorized to wear the Valorous Unit Award and the Meritorious Unit Commendation.

Carter is currently stationed as a staff noncommissioned officer with the 7th Infantry Division.

Captain Florent Groberg Headquarters and Headquarters Company, 4th Infantry Brigade Combat Team, 4th Infantry Division
Medal of Honor

In November 2009, he deployed to Afghanistan as part of Task Force Lethal, with responsibility for the Pech River Valley in Afghanistan's Kunar Province. Upon returning home in June 2010, he continued serving as a platoon leader until he was reassigned as an infantry company executive officer from October 2010 to November 2011. He was then assigned as the brigade personal security detachment commander for 4th Infantry Brigade Combat Team, 4th Infantry Division. He deployed again to Kunar Province, Afghanistan, in February of 2012, with Task Force Mountain Warrior. He was promoted to captain in July 2012. As a result of his actions, Groberg sustained the loss of 45 to 50 percent of his left calf muscle with significant nerve damage, a blown eardrum, and a mild traumatic brain injury. Groberg spent his recovery at Walter Reed National Military Medical Center from August 2012 through May 2015. He was medically retired from Company B Warriors, Warrior Transition Battalion, as a captain, July 23, 2015.

Groberg's awards and decorations include the Bronze Star Medal with one Bronze Oak Leaf Cluster, the Purple Heart, the Meritorious Service Medal, the Army Commendation Medal, the Army Achievement Medal with one Bronze Oak Leaf Cluster, the Afghanistan Campaign Medal with three Bronze Service Stars; the Global War on Terrorism Medal, the National Defense Service Medal, the Army Service Ribbon, the Overseas Service Ribbon, the NATO Medal, the Combat Infantryman Badge, the US Army Parachutists Badge, the US Army Ranger Tab, and the Meritorious Unit Commendation.

Groberg currently resides in the National Capital Region and is a civilian employee of the Department of Defense.

EPILOGUE

Many historians and writers back in the day referred to World War I as the *war to end all wars*, but just 21 years after it had occurred the world was at war again, and this time there would be more civilian casualties than ever before. Writing a 100-year history of one division that participated in both of these and a few others has been a great challenge and an incredible journey.

The more I read about this division the greater my esteem grew for their achievements. Einstein said, *"The world is a dangerous place, not because of those who do evil, but because of those who look on and do nothing."* The 4th Infantry Division never looked on and did nothing. They went where they were sent and always did the job that they were expected to do. Honoré de Balzac wrote in *La Peau de chagrin* (1831):

> *Must not the spell be strong indeed that makes us undergo such horrid sufferings so hostile to our weak frames, sufferings that encircle every strong passion with a hedge of thorns?*

These horrid sufferings are the cement that bonds veterans past and present. The esprit de corps that exists between those who serve and have served in the 4th can only be forged in shared experience. A person in the field would prefer to hear "I got your back" over any command.

Since the end of World War II, around 250 armed conflicts have occurred in no fewer than 155 locations around the world. During the 20th century, 190 million deaths were directly and indirectly attributed to war, which is more than in all the previous four centuries combined.

The nature of war has changed dramatically over the last century and the emphasis of the causes has changed from political or empirical aspirations to those who claim to be waging war because of distorted, bellicose religious convictions. There will be other wars and other reasons for waging war but it won't make a great deal of difference to those in the field. The soldiers don't start wars, they just do what they can to help to end them.

Corpulent port-swilling generals of World War I complacently moved pieces on maps like they were pieces on a chessboard and rarely displayed any altruistic aspirations for the wellbeing of the men in the trenches. Their colleagues may have considered these men as stoic and sturdy patriots, but to those who received heartbreaking telegrams informing of a loved one killed or wounded in battle, these generals were emotionally bankrupt and severely lacking in any tactical erudition. Consequently men died in their thousands.

The emphasis here, as in previous volumes, is not on the opinions of politicians or generals but the experiences of those who did the fighting. They are the ones that matter, they are the ones who selflessly experience things that transcend our own meager existence. There are still people out there resisting aggression and anarchy who have earned and deserve our gratitude and respect. The 4th Infantry Division is much more than just a title for a unit or a military allocation. It is an identity, a commitment that still stirs the hearts and fires the imaginations. So is there any difference between a 4th soldier in WWI and a 4th soldier fighting the Global War of Terrorism? No. They were and still are all prepared to risk their lives, they were and still are heroes, every single one of them. Steadfast and loyal, Ivy men and women onwards!

BIBLIOGRAPHY AND REFERENCES

4th Infantry Museum, Fort Carson, CO, Scott Daubert, Director

4th Infantry Division History, http://www.armystudyguide.com/content/Unit_history/Division_history/4th-infantry-division.shtml

After Action Report, 4th Infantry Division, June 13, 1968

American Battle Monuments Commission, *4th Division: Summary of Operations in the World War*, Washington D.C.: U.S. GPO, 1944

American Battle Monuments Commission, *4th Division: Summary of Operations in the World War*, Washington D.C.: U.S. GPO, 1944

Babcock, Robert O., *Operation Iraqi Freedom I: A Year in the Sunni Triangle: The History of the 4th Infantry Division and Task Force Ironhorse in Iraq: April 2003 to April 2004*. Tuscaloosa, AL: St. John's, 2005

Babcock, Robert O., *War Stories: D-Day to the Liberation of Paris*, Athens, GA: Deeds Publishing, 2014

Babcock, Robert O., *War Stories: Paris to V-E Day*, Athens, GA: Deeds Publishing, 2014.

Balcer, Charles I., *Advanced Infantry Officers Course 1949–1950, Operations of the VII Corps, 1st U.S. Army in the Landing on Utah Beach, Normandy, France, 6–7 June 1944* (Normandy Campaign) (Personal Experience of a Corps Liaison Officer)

Carland, John M., *Stemming the tide: Combat Operations May 1965 to October 1966*

Center of Military History United States Army, *United States Army in the World War, 1917–1919*, Washington, D.C.: U.S. Army Center of Military History, 1998

"Charlie Company Vietnam 1966–1972," Karen Scott, webmasters Michael Belis and Fred Childs, https://charliecompany.org

Congressional Medal of Honor Society, www.cmohs.org

Department of the Army: Office of the Adjutant General Washington D.C. 10 December 1969

Doubler, Captain Michael D., *Busting the Bocage: American Combined Arms Operations in France, 16 June–31 July 1944*. Ft. Leavenworth, KS: US Army Command, 1988

Infantry School Staff, *The Infantry Journal Incorporated, Washington, D.C. Washington*, D.C.: Military Bookshop, 2011

Kent, Major Frederick T., 'The Operations of the 22nd Infantry (4th Infantry Division) in the Hurgten Forest, Germany, 16 November–3 December 1944' (Rhineland Campaign, Personal Experience of a Regimental S-4), Research Paper for the Advances Infantry Officer's Course No. 1, 1946–1947, The Infantry School, Fort Benning, Georgia

Khan Jr., Chief Warrant Officer E. J. and McLemore, Technical Sergeant Henry, *Fighting Divisions*, Washington D.C.: The Infantry Journal, 1945

MacDonald, Charles B., *The Last Offensive*, Washington, D.C.: Center of Military History United States Army, 1993

Marchand, Walter, *D-Day Doctor's Diary*, unpublished book

"Mountain Post Historical Center," http://mountainposthistoricalcenter.org

Port, Jack, *Eleven Weeks in Normandy*, chapter in unpublished book

Posen, Barry R. & the MIT DACS Conventional Forces Working Group, *Breakthroughs: Armored offensives in Western Europe 1944*, Boston: MIT, 2009

Russell, Steve, *We Got Him!: A Memoir of the Hunt and Capture of Saddam Hussein*, New York: Pocket, 2012

Salinas, Antonio M., *Siren's Song: The Allure of War*, Marietta, GA: Deeds, 2012

Steedly Jr., Homer R. "Memories of an Infantry Small Unit Commander in Vietnam with B/1/8 and D/1/8, 4th Infantry Division, Aug. 1968–Mar. 1970," http://www.swampfox.info

The 4th Infantry Division
http://www.history.army.mil/documents/eto-ob/4id-eto.htm
http://www.historymatters.biz/artist.html courtesy of Jared Frederick

References

Material on John Dowdy provided by Karen Scott, and Michael Belis, 1/22nd Infantry webmaster

Material on Bud Roach, Charlie Shyab and Bill French courtesy of Fred Childs, https://charliecompany.org

Material on Homer R. Steedly Jr. courtesy of Homer R. Steedly Jr, http://www.swampfox.info

Medal of Honor citations, http://www.4thinfantry.org/content/medal-honor

Material on Ty Carter, Florent Groberg courtesy of www.army.mil/

INDEX